We all need an escape…

Lost Connections
The Place That Never Existed
A Cold Retreat
Beneath The Whispers
…Just South of Heaven
Noah's Lament
Mr Watcher
The Revenge of Lisa Lipstick
Mystery Island

Hudson Bell Series:
A Lifetime Ago
Come Back Home

Tall Trees Series:
Little Miss Evil

Joel Baxter Series:
The Crazy season

Tales From
The Coffee Pot

?

Question Mark Press

This first edition published in 2021 by Question Mark Press

Copyright © 2021 by Jim Ody

?
Question Mark Press

Tales From The Coffee Pot Jim Ody. – 1st edition

ISBN: 9798509014994

Cover design by: Emmy Ellis @ Studioenp
Promo by: Donna's Interviews, Reviews and Giveaways
Blog Tours by: Zooloo's Book Tours

Contents

The

Reveal

The Reveal was first published in 2018 by Zombie Cupcake publishing, under the title A Case Revealed, in the anthology Madam Scarlett's Circus. It was then republished as The Reveal later in 2018 by Limitless Publishing, in the anthology Carnival Of Nightmares: 2 (Creepiest Show On Earth).

It is one of my most successful short stories.

Chapter 1

My father was known to be a rolling stone. We must have lived on a hill 'cause he rolled out of our lives and never found his way back. I'd heard he'd found solace in the bosom of many a young lady since. Nice work if you can get it, I suppose. Believe me I've tried my hardest.

Perhaps this is the reason why my mother was always bitter and stern. She once said to me that if life gave you lemons, you find an ungrateful man and squeeze them in his eyeballs. It seems my father took most of her goodwill with him. I sometimes wondered whether she could be a serial killer.

I don't need to tell you I wasn't hugged much as a child, although I've gone and done just that. A psychologist may suggest this is part of the reason I do the things I do. Maybe. Or perhaps I do them because they are fun, plain and simple. I've never subscribed to the blame game.

I've always been a little different and I put this to good use as best I can. As an occupation I find people. Sometimes they don't want to be found, and sometimes other people don't want them to be found, but I find them nonetheless. It's not as hard as you might think. Essentially people are stupid.

I have a shoebox office in a shithole part of town. It's cheap and keeps my overheads down. Ifind that to be financially beneficial even if it's not aesthetically pleasing. Dropping a grand at IKEA isn't going to find people any quicker.

Another case is over, so cue the fanfare as I await the gratitude of the city which I will of course modestly wave off. I care not about accolades and awards, headlines, and women swooning at my feet. My only true desire is a small thing called justice. My fight against crime is a long, fitful one, and I bear the scars of battle, to which I emerge victoriously with my fist raised triumphantly high in the air. Okay, so I don't mind a little swooning, but that act has been extinct since the older side of 1970. Today we get what most people would describe as groupies and stalkers. I personally call them friends. Sometimes they are my dates and objects of desire. Other times they cost me cash and leave me with rashes.

I played back in my mind a new client that had chanced upon me a mere hour ago. She was cut from a cloth of beauty. All smooth skin and bright blue eyes. She had a need and I'm the man that can provide for her.

So, through deep contemplation I pulled out a large cigar, balanced it between my lips with no intention of lighting it, and thought about this lady who had graced my presence for all of ten minutes. Her name was Kiki, and she was the sunshine through my rain clouds. Her brother was missing, and I was to be the one to find him.

It would be a hero mission, one which could end up in the bedroom or down the aisle. Some cases were hard to gauge.

I didn't ask her how she came by my name. I'll assume my reputation is rife at the yoga class that she clearly attends and my name was muttered by someone in The Warrior pose, or more than likely the Downward Dog. I'm known around town. Sometimes for good things, occasionally for the bad.

My reverie was brought to an abrupt end by my secretary Mona, a rather apt name if ever there was one, who said sharply, "Quit daydreaming, Caper! She's not worth it."

Through the imaginary pale blue smoke that ceased to float up toward the damp, stained ceiling, I saw her scowling at me. Mona could be very pretty if she didn't scowl so much. However, scowling to Mona is like Batman and crime – always battling but neither is far from the other.

"As you did not witness the fair maiden in question, any such comment should be disregarded by the jury, as it's inadmissible in this court," I replied, and indignantly stuck the cigar in my mouth for another fake puff. I make no apologies for these actions which I consider medium-cool without the health risks.

Mona sighed, and this was a sign that she was about to lecture me so I made a mental note to shut my ears and hide in my mind's own version of Narnia until the wicked ordeal was over. "How many times in the last month has this happened, huh? Three or four times. And that's in the last month! Every time an attractive woman has the misfortune to look at your sorry mug, you get all... all... *weird,* and then what happens?"

I was not going to answer her. I would not be pulled into her web of lies. I stopped short of putting my fingers in my ears and repeating, "Lalalalala!" Mona doesn't favour my brand of humour.

"You'll never see her again! Not even a fleeting glance. That thing in your trousers is not a lucky charm, sunshine!" I thought that was a matter of opinion.

"Is there a point to this or are you just testing your vocal cords?" I mumbled, my mask of Clint Eastwood cool slipping ever so slightly.

She shook her head, and although I looked away, I knew there was some eye-rolling going on there. "And it's that sort of remark that keeps them away, Caper!"

"What the hell are you talking about, woman?"

"You spend most of your time sneaking around with a camera, photographing women having sex. You are basically living a life of actual porn! At least the usual smutty photographers make money from it."

"I had no idea of your expertise in pornographic photographers' wages, but I do bow to your superior knowledge in such matters, Mona." There was more head shaking in my peripheral vision, and as I pondered that this made my job instantly appear better, she was mumbling again.

"I don't know why I work for you!"

"Sometimes I think that I work for you," I said just under my breath, and not for the first time I might add.

"What was that?" She was scowling over her usual scowling now, giving me a full unadulterated scowl-fest. Her gangster name would be Scowlface. Although I've not broached the subject.

I fake-smiled my reply, "Because it works for you."

"Works for me, my arse! Quit stalling and get to it!"

She says these things like my job is easy. But to successfully do what I do you need life skills. This job needed me at my best. It was different. She was different. And this time Caper was going to get the girl.

"You will not get the girl! And why do you insist on speaking your thoughts out loud? Do you not know how annoying that is?" Mona shouted from the next room.

Maybe she was right, or maybe it was time to get a new secretary, one without permanent PMS and with a sense of humour. A younger model with bigger tits.

"You're doing it again!"

"Sorry. Bad habit."

Mona is my cousin. Unsurprisingly, Mona has a history of being dismissed mostly due to her brash nature and inability to listen to authority, so it was a gift of Samaritan-lengths that I offered her a role here on a wage that is somewhere between voluntary and expenses-paid excitement (which is to say she gets paid in refreshments and life-knowledge gain).

So, back to the case at hand. Kiki, the tall and lithe blonde, had requested my services to find her brother who set out to get a job at the circus. Herein lies the problem. The aforementioned circus is one of legends and stories of old.

I've frequented the place on a number of occasions and have been amazed at what I have seen. However, as good as the shows are, the place is bloody spooky and run by a bunch of freaks. I do actually mean freaks; whether or not that is a derogatory comment is not the point. Political correctness has no place around the Big Top.

Whispers have whipped around this place over the past year or so filled with eyebrow-raising suspicion. Folks have a tendency to go missing when this circus rolls into town. And now since its permanent residency has been established, a host of fingers are now pointing in the direction of this travelling band of weirdos. Yours truly included.

Her brother is called Francis, but he's known as Franz. I can see why. I don't have much to go on but that is my remit. I grabbed my phone and headed out.

"I may be gone a few days," I told Mona.

"Try not to die," she deadpanned. It almost sounded like she meant it.

"Sound advice as ever, Toots."

"Never call me that again."

"Noted." Scolded, I left her there to stew. She didn't have much else to do. Well, apart from take messages from attractive single ladies.

Chapter 2

I left my office, went down to the car park and got into my car. It's a 1968 Plymouth Barracuda and possibly the sexiest thing to never have had breasts. It could be a sign of a midlife crisis. There is nothing remotely practical about it. It drinks fuel like a sloppy drunk, handles poorly, and any driven distance is a physical workout, not to mention the engine is so loud any stealth missions are impossible. But it's just so damned cool. It's like having sex with a famously beautiful woman. High maintenance and short-term, and you enjoy her more than she enjoys you. You cherish the moments you have together.

I looked up to the hill with the circus on top. Some say it's always been there, whilst others reckon it appeared on a dark Halloween night many, many years ago and never left. It sounded like the usual bullshit thrown around the local public house after hours, when over-measured spirits had been flowing freely all night and under-the-counter knock-offs had made an appearance. That stuff would make you forget your own name.

The place is run by a dark-vixen called Madam Christine. It sounded more like a whore-house than a circus. I'd be the judge of that.

The winding gravel road crunched under the overly-expensive tyres. Periodically on stakes were realistic looking skulls. Incredibly realistic, in fact. All for the art of the show.

Maybe it was its high location, but as I got up higher thick fog engulfed me. It was the perfect location. Rob Zombie couldn't have conjured up anything more ghostly for one of his movies.

I parked near the black ticket booth that was twice the size of those things that used to house phones before people had them permanently attached to their hands. Inside, a blonde girl made up like a zombie school girl smiled as best she could with bloodied stitches on her face and big black eyes.

"Nice car!" She giggled high-pitched and childlike. She sounded like Rob Zombie's wife.

"Thank you," I replied. Already I looked out of place. I like to wear a black suit for work. It's my way of focusing on the job at hand, and often I gain more respect from people that I interview. I like to play the character of a private investigator, what with me being one and all. Outside of work I remove my tie and on occasion open my top button. Rebellious, huh? But not very often. Smart clothes equal a smart mind as my old mum used to say – before putting lemon juice in men's eyes apparently.

"You want tickets?" She waved a handful just in case I was simple. A standard conclusion when looking at me. A good suit can still sit nicely on an arsehole. Some say I look like an American Bible salesman. Personally, I've never met one so I can't comment. Perhaps they have black hair parted at the side too. Though I suspect they carry a Bible or two. It's not a book I possess.

"Not right now," I said, fumbling in my pocket. She looked slightly worried. I have that effect on women. They tend not to fancy pocket-fumblers, and often call the authorities. Occupational hazard. I pulled out a picture of Franz and showed it to her. "You seen this guy?" I said it with authority. I'm good at that.

A sadness washed over her momentarily, and she was shaking her head before she'd even glanced at the picture. My sixth sense was going crazy. I tried the beady-eye approach like I was Eastwood again to show she'd been rumbled. I thought about speaking through gritted teeth, too.

"No. I mean, he might've been at one of the shows… but outside of here, no."

I nodded and let an awkward silence build up between us. I've had many dates where this hasn't been deliberate, so my method acting was on point.

I pulled out a cigar and placed it in my lips, unlit, and it bobbed. I glance down at the picture, fingering the corner like I might be sad. I then lifted it and showed it again. "You sure?"

She was back with the nodding again. She was good at it.

"What's your name?" I held the cigar between my first two fingers like I was the author/singer

Kinky Friedman. I thought it made me look distinguished.

"Dedna." She smiled but looked a little worried now.

I had to grin at that. "I like it. What's your real name?"

"That is my real name."

I winked. "Right you are, Toots."

We were then left a little awkwardly looking at each other. She was probably thinking how much of an asshole I was, and I couldn't blame her. It was nothing if not a fair conclusion to be made. "Anyone else here I can speak to?"

"What about?"

"Tickets," I said sarcastically.

"But I… *Oh,* I see. Let me go and see who's around." I nodded, and she walked off.

I wasn't comfortable with her wearing a school uniform. She was over twenty years of age, so to dress in a provocative way in a recognised uniform of a minor just didn't sit well with me. The outfit was asking me to look at her, but it felt like she was taunting me by suggesting what she was making me think was wrong. I didn't like that. It seemed cunning and wily. Traits of my ex-girlfriends. I wondered if she'd had therapy, too.

I looked off into the distance and saw who I assumed to be the stunning Madam Christine. I actually took a breath. She was a legend. An enigma. There was something about her that showed enough to appear real and almost attainable, and yet like a human mirage was always just out of reach. I'd not met a man alive who hadn't had some sort of fantasy about her. That shows the breadth of her appeal. Some of those men were openly gay and still spoke lustfully of her. A real-life cougar.

It was no great leap to suggest that young Franz had been drawn in by her too. She glided rather than walked and she would catch your eye for a split second and make you feel like the most important man alive. Then as quick as a bad thought she was gone, and you were left paralysed with a mix of desire and disappointment. These feelings are second nature to me.

Before me were large tents. Strange looking people threw me a glance then went back to their work. So many things had to be done in order for this place to run smoothly. The show must go on!

"'ello?" A gruff voice slapped me back to reality, one at which an auburn-haired siren was no longer greasing her naked body with lotion but instead had morphed into an aged and heavily tattooed figure with large rings in her ears that made the lobes sag. There were very few bare bits of skin that didn't display faded tattoos. I couldn't be sure whether this person was male or female. There was the suggestion of small breasts but my mother taught me never to stare.

"Good day," I said. I'm not sure why, I'm never usually that formal. It was because my top button was still done up.

"Is it?" the figure replied. One eye closed quickly then opened. It didn't seem to be a wink, more irritation. They might be allergic to me. That would certainly confirm them to be female after all.

"It's a good day to be alive." I grinned. That didn't work. I was met by silence. I looked over to Dedna who was shaking her head at me. It was a bit too early to be showing signs of disappointment toward me, but I've been known to be a quick mover. I've disappointed women before they've even met me, such are my skills.

I held up the picture. "Have you seen this person?"

"Who said I had?"

"Nobody, it's just a question. This guy is missing and I was told he'd come here. So you've not seen him?"

"I don't reckon. You the police or somethin'?"

"I'm a private investigator. A detective, if you like." This was my standard line. Part of me thought it was cute.

"*Really?* For this missing person?"

"I'm working on a couple of angles. I'm a multi-tasker. You know the story, grew up in a poor area, drink and drugs in the family, suddenly the mum is wondering why junior has left..."

Total bullshit. Franz came from a nice family, and by all accounts this was completely out of character. However, experience tells me that if you make out the victim is best off away from the family, they open up warmly, confess to having seen them whilst feeling good that they have done a good deed in keeping them away from the horrors of home. Human nature can be such a strange thing. If they knew the lad came from a good family then panic kicks in, and more often than not when we find the person, they are no longer alive.

"The other angle I am interested in is the carnival, and specifically the success of yours. On a non-professional level, of course. In the fluctuating economic climate, specifically one that is currently on a downturn, it is surprising that a business such as this survives."

"What else would we do?" It felt rhetorical, and in all honesty, there was little else these people *could* do. Although I'm led to believe the government is often on the lookout for new clowns.

"Without seeing your CV, I couldn't possibly comment."

"You some kinda smartarse?"

"Not especially."

"I'll bet. Sorry I can't help you," she concluded and turned away.

"Hey… okay. Look, can I run something by you?" I said when she turned back around to face me again.

"Shoot."

"I'd like to hang around for the day, interview people, see how things are around here?"

There was a shake of the head. "She don't like people hanging around."

"I have a writer friend. He would love to do a piece on you all. I said I'd check the place out for him. It would be great publicity," I tried with a weak smile.

"Hmmm. Wait here." And she was gone.

Dedna giggled. "She likes you."

"Really? She didn't appear very warm."

"The last outsider she talked to ended up in the hospital."

"Good to know."

Chapter 3

It was a good ten minutes before she returned. In that time, I had pondered a short list of her female traits. I was beginning to think I had more than her.

"Looks like you caught a break," she barked at me.

"I'm sorry?" I said.

"You and me both. She says you can hang around. You are also welcome to spend the night in the cabin if you want. Give you a chance to get the real story."

"Really?" I said, not trying to hide my surprise.

"I look like I joke around?"

"No, I would think you wouldn't ever be considered a joker."

"Likewise. Well, quit gawping at Dedna's tits and follow me. There's a cold shower that you could make use of."

I followed behind trying not to be distracted by faded tattoos that looked like scaly skin in their greenish haze. Symbols and crudely-drawn faces wobbled slightly with each movement. She was distracting for all of the wrong reasons. I didn't want to think about her anymore just in case she could read minds.

I didn't think that I was supposed to walk next to her, so stayed a few steps behind. A pretty good analogy of our relationship so far, I'd wager.

To the right I could see the giant big top. It stood powerful and erect as the centrepiece, a number of smaller tents and buildings tunnelled off in various directions.

When we turned to the left following the path away from the tents, I saw a human ball of a woman. Her hair hung down, and her body bent around the painful way like a human letter 'O'.

"Who's that, Ink?" she called not even bothering to untangle herself.

"Never you mind, Leah!" was the response from in front of me, not even looking her way. Being observant is key to my work, so with that skill I'm guessing that Ink was a nickname.

I glanced back and saw a smile on a face with bare feet touching either cheek. I wondered whether she chewed her toenails. And looking at how supple she was, I wondered other things too. But I had to stay professional. It's how I crack cases.

A line of cabins with trees hanging overhead appeared in front of us. They looked like they had been plucked straight out of a *Friday the 13th* movie set. Functional and adequate, but with a chance of ending up on the wrong side of a machete fight.

She pulled out a key and unlocked the door to number three. I liked that. Three was my lucky number.

"There you go."

I stepped in. "Thanks."

"Don't thank me. I would've sent you packing. What's your name anyway?"

"Caper."

"Caper? What sort of a name is that?"

"A proper name is what it is, *Ink*."

The muscles in her jaw clenched. She wanted to do bad things to me. Not in the kinky way, either. "Stay away from Madam Christine, *Caper*. And don't speak to the twins."

"The twins?"

"You'll know." She looked me up and down, snarled, and was gone.

I shut the door behind me and thought that I should have brought my bag from the car. I didn't have much in it, certainly no toiletries or anything for overnight, but I did have my laptop and a few other items that may come in useful.

The bed was large and covered in a floral bedspread. I had to wonder at the state of the cleanliness here. It was hardly a hotel, and I couldn't imagine cleaners making a daily appearance, but perhaps I was just being a little mean.

I'd had a few hard weeks and they were taking their toll on me. I'm no spring chicken anymore. Cases don't stop coming and like a crime-whore, I don't turn anyone away.

I'm not sure what the plan was, if I was honest. I had not seen Franz walking around, nor had I heard the cries for help from a teenage boy tied up in a barrel somewhere. I could say that everyone here was a little strange, but surely that was the requisite for being part of this place, *right?* It was a full-time show. A graveyard for student actors who had tried the big time and failed miserably. Here they could play the role permanently, the world outside of their eyes a constant audience.

The bed looked comfy so I lay down, lacing my fingers together behind my head.

A faint smell of lavender perfume danced its way to my nose, and my eyelids gave up the ghost of staying open. My final thoughts before slipping into a deep sleep were hopes that this would be some *Scooby-Doo* mystery that would sort itself out. Some janitor, relative, or jealous competitor would be the monster. It might end well, and we'd all live happily-ever-after, or if nothing else I'd end up naked with the beautiful Kiki as a token of her appreciation. I'm always accepting of such a gift of thanks.

"What're you looking for here?" a voice whispered to me.

I opened my eyes but everything was bright. I could barely make out the figure that owned the voice.

"What?" I said, still getting my bearings.

"You seek answers, but tell me, do you really know the questions yet?"

Something inside gripped me tightly. The figure got clearer, the lights dimmed slightly, but she still appeared as if in a spotlight.

"I'm looking for a teenager called Franz," I said, aware my voice was small and missing its usual bravado.

"So you say, but is that the real reason that you're here?"

"I've been asked to find him. That's my job."

She got closer to me. "I didn't ask you about your job," she whispered in my ear.

Her pale skin was flawless, her eyes penetrating, lips full and purple, and her fiery hair fell down the sides of her face. At times she was youthful, and others a flash of age like a seductive older woman. Yet there was something wise and incredibly dangerous about her that had my heart beating hard and fast. It was excitement and fear all mixed together.

"I'm looking for the lad…" I'd lost all conviction in my words.

"We both know that's not the case."

A flash of bright light had me turning away and shielding my eyes. When I looked back, she was gone.

I was there alone. I sat up and stared at the wall. I must have been dreaming, right?

Like most times when I'm confused and bored, I grabbed my phone from my pocket and rang Mona. On the third ring she picked up.

"Ooo, you almost got a fine for breaking the three-ring-rule!" I said.

"You rang my mobile," she said flatly. Would it hurt her to pretend to be pleased that I'd called?

"I'm well aware of that," I lied. I suppose she was allowed to answer her personal mobile in as many rings as she saw fit. In fact, I could count myself lucky that she'd answered it at all.

"You should count yourself lucky that I answered it at all," she said.

See, I told you.

"How're things?"

"You never ask me how I am, what's up? You left about three hours ago. You home sick already?"

"Did I?" I looked at my watch. It was indeed three hours later. "Blimey!"

"Are you screwing her?"

"Who?"

"Kiki Dee."

"Don't go breaking my heart!"

"Not going to happen, Elton John."

"Haha. No, I've not even seen the fine woman. I'm staying here at the circus overnight to get a handle on this one. I think there is something a bit strange here."

"It's a circus with freaks and sideshows. You can be sure there is something strange going on. Not to mention the weirdo holding your phone."

"Ah, a joke."

"Indeed, you are."

Mona sounded annoyed and sarcastic. She was no fun when she was like this. Actually, she was no fun at any stage. She needed to get her head out of those romance novels and find a handsome stud to fuck her senseless. She might find a ray of happiness then.

"Right, well. Speak soon. Goodbye, yellow brick road!" I heard her groan before I pressed the button to end the call.

And then I saw the note:

Ticket booth – 5pm

I checked my watch—it was ten past five.

Dedna?

I grabbed the key and left the cabin.

I surveyed the large sprawl of the circus area. It was a domineering place that wasn't meant to be welcoming. Like horror movies and roller coaster rides the point was to entertain you and take you to your limits rather than comfort you. You were meant to come, be entertained, and leave on shaking legs.

I've stayed at very few places where people have disappeared, mainly because they are public places and the leads are woolly at best. But I wasn't lying when I'd said this was more than Franz. Franz was an excuse. I'd hunted down enough people to know the difference between a kidnapping or abduction and a conscious decision to hide.

Franz was a teenage boy. A loner. He had visited the circus four times in the past two weeks. One of those times he had tried to sneak in and had been kicked out. He was desperate to go there, and I could see a number of reasons why that might be. Staying the night seemed logical. I'd conducted enough interviews to know that people lie easily when prepared, or for short periods, but watch them over any length of time and the truth will appear.

I got to the ticket booth and walked around the back.

"In here!" a high-pitched voice hissed.

"So what's with the secrecy?"

"You can't tell the time?"

"I was sleeping."

She shook her head, which made her blonde pigtails wiggle. Through the make-up she looked cross.

"You say you're looking for someone and yet the first thing you do is have a nap? Are you sure this is your job?"

"I wasn't planning on it, but that's what happened."

"Well newsflash! I wasn't planning on living here and giving strangers the willies full-time, but guess what? That's what happened!" Her serious face broke. She was the sort of person who tried to be positive.

"You give people the willies?"

She rolled her eyes. "You belong here more than I do!"

"Okay," I said. "So, what's with the clandestine meeting? I presume it has nothing to do with one of us giving the other the willies, right?"

She punched me playfully on the arm. "Not yet!"

I tapped my nose. "I get ya!"

She stopped and composed herself. "I know where he is. The guy. Franz."

"Go on," I encouraged.

"I first saw him a few weeks back. He was always one of the last to leave the big top. He looked mesmerised by it all. At first it was cute. This lad was in awe of the whole show and the place itself. That's exactly what we want. Then he started to appear more and more. Last week, Ink caught him sneaking around."

"I don't imagine she just waggled a finger, smacked his bum, and sent him packing."

Dedna shook her head. "No, she punched him in the face and threatened to do something unsavoury with his balls."

"Nice. So d'you think he came back to get revenge on her?"

Again, she shook her head a couple of times. "No, it wasn't like that. It was like he was obsessed to the point of addiction, and even the threat of castration wasn't enough to stop him."

"So what kept bringing him back?"

"Not what. Who."

"Madame Christine?"

This time she seemed non-committal, but she looked up at me and her eyes told me all I needed to know.

I ran my hands through my hair. "I had a dream," I said.

She grinned. "What was it, Martin Luther King?"

I was beginning to really like this woman. She made sarcasm fun again. To me it should be an Olympic sport.

"Madame Christine came to me earlier. It seemed so real. It must've been a dream."

Dedna looked serious. "She is not what you think she is. She is powerful. I can't say any more than that."

I nodded. This told me everything yet nothing at all.

I should go to my car and get the hell out of here. I should probably go back to looking for husbands who'd run off with their fancy young ladies. Wives who'd had enough of their husbands and left the country in search of their foreign prince. Or the odd heart-wrenching abducted child that ends in heartbreak and an ending that doesn't bear repeating.

Still, something kept me here. I wanted to know what was bringing the likes of young Franz back, even with the threats of his balls being ripped out and used for a game of table tennis. I wanted to know more about Madame Christine and the carnival.

Who knows, maybe I was beginning to get addicted, too?

"You said you know where he is?"

She stopped, deep in thought like she was toying with whether or not she should tell me.

"I'm a big boy," I said, hoping to move her on. "That's what I'm here for."

"I know, but if I tell you then you might go..." She looked at me, and I'm not sure what it was I saw. I wanted some hint of desire, but all I saw was pity.

"Not necessarily."

"That could be even worse."

I reached up and smoothed her cheek.

"Don't, you'll smudge my makeup," she said, grabbing my wrist.

"Is that what you're most worried about?"

She touched my cheek, too and bit her lip. "Things are complicated." She leaned into me. At first, I thought she was going to kiss me, but instead she whispered in my ear. "Go to The Green Room. It's behind the Big Top near the psychic tent."

"Thank you," I said.

She blew me a kiss, turned, and was gone.

Chapter 4

It was a little unnerving to be walking around on my own. I felt like I was trespassing. The odd person – and when I say odd that's exactly what I mean – would look at me like I was an abnormal growth on the face of a beauty queen. I'd raise a hand which did the job in moving them on. They didn't want any interaction with me. I was used to that.

I nearly walked into a wooden post when I saw Siamese twins bickering. It's not something that I see every day. Imagine having another living person with you 24/7? It didn't bear thinking about. These two were really going at it! What a bloody fascinating spectacle.

I walked on past a bearded lady and pondered what these people did for fun when not performing? Did they go into town? Hang out at Starbucks? It seemed unlikely.

I heard a scream that was abruptly muffled, and I was drawn to it. It was a desperate sound that someone was trying to hide. I walked quickly toward the tent it had come from and tentatively slipped inside. I saw the body being dragged out, the blood pooled below leaving a smudged trail. A clown was pulling it, and another figure walked beside carrying an axe.

They turned and looked at me.

I was about to run but was frozen with fear.

The clown nodded and tipped his bowler hat at me, then turned and they were gone through another tent flap. Just another oddity.

I tried to process what I'd seen. Perhaps this was a practice run for the show. An elaborate dress-rehearsal. But everything looked so real.

So very real.

I backed out of the tent and was met by a tall, skinny man in a top hat who stood on stilts. "Tonight's show is sure to be the best!" he proclaimed as if addressing a huge crowd and not just me. I guess he always spoke like that. I assumed he didn't get invited to many funerals.

"I'm sure," I replied, still a little shaken.

"Mark my words! Thrills, chills…" he bent down close to me, "…blood spills!" He straightened up and walked off still shouting, "Roll up! Roll up! The greatest show on Earth!"

I walked past the painted arrow pointing to the psychic tent. Presumably this was for those without these specific abilities. At the opening of the psychic tent, I slipped around the side and saw a huge green box. It really couldn't be anything but The Green Room.

I pushed the door but found it locked. I was then startled by an accented voice behind me.

"What ya doing, lanky?"

I spun around and immediately looked down to a small person. I'm not sure what the politically correct terminology is, but being called *lanky* would sure allow me to call the little shit whatever I wanted to.

"Your mum, she around?"

"You trying to be funny?"

"You tell me."

"You're not."

"Everyone's a critic."

"*Critic?*"

"Yeah, like cricket but more fun."

His face scrunched up like he was chewing stinging nettles, and he lunged at me, punching me hard in the stomach. I kicked out and sent him falling backward onto the ground. It wasn't my finest moment. It was funny, but I'm still not proud of it.

"Hold on," I said as he jumped up ready to punch me again. "Look, I'm not looking for a fight. I'm Caper, and I'm looking for a missing teenager."

"So why you kick me?" he whined, then muttered something that could've been in Russian.

"From what I recall you punched me in the nuts."

"Stomach."

"You've not seen the size of my nuts."

He seemed to be sizing me up again. I tried again.

"Have you seen him? The teenager? His name is Franz."

"You're fucking simple. You know that, right?"

"And you're fucking rude! Have you seen him or not?"

He sighed. "Look, we have many kids hanging round. They're obsessed with things that are different. You can't blame them, no? That's what we sell. But they get bored, you know?"

I nodded. "You think that's what happened here?"

"Sure, why not? If I was taller, you think I'd be here?"

I shrugged. I had no reason to speculate what he would or wouldn't be doing by way of an alternative vocation. It was really of no concern to me.

"I grew up in circus. Me and my brother. We came to this country ten years ago. Our circus was no more but we found Madame Christine, and here I am." His broken English was spoken with deep sadness.

"You and your brother?"

"No, my brother died a few years back." He looked down. Which in truth, wasn't that far.

I felt uncomfortable. I also felt a bit sorry for him, but my stomach still ached from his punch. What was it kids said nowadays? Sorry, not sorry.

"We performed this act a thousand times. I shot egg out of small cannon into the air, and Priski, my brother, would catch in his mouth. But one time he caught it he was distracted..." With tears in his eyes, he held up the thumb and forefinger on his left hand. "Centimetres. Five-degrees in tilt of neck was all it took to lodge. It ripped his windpipe. It was most sad time."

"I'm sorry," I said, noticing he sounded more Russian than he had a few minutes ago. Killed by an egg? Was this guy for real?

"You not know him."

I fumbled in my pocket and pulled out the picture. "You've not seen him?"

He stopped for a second, looked at me, and almost said something, and thinking better of it he shook his head, and said, "We have hundred people here for a show. We have many shows. I don't remember everyone."

I nodded. "Okay. I'll leave you to do whatever it was you were doing."

He glanced at The Green Room and then at me. I got the hint. I walked off, fully expecting him to shout at me or perhaps try a surprise attack.

I planned to catch a show tonight. I'd find Dedna and get a ticket. It was a good excuse to see her and to scope out the place. I also wanted to see if there was an act involving a clown and a man with an axe.

I walked up and around the side of the next tent away from the psychic tent. The dark veil of night was beginning to float down upon the circus. Small lights glowed and only emphasised this point.

I heard another scream but it was unclear whether this was in pleasure or pain. They sounded very similar at times.

I scanned the area, unsure of exactly where I was going when I saw a tent with a glass window in the side. Tents had come on a long way since I was a child wrestling with guy ropes and main poles as a Cub Scout.

I saw movement in the window.

She stood with her back to me slowly undressing. Like some sad Peeping Tom, I was mesmerised. I'm not proud of this, but there you go. It was a tantalising private show that I was drawn to. I realised I was now walking toward the tent. The last item of her purple clothing hit the floor, her flame hair bright against pale skin. A hint of a breast was visible.

I was a few feet away, my mind teasing me with thoughts of my touch on that skin, my hands on – *Smack!*

Out of nowhere something hit me in the back of the head, flashing a bright light in front of my eyes. I fell to the ground feeling incredibly stupid and vulnerable.

A silhouetted figure was behind me.

"Caper!" a female voice hissed at me. "What the hell are you doing?"

She stepped into the light, dropping shadows in an eerie way over her zombie face. It was Dedna.

"I was…" I started, but I really had nothing sensible to say.

"I know." She yanked me to my feet, and I dusted down my suit.

"What hit…"

She picked up a stone. "This!"

"You threw a rock at me?"

"It's a stone."

I shrugged. "Really, it's more of a rock. You could've killed me."

"Is definitely more of a stone, or a pebble perhaps. Unlikely. You were…"

"What? I was what?"

"Look, I've seen it before. Come on, Caper." She grabbed my hand, which felt good. "Madame Christine draws people in. She's hypnotic. Sometimes…" she paused, took my other hand and faced me. I wondered what she looked like under the make-up. "Sometimes they don't come back."

"What d'you mean?"

"I've seen them disappear to her trailer or her tent and *poof!* They never appear again."

My eyebrows rose. "Ya think that's what happened to Franz?"

She shrugged. "I think that little puzzle will work itself out."

We walked on. I looked around again. The conjoined pair stood oblivious to the world with the dominant one extremely animated as the other was silent and looking royally pissed off. This place was familiar in a strange way.

"Oh," I said. "I wanted to buy a ticket for tonight."

She grinned. "You don't need a ticket, Caper!"

That was fair enough. I never turn down a freebie.

"You hungry?" She pointed over to the kitchen area.

I nodded. It had been a while since I'd last eaten, and actually I couldn't remember my last meal. This was totally unlike me.

"What's on offer?"

She grinned knowingly. "Sit here," she said, pointing to a wooden bench outside. The aroma of spices danced in the breeze around me. "I'll get you something."

I started to say something, but she held a finger to my lips and grinned. Off she skipped, all long legs and swinging bunches. I wondered what it would be like to pull them gently whilst taking her from behind. I was then a little shocked I'd thought it. This place was making my thoughts more sordid than usual.

Darkness had already fallen and the lights shone brightly, twinkling and adding a touch of magic to the place. I felt a sharp pain in my head, a flash, and a vision of blood. I grunted and grabbed my head, but just as quickly it disappeared.

"She getting you a burger?" a familiar gruff voice said, startling me. *Ink.*

"Yep," I said.

"You found Franz yet?"

There was a softness in her features now, different to how I'd seen her earlier. It was almost compassion.

"No, any ideas?"

"Sometimes the answers are right in front of you," she said. "We can't always see all that is too close. I'll see you later."

I know this is a circus filled with carnival freaks, but these characters were something else. They made odd look normal. I couldn't help but wonder whether they derived from a day release program from a psychiatric ward somewhere. They either spoke to me in a condescending manner, in tongues, or in riddles.

"Here you go!" Dedna giggled, handing over a huge, fat burger. A napkin did its best to keep in the juices from the meat, but it was a losing battle. Pineapple and onions peeped out from under the sesame seed bun.

"This looks amazing."

"Oh, it is that and then some!"

I took a bite, enjoying the sweetness of the fruit mixed with the meat and onions. Then a fiery jalapeno chaser ran through and abused my taste buds, just the way I liked it! This was pure heaven.

"How did you know?"

She winked. "Lucky guess." She was eating some fries and nothing else. I guess that's how she maintained such a fine figure.

After a while she looked at me in a serious way. "What's your next move, Detective?"

I shrugged. I suppose I needed to get into The Green Room, where she had originally told me to go. Whenever I talked to anyone, I was given nothing but riddles in return. It was frustrating and getting me nowhere. I had a feeling they all had something to hide. Even Dedna, although her seduction tactics were extremely good.

"The Green Room?" I said as a question.

She nodded, as if she had led me to this answer.

When we'd finished, she took my hand. "Shall we go now?" she said, and I was ready to follow.

"Yes, if you think I'll get answers."

"I think you will, Caper. I think you will."

And off we went.

Chapter 5

We walked back to The Green Room, past a woman with a knowing look about her who nodded a greeting to us both. She was a psychic. I didn't know for sure, but it was just a strong feeling I had.

Again, there were sounds that escaped into the night. At one point I stopped.

"Something isn't right here, is it?"

She looked at me sympathetically. "I know it seems like it now, Caper, but soon you'll see. Everything will be alright, I promise."

I guess I had to trust her. I mean, I'd already invested a certain amount of trust to follow her around here. I couldn't be certain whether I was to end up being dragged into a darkened tent by a clown or into this beautiful woman's bed. The coin was already in the air and spinning. Soon I would learn my fate.

"The door is locked," I said when we got there.

Dedna produced something from her pocket. "The key," she said and handed it over to me.

"Why didn't you give it to me the first time?" I asked.

"I wasn't sure that you really wanted to come here."

"What? To The Green Room?"

She nodded. "You might not like what you see inside."

I let the words settle in my mind for a second. I wasn't sure what she meant. I took the key and unlocked the door.

My mind flashed through a montage of corpses and mutilated bodies, horrors and evidence of missing persons gone by. This could be a hundred cold cases ready to be solved.

Pushing down the handle, I opened the door tentatively. The old musty smell hit me instantly. Inside was a car covered in dust.

A click exploded light onto it. My stomach dropped as the familiarity struck a chord.

I turned and looked at Dedna. She had a shocked expression on her face.

"I d-don't... W-What has this got to do with Franz?" I stammered. My mind was spinning around, words, pictures, and thoughts flashing as I struggled to piece together all of the data.

"What are you thinking?" Dedna asked quietly, her words thick with sadness.

I stared at the Plymouth Barracuda. The one that was identical to the car I owned.

"This looks like my car." I started walking over to it. "I mean, I don't know of many others like this."

She was nodding slowly. "It is yours."

"Who put it here?" I asked, but it all seemed a little unbelievable. Were they trying to keep me here? I thought about Madame Christine. She was never going to let me leave, was she?

"Let's go back to your cabin," Dedna said. "I'll explain."

I had so many things I wanted to say, but I couldn't string any words together. Every time I tried, nonsensical noises escaped instead. She took my hand.

We walked back. Every person we met seemed to stop what they were doing and look at us. For the first time I felt like I was part of some cult. They knew.

They fucking knew.

Using my key, I opened the door to my cabin and walked in. Dedna followed but bumped into me when I stopped abruptly.

It looked different. The things were arranged the same, but there were more things there. A movie poster of *Pulp Fiction* was on the wall above my bed.

"What is this?" The words slipped from my mouth, but I'm not sure where they'd come from.

Dedna gently pushed me forward, encouraging me to walk in. "It's your room," she said. "Everything here is yours."

I walked over to the wardrobe and opened it up. It was full of black suits and white shirts. They were all my size. Of course, they were my size.

"I don't get it." I walked up to a well-thumbed novel on the side table. It was titled *Missing Miss Legless* and the cover depicted a stripper and a detective in a black suit. My stomach dropped when I saw the tagline on the cover: *A Caper Juggins Mystery*.

"It's alright," Dedna said and pointed at the mirror.

I walked over and looked into it.

My face was nothing like I remembered. Specifically, as it was covered in clown make up a lot like the more contemporary Joker look. My hair was bright green and stuck out at all crazy angles.

"What the… how…?"

"You work here. Do you remember now?" Her voice was filled with sadness and twin lines of tears had messed up her own face paint.

"No," I argued. "I'm a detective! I've come to get to the bottom of a mystery. I have to find Franz."

Someone else appeared behind us. "Then congratulations are in order." Her voice was loud but still seemed like a whisper. It was a contradiction.

I turned and saw Madame Christine.

"I don't understand," I said again. This was going to be written on my epitaph.

"Dedna? Care to explain to the detective?"

"Come to the bathroom," she said to me. Really hoping that Franz was not going to be there bound and gagged in my bathtub, I followed her.

She took a washcloth from the side and ran it under the tap. She handed it over to me.

"Wipe your face," she said forcefully, unable to look me in the eyes. I wasn't sure what this would prove, but I did as I was told.

I rubbed once, then twice, then I scrubbed back and forth a number of times.

Dedna came up behind me and slipped an arm around my chest. She kissed me on the side of my face, and as she turned me toward the mirror, she pulled out the photograph from my pocket.

I looked long and hard at the face of Franz that stared back at me in the mirror.

I had found him. Because I *was* him.

"You've been here for a few years now, Franz. Your car was put in The Green Room for whenever you wish to leave. You've never wanted to. Although once in a while you want to be someone else."

Then Madame Christine was there kissing the other side of my face.

"Always Caper Juggins, the great detective. Welcome home, Franz," she said. "Every once in a while, we lose you but we always bring you back."

"You don't want to go anywhere, do you?" Dedna said unbuttoning my shirt.

"We want you here," Madame Christine whispered, now naked and unbuckling my belt.

I was still confused, but for now I was happy to comply.

The End

A trapped man's tomfoolery in the gigantic big
top,
Soaked to the skin as water balloons go *POP!*,
Anonymously hidden, the make-up's just for
show,
Entertaining the fickle folk in each and every row,
But, through the laughter, all the highs and the
deepest lows,
Sits a child with a pained face, and a heavy heart
that knows,
Whilst I'm squirting my flower, and stupidly
tumbling to the ground,
I'm oblivious to the laughter, I just hear heckles
all around,
You see, I was born into the circus, and forced to
be a clown,
And made to entertain the strangers in each and
every town,
The kid stands up, turns and leaves, he knows this
show's my last,
Heckling turns to gasps as unexpectedly there's a
gun blast,
But there's no flag-with-bang that flies from a toy
gun,
The gun is real, I no longer feel, Bullets chase out
my life
Job done…!

The Moth in the Jar

The Moth in the Jar was first published in 2017 by Bloodhound Books, in their charity anthology Dark Minds.

I squeezed the joke stress reliever as I sat in my office. It was in the shape of a boob and had been a Secret Santa gift the year before. I'd bought a nice bottle of wine for the person I'd been randomly assigned. In return I'd received this memory-foam boob. Not even a pair. I felt short-changed.

A surreptitious glance at the computer screen clock told me I was free to leave for the day. I'd earnt the right to down tools and leave now. Outside my office was a sea of minimum wagers. All doing a wonderful job of pretending not to look at the clock. A silent hooter sounding in their corporate bedlam.

A couple with a slack work ethic and no ambitious tendencies got up almost triumphantly; a rebellious act that all but stuck two-fingers up at anyone with roving eyes.

My time as a clock-watcher had ceased years ago. I'd sniffed the right crotches to be the keeper of my own weekend. I'd gained promotions, responsibilities, and a couple of extra noughts to my wages by way of thanks from those above me.

The memories were still fresh of wearing their shoes, counting down the minutes, and leaping up as if receiving either an electric shock or some sort of epiphany just as soon as the magical 5:00pm appeared. However, at some point the revelation hits you that a little extra effort results in promotion, pay-rises, and a better standard of living. A hushed voice in a quarterly performance appraisal had woken me up to smell more than the roses on offer. Perhaps the gentle tap from Lady Luck helped too.

I looked at my lonely office. I was not the sort to adorn it with my academic accolades nor pictures of my handshaking of celebrities, so apart from a couple of family photographs, the walls were uncharacteristically sparse. I learnt a long time ago that nobody wants to see my certificates.

Having earned my stripes, I was able to leave when I wanted to. I had hit, and smashed through, the threshold that silently winked at me and with a secret handshake said: *get the work done to a decent standard and you can come and go as you please.*

So that is what I did. With little care I left an open-ended Out Of Office message that was vague enough to suggest I may be checking emails up until midnight, or may also be deciphered as: *I might never check them again.*

It was three in the afternoon on a Friday. My hours no longer applied. I had overseen the winning of a large contract so could negotiate as many free Friday afternoons as I wanted. This contract was worth millions. I was suddenly a corporate king with the meal ticket that everybody wanted.

I looked down at the picture on my desk, taken in the Caribbean last summer. My wife Laura, as slender as ever, blonde and showing her bright white teeth as she smiled, looking gorgeous in a sprayed-on dress. Next to her my eight-year-old daughter Bobbi grinned, an ice-cream melting in her hand. It was the picture I wanted people to see, not some acknowledgement that I attended a compulsory course, gaining the signed congratulations as a reminder that I stayed for the duration of the biggest borefest of my life.

"See you soon," I said under my breath to the picture, wheeling back on my chair.

I grabbed my jacket but held it over my shoulder as the weather was seasonably warm. I raised a hand to a couple of my team as I left the office. Mainly the ones that weren't jealous of me. These were not the ones silently thinking of ways to murder me without ever having the balls to follow through with their morbid fantasies.

One of the women, a pretty brunette called Mel looked slightly concerned as she waved fingers at me. I smiled back; she deserved that at least.

I had just gone through the exit doors and slowed for the lift when I heard a voice call my name, "Tom?"

I looked round to see Mel stood there straightening her skirt. "D'you fancy going for a drink?" A proposition from an attractive young lady was another benefit.

"What? Now?" I replied, my jacket still clung to my shoulder as my right hand automatically went towards my left hand.

"Now. Or later. Whatever?" She was trying to be dismissive.

I was turning around the wedding band on my finger. I don't know whether this was through unspoken love or perhaps some illusion that I was trying to make disappear. "I would like that Mel, very much, but..." I couldn't say any more and let the words hang there. Their weight too heavy to follow with anything flippant. Even a joke seemed grossly inappropriate. She knew. She had to know though, right?

I saw her eyes glance to my fumbling hands. They were filled with a sadness that was disappointment, as much for me as it was for her. This was perhaps a joint burden that we silently shared. In another world and in another place.

"I understand... *Laura*." I nodded at her words. My lift arrived. The doors opened to show another member of senior management. I nodded at him, and of course he reciprocated. Big dicks united. He was off home, too.

I turned back but Mel was gone. A guilty thief merging into the crowds.

How did I feel? How *should* I feel?

Love wraps you up tightly, engulfing you in emotions so strong you almost suffocate. Perhaps it was possible to feel the light touch from another love, whispering upon your cheek like a breath of fresh air.

On the way out, I nodded to the security guard who is polite but with little charm. I wondered again whether he provided any real security here, other than the jurisdiction to slightly man-handle unauthorised personnel or escort employees on their dismissal walk of shame from the premises –

the latter I always thought to be a real perk of the job. He seemed bored and acted like this was community service. Perhaps it is.

My car was less than twenty-feet away from the building, another proof of my status. Up there with the disabled and heavily pregnant employees, senior management get to park their flashy cars like a game show reveal of *look what you could've won*. Perhaps our portly figures from rich food, or the weight of our thick wallets, give justification to us not having to fight for a space like the rest of the employee-cattle. My car is a Range Rover. I don't need a Range Rover, but it costs me nothing but a small amount of tax per month, so why not? It is slightly more palatable in silver rather than a Chelsea-wives White or a footballer's black.

The sun could not hide in a cloudless sky, and so I was forced to put on my sunglasses. I often shy away from their usage, this being one of a few acts of self-consciousness I have, often happy to roll the dice with my eyesight and a life of crows' feet in order to feel at ease. Some consider dark-glasses to be cool, which says a lot about our society today. When we feel covering up the part of us that sets us apart from others is considered aesthetically pleasing, then it could be said that we are losing our grip on the important things in life. It is also said that cool is but one letter away from fool, so think about that.

Before I started up the V8 motor, I sent off a text to Laura. 'Just leaving x'.

Now in our late thirties, we had been married for a vast number of years, but I still felt I was an incredibly lucky guy. I am not always struck with random acts of romance, but today something told me that I should do it. A few streets away, I pulled in next to an independent florist, and made a fuss about choosing a small selection of flowers I knew not the name of, only how beautiful they complimented each other – the same way I felt a family photograph of Laura, Bobbi and I did.

I sang along to The Stones on the radio whilst drumming my hands on the steering wheel to 'Honky Tonk Woman' and grinning like the village idiot. I lived only another ten minutes away in a new housing estate on the edge of town. It was on what was once a green belt of land that for fifty years the council had promised would not be built on, but finally the financial pull had been too much, and a handful of years ago a dozen houses, including our Victorian copy was erected. Money and over population once again trumping the environment. Everyone cares about the environment just as long as they don't have to change their ways.

I opened the front door and called to Laura, part of me knowing we had a couple of hours before I had to pick Bobbi up from school.

"Laura? I'm home!" I called, slightly in a sing-song fashion but got no answer. Of late she had not been herself, so perhaps this was the real reason for this off-of-the-cuff romantic gesture. It's funny how you do things to later realise that there was probably a reason for it.

The place seemed empty without Bobbi running around, the sound of her giggles bouncing off of the walls.

I walked up the stairs, clutching the flowers to my chest, my heart rattling my ribcage the way it had done a lifetime ago when we had first met. Anticipation meets anxiety.

There was almost an eerie feeling as I walked slowly down the landing towards our bedroom. I peaked in the door and saw her laid under the covers, a single crisp white sheet over her lithe naked body. She smiled coyly, then grinned at the flowers.

"For me?" she said in a half whisper. I nodded and pointed to her, "For me?" I whispered back. She nodded and drew back the sheet.

Liberated from my clothes, she welcomed me warmly as we were entwined as one. This tender act seemed even more poignant than normal, and at one point she smiled as a tear escaped onto the pillow below. This wasn't just love but something I couldn't believe others had ever experienced so intensely. The clichés are there, dog-eared, creased and stained, but this doesn't make them any less truthful. A Polaroid of passion, this was a teenage fantasy that I never thought would come true.

Between the love of my wife and the love of my daughter, I had no room for anyone else.

Afterwards as silence fell upon us, Laura closed her eyes and drifted off to sleep. Her breathing rhythmic and deep, she was an angel sweetly off somewhere else. I left her peacefully recharging her batteries, as I went downstairs and put on a pot of coffee.

The doorbell rang.

I did up my jeans, and slipped on a T-shirt. I opened the door to expect to see the postman with a parcel for me to sign. He or she certainly didn't need to see any of my naked body. They weren't paid enough.

It wasn't the postman. It was Mel. She stood there as a picture of sweet innocence, like a dessert that turns up when you're full but you just want to take a bite.

"Tom?" she said in a way that she almost sounded like she required me to confirm this for her.

"Mel. Hi, I… Are you okay?" I glanced behind me out of habit, then back at the attractive lady at my door.

Ignoring my question, she said, "Is everything alright, Tom?" I paused, which made her look all the more concerned. If this was her way of coming on to me then it was certainly one of the more unorthodox methods and not one most people would choose.

When I didn't respond, she added, "Can I come in?"

I took a step back, looked up the stairs, and then ushered her into the lounge. My head was spinning, and a kick-drum had replaced my heart. What was I doing? Nothing good could ever come from this situation.

"Look, Tom," she touched my arm, which made me freeze. "Things have been difficult. I know that, but I am here if you need someone to talk to."

We both sat down. Mel on the side of the sofa – Laura's side – and me perched in my chair looking at her, not knowing what to say. I was unclear of her intentions; or perhaps deep down I knew.

The air became thick with tension, and a wave of vertigo had me suddenly grabbing for the arm of the chair. Her lips moved in slow motion, and the tip of her tongue came to rest in the corner of her mouth, possibly in suggestion.

"Sorry?" I said, realising I had missed what she had just said to me. The words floated over my head, never making it anywhere near my ears. Above her, a picture of a smiling family looked over our illicit liaison.

"I didn't know whether I should've come here." She glanced down at hands that trembled, wringing with nerves, maybe a little adrenaline pulsing around her body.

"It was very thoughtful of you," I said, glancing up out of the lounge door again. I hoped Laura would remain upstairs.

She ran her hand through her hair, then in a quick movement she must've felt vulnerable and tugged a few strands back down by way of a shield, or a comfort blanket of hair follicles. "It's just. You never talk about it."

"I… I'm not sure I, er," I got up. "Excuse me for a minute." I strode up the stairs, wondering just what I was getting into. I walked towards our bedroom, suddenly filled with dread and guilt.

Laura sat in her trousers and bra, buttoning up her shirt. "And what, may I ask, is she doing here?" She spoke. At first, I thought she was cross, but then I saw the side of her mouth twitch. I think she was amused because she saw me squirm.

"Laura, I… I, I don't know," I stammered, placing a hand gently on the side of her neck and sliding down her shoulder and clavicle.

She looked up suddenly with cold eyes. "Yes, you do, Tom. She wants you."

"I… I… but…" I started but was unsure just what to say. "Go to her," she said shooing me away. She lay back on the bed, suddenly purring with seduction. "I'll be here when she's gone."

I walked away, backwards at first, and then spun around and headed back downstairs.

Mel was sat more comfortably now, and I swear that she had undone one of the buttons on her blouse. Her breasts appeared to be straining the buttons more than I'd remembered. I looked away, my eye catching the clock, and without even being completely conscious of it, I knew there was still plenty of time before I picked Bobbi up from school.

"Everything okay?" Mel asked again. This was a recurring obsession for her. It was also odd that she didn't think it strange to come to the house of a married man, lounge out on his sofa like some truck-stop whore, and then ask him whether everything was okay. For a second I wondered whether this was some elaborate set up that Laura had coordinated to gauge my reaction or perhaps some sort of spicy threesome that she'd orchestrated. Deep down I knew I was far off the mark.

"I heard voices," she said. "Is someone else here?" I felt my heart sink. To lie would do me no good with either woman, but was this really a time for the truth?

"Look, I was talking to Laura. I'm fine, so... you know, maybe you should go."

Mel looked up and swallowed hard. "Tom," she said shuffling forward and grabbing my hand. "You know that Laura is dead, don't you?"

If it wasn't for the look in Mel's eyes then I might've thought she was joking, except people don't joke about that sort of thing, do they?

Something was happening in my stomach. A deep hole was appearing. My throat was contracting, and I was gulping for air.

"No," I muttered barely audible and with no conviction. "I was upstairs talking to her. We were... she just..." Mel was up on her feet and pulling me close to her before I could fully understand. My legs were weak twigs, and my body a dead weight unable to stay upright. Colours flashed like a kaleidoscope being twisted by a child. I couldn't make out any of the shapes, my world was unrecognisable, but the feeling of her body against mine was familiar.

"Laura!" I shouted, my eyes filling up. "Come down here!" I ran to the stairs calling her name, now a child without control of his emotions. I stomped up the stairs and towards the bedroom.

"Laura!" I screamed.

Laura was laid on the bed, her skin pale and her eyes lifeless. Slowly her head turned towards me, her dark eyes looked almost hollow. "My poor Tom," she muttered resignedly, blood trickling from the corners of her mouth.

"What… when…" Laura raised her finger to her lips. "Let me go, Tom. Later on we can be together."

I sat on the bed with my back to her, my head heavy in my hands and my heart broken into a thousand pieces.

My heart suddenly leaped, and my eyes shot open, and I turned back to her fading body, "Bobbi?! What about Bobbi?" I said desperately. Laura's body finally faded away with her shaking her head. "Nooooo!" I screamed loudly. My throat raw as I punched the wardrobe door. The door swung open to reveal its empty contents. All of Laura's clothes were gone, cleared out long ago.

I heard Mel before I saw her. She grabbed me again, but I shook her off, pushed past and went into Bobbi's room. Her things were there, but it was too clean and tidy. Everything looked about right, so maybe she was still here.

The calendar was two years out of date, and the month was wrong by a couple, but kids aren't as bothered about time as adults, are they?

"She's gone too, Tom," Mel said quietly. "That was the month and year it happened."

"This cannot be happening!" I said holding the top of my head with both hands, worried that it might explode with over sensory reaction. "But, I saw them, I have… I know…"

"It's not unusual to be like this, Tom. Our mind is a very clever thing, and yours has been protecting you for over two years."

"No, look, wait." I fumbled in my pocket for my mobile. "I took this last week when we were at the park. Look, it…" but of course the picture showed the park with no one else in it. Another showed an empty seat on a park bench. Three pictures in fact, and a small footbridge that I had taken five shots of because of the wind, then the sun in Laura's eyes, and Bobbi distracted – but these were now five very similar photographs of a bridge. Nothing more.

It was hard to imagine that I could ever feel a worse feeling in my life. This had to be rock bottom, and I could see no way out.

"You took a few months off after it happened. Do you remember that?" I shook my head.

I walked slowly down the stairs. Mel followed close behind. I almost wished she would push me. Let me tumble down headfirst and land like a discarded action figure, limbs bent in positions only yoga masters could successfully execute.

I was now in a thick daze, completely numb. I walked out of the back door and down to the bottom of the garden. Ignoring the dead flowers, and the unkempt grass neglected years ago, I strode forth; the magnetic pull was too much.

"You had feelings for me, Tom. That is why we were here."

I turned to her, and suddenly anger was firing through me, burning in my veins. "I should have been with them!" I spat. "It was all your fault!"

The door to the shed was locked. The key remained close to me at all times, hung around my neck. I pulled it out.

"And this helps, does it?" She said loudly. "You blame me, because I knew how to treat you better than your wife!"

"You were nothing more than a whore!" I spat and swung open the door. I pushed my way to the back of the large brick building, past memories idly sat or leaned against other unwanted items that once had a use before my life changed forever. The large hemp sack lay hidden behind old boxes. I was no longer put off by the smell or the flies, as I reached over and pulled off the top of the sack.

The dried-bloodied face of Mel stared back at me. Lifeless and shocked.

I looked behind me, but Mel had now disappeared too.

I rubbed my hand through my hair and felt the tears in my eyes. Flashes of memories switched back and forth between naked passion with Mel in a hotel room and my family in a car surprising me with a visit at work... stolen kisses and quick breaths as a lorry ploughs into the side of the car splitting it in two, killing my wife and daughter instantly. The agony and the ecstasy.

I stumble back to the house sobbing uncontrollably, remembering the doctors shaking their heads at me, the policemen offering me useless condolences, and the months of therapy and mind-numbing drugs.

Tears drip as I reach into the back of the cupboard in the kitchen retrieving the bottle of the illegal tablets. I had promised a number of people that it would never come to this, but I always knew that reality would bite and I would have no choice.

I swig down a glass of ice-cold water to speed up the effects rushing the tablets into my bloodstream. I sit down and look at the two pictures in front of me. I rip up the photograph of Mel in anger; the pieces rain down onto the floor like confetti.

My vision begins to blur as I look at the picture of my wife and child. My thumb caresses their faces without feeling. My breathing is suddenly strained, and my head is swimming. The darkness engulfs me.

"See you both soon…" I barely manage, and like a moth in a jar I give up the fight for oxygen and accept my fate.

The end.

I've run out of all honesty's and white-lie, blind-drunk truths,
Another evening of verbal attacks and physical abuse,
Metaphorically hair-pulling at a crossroad I can't decide,
Should I stay or should I go and hide a smile worn as a disguise?
My being is all battered, our poisoned love's now rotten,
Head shaking at poor decision making. *What's happiness?* I've forgotten.

Start the meeting for peace talks, drink the coffee, and eat the cake,
Questions go unanswered and all discussions turn to hate,
The lift of my life keeps sinking me lower into hell,
My slapped cheek represents the licking flames; the final bell,
I've conceded more than two falls and it's a relief when I'm knocked out,
My voice was never meant to be heard, there's no reason to scream and shout.

The truth is, the cold nickel lollipop will make my pain stop,
I'm so lonely but at the bottom have no further floor to drop

Finger poised, chin up, "Think of God," is what
they said,
Yeah, well fuck him with every piece of my brains
soon shot from inside my head.

Kiss, kiss,
Bang, bang ,

Trigger pulled,
I'm dead.

The I-Scream Van

The I-Scream van was previously unpublished. It
was written in 2018 for an anthology that
eventually never happened.

Part one:
A week ago

The sound startled me. I snapped my neck to the side as I heard the rustling in the dry leaves followed by scurrying scared small feet.

I was crouched down low behind a bush, its branches tickling my cheek with the breeze. My torch was off, and only the light of the moon shone to reveal the empty road ahead.

It was nearly three am. I was alone and scared. Part of me was excited at the prospect of what I might see. I felt a pang of guilt that my parents would think that I was sound asleep, all of us looking past the fact that a fourteen-year-old boy still held a bear closely at night for comfort. It was a habit, what could I say?

The tales of it were all over the school. We had talked about nothing else over the past few weeks.

The story of the Ice Cream Van that drove around the villages. I had thought that it was bollocks to start with, but so many people had seen it that it had to be true. I'd been caught by my parents searching for details on the internet. At first my dad had laughed it off, telling me his own stories from his youth about the ghostly school caretaker that roamed the corridors at night. Dad was of a time before computers. Probably before television and cars too, so he was not a reliable source in my book.

Later on, though, when he saw that I was in chat rooms talking about it and then watching various videos on YouTube, he got all cross and talked about kiddie-fiddlers and stuff and us kids being hooked in on it. He tried to make out that we were just naïve. We'd follow anyone offering to show us their puppies.

So now this made the stories even more exciting. I'm not sure any of us really believed in it, but then why would I be here having snuck out of my house and cycled all of this way if deep down I didn't on some level believe it to be true.

And then I heard it.

The eerie sound of a lullaby played at a slowed down tempo making what should be a jolly tune now seem haunting.

It got louder and the twin beams of the headlights cut through the night like blades. I could then see the huge clown face lit-up on the top of the van. It smiled but without happiness. It looked like it was a predator that had just seen me.

My heart beat hard and fast in my chest. I felt like I had just discovered for the first time that Santa Claus was real, and instead of him being a nice guy, he wanted to take my soul in return for presents.

The fear tickled up my back like icy-fingers, and I felt myself step back into the bush. I was crouching down and pulling my hood up over my head. I was the ostrich burying my head.

And then the van stopped.

"What will it be, lad?" an overly jovial voice sang out.

I held my legs and kept my face down praying that the van would pull away. I knew that he was talking to me, but for a second I hoped that I was not alone.

"Don't be shy! We have everything here! Scream, scream, scream!"

Everything went quiet. I slowly looked up.

"Ah-ha!" The face was there almost touching mine. His pointy features sneered at me. Spots of blood splattered his white outfit.

"Peek-a-boo! I see you!" There was a brilliant white light as something smashed against my skull. I felt my body being dragged towards the van.

The music started up again.

I never got to tell anyone about what I had seen, because I never got to live another day.

The stories were true. I know now because they are what killed me.

He is what killed me.

Part two:
Tonight

We were all excited. Filled up to the brim with hysteria and it spilled over into silliness. Fifteen-year-old boys all drunk on fizzy-pop. We had talked about nothing but tonight all day at school. Davo and Tez had just cycled over to my house for the night. My dad was away with work and he often left me alone on a Friday night. I didn't mind, I was fifteen and had full access to the internet. What more did I want?

"So, what d'you reckon?" Davo said grabbing Tez by the head and rubbing his knuckles over the fat kid's buzz cut.

"Cut it out!" he almost squealed, pulling his head free and glaring at my skinny mate. They could go on like that for hours.

"That kid was taken by him, wasn't he?" I spoke. We were convinced that the recent story of the young lad missing in the night could be attributed to that of the ever-growing story surrounding a mysterious Ice Cream Van. One that roamed around taking innocent children into the night never to be seen again. It sounded pretty ridiculous. Of course it did. That's how all the great stories started, didn't they?

"Tomkins reckons it's some sort of Slenderman hoax!" Davo said.

"For one thing, Slenderman is not a hoax," Tez said. "He's real. You've seen the videos, yeah?" It was true. We had indeed seen videos, but as to how true they were well, who knew? Davo was right though, this local legend called I-Scream suddenly appeared about a year ago. Someone knew someone else who had seen the van in the early hours of the morning. As these tales grew legs and the stories were embellished, they began to scuttle around from group to group until there was no one at school who hadn't seen, or known someone who'd seen, I-Scream.

"It's bullshit!" I said, and I didn't mind calling it either.

"Shut up, Duke," Tez said, slightly hurt. He loved the story. He couldn't get enough of it, in fact.

"Calm down, Tez. Don't go piddling in your pants!" Davo laughed at that. "I'm not saying I-Scream is bullshit, I'm saying that all of these people who claim to have witnessed him are full of bullshit. He would've been caught by now, right?"

"S'pose," Tez conceded.

We huddled around my PC again. I fired up the chat room for us to watch and read the bullshit that everyone else was talking about. All of these people claimed to have knowledge of who I-Scream was and why he was doing what he was doing.

Tez glanced at his mobile. It was some shitty pay-as-you-go thing. We laughed at him and said that it was his baby monitor, but Davo and I didn't have one, so I guess our teasing was born from jealousy.

"You waiting for your mum to come and sing you a lullaby?" Davo said in a patronising voice and grinned.

Tez shook his head after a roll of the eyes. "Look, if my mum knows I'm here and there is no parental supervision, then I am gonna be grounded!"

"*Parental supervision!*" Davo and I said in silly high-voices.

"Take the piss all you want, but Duke's dad is never around, and Davo, your dad is always drunk!"

"He speaks the truth, this young man!" Davo said in some mock generic American accent that could've been from any state. It was true. His dad had lost his job six months ago from some factory near town, and since then Davo reckoned he'd not spent a day sober. It didn't seem like a good way to get another job. His mum had left not long after Euro '96, though it was unclear as to whether England's loss was a factor in her decision.

"Look," Tez carried on. "I said that I was over Davo's house, which didn't go down well. What if they check up on us?"

"Why say you were over mine?" Davo said and gently punched him on the arm. "Numb-nut! You should've said that you were over here, and that Duke's dad was around."

I nodded. That made better sense, but Tez and common-sense parted company many moons ago. You had to love the simple lad.

"Yeah, I suppose that would've been better," he conceded.

We rolled our eyes at him. Some days he truly was thick as shit.

"So, Duke, you gonna tell us your news or what?" Tez said.

"What? That he's gay?" Davo grinned.

"Good one." I rolled my eyes at the standard homophobic put down.

"Let him talk," Tez said. He was smiling in anticipation. He was a believer. He loved the mystery surrounding I-Scream more than anyone. He still thought that the tooth-fairy existed and that America had put a man on the moon.

"I found something," I said, instantly grabbing the attention of my two mates.

"Really?" Davo added. He liked to feign machismo, but really, he was dying to find out more.

"I cracked a code to where I-Scream comes from."

Tez and Davo sat up and inched in a little closer ready for a revelation.

Davo then said sceptically, "How? And why would *I-Scream* put his whereabouts online?"

"He wants to get caught, doesn't he, Duke?" Tez said through a mixture of excitement and fear.

"Bullshit!" Davo said.

"Well go home if you want," I said to him.

"Go on, then," Davo said. "I'm listening."

"Look," I began. "I admit, I don't know whether it's real or not, but last night when I was about to turn off my tablet, I received a message." I fumbled with the laptop to bring up the messenger app that was also on my tablet.

I brought up the message and showed them that there was a link next to the words *Find me*.

"So someone sent you this link?" Davo said. "Some random person?"

"Yep, so it seems."

"Where d'you think it came from, Duke?" Tez asked.

"I reckon it was from one of the chat rooms. You know how you sign up and sometimes add details like your contacts. I have it linked to my messenger. So maybe it's someone else trying to find him or…"

"I-Scream *himself!*" Tez exclaimed.

"I call bullshit again!" Davo said. "The guy takes children in the middle of the night but sends you a message so you can find him?"

"Why not?" I said.

"Because it's dumb!" Davo sneered. "It's probably attached some virus to your tablet! And your balls'll fall off!"

I raised my eyebrows. "Really? You send a location to teenagers. The very type that you have been looking to take so they will come to you? Doesn't sound dumb to me!"

"So, where is he then Einstein?" Davo said still not buying it.

"The bus stop out on Church Road," I said.

"That's where he is?" Tez said in a small voice.

I shook my head. "No, that's where it starts."

"What?"

"The treasure hunt."

"I thought you said you knew his location?"

"I know where to start. All we have to do is follow the clues."

"Are you sure it's not someone winding you up?"

"What have we got to lose, huh?"

"Let's do it then," Davo said, clapping his hands together. He was finally on board. He loved a bit of excitement. "Tez, you in?"

Tez nodded, but slowly and could barely smile he was so nervous. "I guess." I could tell he was contemplating whether or not to ring his mum and ask her.

So that was that.

*

It was dark, and there was a summer breeze whipping around us as we walked up towards the bus stop. A silence had fallen among us, not one of us wanting to admit to the others their nerves were on edge.

"Go on then, Tez. Go and see if it's in there," Davo said, ever the bully trying to coax the fat lad into the dark bricked bus stop. I was going to say something, but sometimes knowing it deflected similar comments aimed at me was enough for me to hold my tongue.

We all walked in, tentatively flashing our torches into the corners. Creatures ran off, and cobwebs glistened.

"There!" Davo said, and I reached up to find a small envelope. He pulled it free and slowly opened it up.

We gathered around behind him and looked at the typed line:

1000 steps down the road by feet,
Why not take a rest under the seat!

"What?" Davo said. "Which way?" Which was a fair comment. If you had your back to the bus stop it would be the opposite direction to that of facing it.

"Right," I said trying to add some logic. "The hill goes down. I bet it's the seat next to the green."

Tez was nodding. "Yeah, that's probably about a thousand steps, right?" We nodded.

So off we went down the road. The stream was next to us and the moonlight shone off of it, sparkling through the gentle ripples. Nobody was around. It was as if the world knew something was happening outside, and nobody else wanted a part of it.

Davo ran towards the bench, ignoring the steps, and felt underneath. He grinned as he came up with another envelope.

"Look!" he said, triumphantly flapping it around in the air, just in case we'd suddenly lost the use of our eyes.

"Don't just wave it around! Open it up you knobhead!" I said grinning.

"What does it say?"

Behind the pub you'll find your fate,
get down and look beneath the gate!

The *Pig In The Blanket* pub was the other side of the village. It was a popular hang-out for teenagers of drinking age and also of those coming up to it, as we tried to bum a sip or two of alcohol. Last summer, Davo took half a pint that someone had left in the beer garden, and we'd sat in the hedgerow passing it back and forth like we were kings. Looking back, it all seemed a little embarrassing, but that's what growing up in a village will do to you.

We found ourselves jogging at one point, the adrenaline providing us with the energy required. It was exciting.

"D'you think he's trying to tire us out?" Tez said, puffing. His cheeks were now ruddy. "I mean, we now seem to be going all over the village?"

"That's your chubby frame that's tiring you out! Some of us are built like runners!" He sprinted off before stopping abruptly outside the pub. He glanced over as if being watched and tried to look innocent. Something that was extremely hard for him.

It had closed an hour or so ago, but there was still the sound of the odd local. Drunken laughter and clanging glasses soundtracked the night, along with some Lynyrd Skynyrd that was playing on the jukebox. In the country the rules are different when it comes to leaving times. Some locals stay until morning if they want.

We snuck around the back, through the car park, and toward the adjacent field. The gate sat there unaware of its importance tonight.

"Go on then, Duke," Tez said. So reluctantly, off I went striding out towards it. I bent down and slid my hand tentatively along the bottom.

And there it was. A small envelope.

I pulled it free and again pulled out the note.

You are so close, and nearly there to win,
take a right, and then go left, and look at the
shed within!

"Let's go!" Davo said jogging again.

"Slow down, Davo!" Tez called. Thankfully he did.

We went right at the road as the houses got sparse. More trees lined each side and made it seem darker. Only by the light of the moon did we now walk on deeper into the night.

The place was filled with memories. Lots and lots of them. We'd cycled out here, and once when it was thick with snow, we'd pulled a homemade toboggan along the icy road as we made our way to the huge hill three fields over. It had been cold and tiring but probably the most fun I'd ever had.

We took the left and followed the road down towards the first house.

We had all begun to slow down, and no one wanted to speak first and say the obvious. We approached the only house that was there. It did indeed have a shed.

"Duke?" Tez said.

"Yes, Tez," I replied.

"Is this right?" he said nervously.

"What's going on, mate?" Davo added.

"This appears to be the place," I said. "It's led us here, come on." They followed me to the large shed, which was more of a barn, and I opened the door and walked inside.

"This is your house, Duke," Tez said.

"And your shed." Davo mumbled, noticeably scared.

I nodded and walked further in. They still followed. "Weird isn't it," I grinned.

The shed door slammed behind us. Tez and Davo jumped at the noise and looked at each other, puzzled.

"Is this a joke?" Davo said.

And then the music started like a slow lullaby. We all looked at the large tarpaulin-covered-vehicle.

"Duke?" Tez said almost sobbing. "What's going on?"

The tarpaulin slowly came back on its own to reveal the wonder and beauty of my dad's unique ice cream van.

Then a loud laugh amplified out, and the blood drained from my friends' faces.

"What'll it be, boys!" The sneering voice of my father rang out as he appeared to spring back and forth, skipping from foot to foot. Hyped up as he was by youngsters.

I edged to the side and sat down. I loved my father, and this was my gift to him.

Jim Ody

They never found the bodies of Tez and Davo. Or any of the other bodies of the missing children past and present, for that matter…

Dad told me this morning we're moving. A fresh new start in a new area.

Fresh new kids.

I can't wait.

Let the fun begin.

The End

Teaching
Tom

'Teaching Tom' was first published in 2018 by Crazy Ink. The anthology was called A.W.O.L. A.I.

Chapter 1

Tom's luck had finally run out. He knew it would eventually, but that still didn't make it any easier to take. She was older and way too good for him. She was the sort of woman that was strong and feisty on the outside but had an evil twinkle of mischief that fuelled male fantasies.

Although they were both single it had felt like an affair. It was too good to be permanent, so when the end came it was inevitable but still no easier to take.

Tom stood next to the large coffee machine and wondered why he drank the stuff. It tasted like shit. But it was free. I think he had his answer.

He thought about punching a hole in the huge picture depicting a gorgeous model with a wide satisfied smile. *There is no way she was drinking this crap,* he thought.

"Good weekend?" A loud booming voice shouted at him with all the warmth of Greenland. He was a tall and looming person who loved himself a lot more than anyone else did. His blue suit was pinstriped, and there was a sudden waft of expensive cologne. But a dickhead was still a dickhead no matter how good he smelt.

"Not particularly," Tom replied knowing the guy couldn't care less about his reply. It was typical management, not worth their salt, and said purely for the eavesdroppers around them.

"Good, good," Mr Management responded. He really couldn't give a flying-flapjack.

Toni had been the name of Tom's desire and the cause of his sudden depression. He hadn't seen it coming which made the words more painful. In hindsight the fact he'd gone down on her for twenty minutes but only received a half-hearted hand job should've told him something was wrong.

Fifteen years his senior, Toni was upper-management in another company, and since leaving her husband, had left a trail of broken men in her wake. He'd paid no attention to the stories he'd heard. She was the one who had come on to him a few months back, and he'd felt like the luckiest man alive when she slowly removed her power suit. His jaw was fully open when she stood in her expensive underwear and proceeded to tell him exactly what she needed him to do to her. Ever the domineering manager.

Now that was all over.

He compromised and kicked the coffee machine instead. A couple of people looked up accusingly but shrugged in agreement. Nobody liked the coffee from the machine. The thing should be launched out of the office window!

He headed to his desk with as much enthusiasm as a man walking the green mile to their execution. In fact, probably less so.

"Hard night last night was it, Tom?" Ed said winking at him as Tom threw his bag under the desk and placed his laptop on the docking station.

Tom sighed, frustrated with the knowledge that even if he stood up and called a team meeting and tried to tell them the God's-honest-truth it would go something like this:

Tom: Look guys I just wanted to say that Toni and I are...

Trish, the young teenager: You're getting married, aren't you!

Tom: No, I...

Doreen, the older, and self-appointed wise member of the team: Marriage is a waste of time and money. Look at what happened to my Pete?

Ed, my best mate: Shit, I hate speeches! The best man speech has to be funny, doesn't it?

Tom: Look, Ed, I really wouldn't...

Ed: Am I not your best man?

Tom: I'm not saying that.

Rex, the joker of the team: Why? Am I the best man? Or are you about to propose to me!

Trish: Are you going to propose to Rex? (she seems confused.)

Tom: I'm not proposing to Rex.

Rex: I'd treat you well!

Tom: I'm sure you would.

John, my boss: So what was the point of this meeting again?

Tom: I was just trying to…

Doreen: Marriage, apparently. I just don't understand youngsters these days.

Trish: That's 'cause you're old!

John: Trish!

Trish with a nervous giggle: Just joking.

Doreen, under her breath: Little tramp! Toni's no spring-chicken either!

Tom: Look, can't you just listen for a second?

Ed: When's the date? You don't want it in the winter. And then there's the stag-do to organise!

Trish: Can I go?

Rex: Only if you have a sex change!

Trish: That's sexist! I want to go!

Ed: You could be the stripper.

Doreen: Slapper more like!

Trish: What did you say?

John: Tom, congrats and all that, but when's the date, as we all need to get back to work?

Tom: There's no bloody wedding!

Rex: So is this just a big joke then?

Tom: No, I…

Doreen: All men think that marriage is a joke.

Ed: Not true. It's the only night of guaranteed sex!

Doreen: And with that the prosecution rests, your honour.

Trish: So am I going on the stag-do?

Rex: Not if there's no wedding, you blonde bimbo.

Ed: You can still strip for us though, Trish.

Doreen: That sounds like an HR disciplinary, Ed.

Ed: She wouldn't look that bad.

Doreen, shaking her head: Men!

Rex: Why don't you just ask her out, Ed?

Trish giggles, and Ed looks up to heaven.

Tom: So anyway, what I wanted to say…

Doreen: Just say it, Thomas, I've a lot to do before I go on holiday.

Ed: Where are you going now? I thought you only just went away.

Doreen: Well, Jeff and I wanted to go to…

Tom: HELLO!

Doreen: Youngsters are so rude! I was just speaking to Edward.

Ed: Don't call me that. I feel like I'm in trouble.

John: Look, Tom, tell us what's on your mind later would you, you've been babbling on for too long. (He claps his hands.) Back to work everyone!

So that is why Tom just replied, "Something like that," instead.

"You old dog, Tom!" Ed beamed thinking that Tom had been working his way through the dog-eared pages of the karma sutra all weekend (he'd tried once and pulled a muscle in his hamstring thanks to the one on page seven).

The morning was a strain. Tom had sent seven unanswered text messages to Toni, sent her messages on a couple of her social media pages, and one long email. It was pathetic. But deep down he felt like he'd fumbled his last pair of tits.

His work output was on the lower side of zero. People were beginning to mumble about him.

At lunch time, and in defeat he pulled out a battered copy of the latest Joe R Lansdale novel to read. He held open the book, but the turn of the century nostalgia failed to hold his interest when his mind was fixated on a woman who never wanted to see him again. She hadn't said that, but instead had suggested they just be friends. He didn't want her as a friend unless it came with benefits. Even an uninterested hand job was better than nothing.

Tom did another round of checking his phone just in case he'd missed something in the last five minutes. He'd not. Although she'd not responded either to tell him to stop texting or threatening him with harassment. That was a good sign

Like any true male friend Ed didn't pick up on any of this and instead decided that it was as good a time as ever to ask Tom another of his stupid questions that not only could've waited until later but could've waited for another lifetime.

He was very serious when he suddenly asked, "Do you think that Bert & Ernie were gay? You know, from Sesame Street."

Tom put his book down and wondered how many other Bert & Ernies he knew. Ed looked to be wrestling with this incredibly seriously. In a world comprised of natural disasters, famines in third world countries, oppression of race and gender, finance cuts and job losses, and poverty on our own doorstep, Ed never ceased to amaze Tom with questions on topics the media have foolishly and quite flippantly managed to miss.

"What do you mean *were*? They're not dead, *are they*?" Tom replied deadpan and with only a hint of sarcasm.

Ed was now frowning and looking more perplexed than Tom had ever seen him. This appeared to have come as a bit of a shock to him and put the cat amongst the proverbial pigeons, so to speak.

"Shit, I never even thought of that?" he stopped for a beat and then rolled his eyes smiling. "Nah, we would've read about it in the papers, *wouldn't we*? They were huge in the 80s."

Tom was suddenly wide-eyed. The guy was serious. "They're also puppets, Ed. You know, hand up their ass, controlled by strings, puppets."

Ed stopped and stared at Tom, clearly gauging whether he was joking, and then the penny dropped. "Er, yeah, I know. So what d'ya reckon?"

Tom sighed, sometimes it was easier to just play along. "I think that Bert married one of those puppets that doesn't have a name but always ends up in the singing bits…"

"The chorus girl puppets."

"Yeah, the chorus girl puppets. They have a son called Bellamy who is studying law at Harvard. Now, Ernie, he fell on hard times. Partied a little too much with Big Bird at *The Crazy Horse* in Vegas before he was caught sniffing nose candy with Oscar. He was last seen in a Kentucky trailer park after 5 years in rehab."

Ed puffed out his cheeks and shook his head. "Shame. Where'd you hear that?"

"Wikipedia." Tom picked up his book again and wondered what sort of a childhood Ed had endured.

Within seconds, Ed was drumming his fingers on the desk, a sure fire sign that although he accepted the answer Tom had provided there was something that just wasn't sitting right with him.

"But were they gay?" He asked.

"I don't think we have a right to ask that sort of private question, mate," Tom replied without even looking up. "Personally, I'd say they were brothers with an undetermined sexual preference."

Ed made a clicking sound with his tongue. "Apart from being yellow, with black tufty hair, they didn't much look alike."

"That don't matter," Tom said, turning over a page. "You know Kelly in accounts? Her sister is twice the size of her and has ginger hair. They're sisters. Mark my words, those boys were related."

"If you're sure?"

"What? That Kelly has ginger hair?"

"No, about Bert and Ernie."

"One-hundred percent." And they left it at that.

Tom wasn't looking forward to leaving work. His car was filled up with everything he owned, having been kicked out of Toni's that morning. He was going to live in his grandpa's house. It was said to be haunted, but that aside it still smelt of puke and piss. As far as he knew ghosts were unable to produce the smell of bodily fluids.

He had gone from flat-screen TVs, huge waterbeds and wetrooms, to a huge old TV a stained mattress on the floor and a room wet with urine. I guess progress was working backwards on this one.

Chapter 2

Tom pulled his car up to the kerb outside his grandpa's house. He turned off the engine and sat there looking up at it. It was a small but foreboding property that had seen better days. Set back from the road and hidden behind a couple of trees, it was the ugly house of the street. Unkempt and unloved.

He almost thought about going to Ed's house, but the thought of paper-thin walls and enduring the sound of another man masturbating was enough for him to take a deep breath and give this a go.

His car was full of his crap. All piled up in a haphazard way. He'd not wanted to wait around, carefully arranging everything whilst she was there at the window with a scowl on her face and proving she didn't want to *just be friends*.

He grabbed his rucksack and glanced at both sides of the street as he went up to the front porch. He took the steps tentatively, not knowing whether they would take his weight, and then looked back at his car.

As he turned and forced the key into the lock, he heard a noise from next door. He turned quickly and saw a head duck down. He didn't fancy playing a game of hide and seek so ignored them and walked into the house. Knowing his luck there would be a houseful of kids next-door.

Tom stood and stared thinking it was like going back in time. A pang of guilt washed over him as he remembered just how long it had been since he was last here. His grandfather had been sitting in the corner attached to some breathing apparatus, and he had perched on the edge of the sofa, uncomfortable both physically and mentally. The conversation had exhausted quickly, and he'd tried hard not to keep staring at the clock. He knew then he never wanted to be in the position of his grandfather, with people reluctantly coming to see him without a thing to say. *How awful*, he thought. *To be such a burden.*

He glanced at the same clock now. The white face was tinged a mild yellow with time, but the mahogany case was still just as dark.

He ran his hand through his wavy hair, a usual pose of thought, and took a deep breath. He glanced from the house and back to where his car was and without further ado started the many trips back and forth to unload his car.

Having dumped it all in the lounge, he rang for a pizza (almost by habit giving Toni's address) and set about trying to integrate his things with his grandfather's.

An hour later he was eating the takeaway and watching TV on his phone having given up on his grandfather's large useless box that no longer even got the basic channels. He'd already purchased a new one online – along with a host of things…

He was still caught in the past. Aside from the house, he constantly thought about Toni. He knew the minute he had pressed *SEND* on the text message that it was a desperate act. Any person who has been dumped will know texting a pleading message turns very quickly from a good idea into a sad and embarrassing mistake – all too often after the *SEND* button has been pressed.

After ten minutes he knew his message had been ignored. He scrolled to his pictures and looked at the many taken of Toni. He smiled in defeat and stopped scrolling when he found a couple of naked pictures. They had been taken as a bit of fun. It had been her idea. And now looking at them it felt voyeuristic and wrong. His thumb hovered over the *DELETE* button, but he couldn't do it. Not just yet.

Tom chucked his phone to the side got up and walked up the stairs. The house was as he remembered, although some of the bedrooms he'd never been in, and the smell of urine was stronger now. His grandma had died years before, and so he'd had no reason to wander around. His visits had been confined to the living room.

Tom had already gutted out the bedroom of his grandfather's things and had added as much of his own as he could. He'd emptied a can of body spray in the hope of masking the dank smell, and he'd added books and music to the shelves. It was going to take some transition to make it feel like his own. But his parents had given up the opportunity of a sale to let him stay there, although they were still negotiating rent. His mouth was tight-lipped over his mum's feelings towards his relationship with Toni, although his dad just grinned and winked. He got it.

Tom opened the spare bedroom and walked in instantly overwhelmed by the junk. The beginnings of hoarding. Things were piled up at the sides to give the impression of more space. The sides were more of a health hazard instead.

Suddenly he saw the head and jumped!

He walked forward and realized that it was some sort of dummy. The face had incredibly detailed features. It was sitting in a chair and appeared to be staring at him.

A large, life-like doll of a beautiful woman. Tom had to wonder what the hell it was doing there. He was no expert, but it looked like it might be one of those fancy sex dolls with latex skin and moving parts.

What the hell was his grandfather doing with this doll? He was hooked up to oxygen tanks for as long as Tom could remember so to have the desire and the ability to go at it with a sex doll was both unbelievable and disturbing in equal parts. Then he started to think about the logistics of it, and what was under the clothes. It looked so real. This wasn't one of those generic inflatables with a constant puzzled look on her face, as seen on stag-do's up and down the country, nor was it a flimsy thing being tossed around by sports fans at stadiums for a laugh. No, this looked like a half-baked, gorgeous woman.

Tom chewed his lip and reached out to touch her face. Just to see what she felt like.

Her eyes suddenly came to life, and she moved into a new position.

He leapt out of his skin as she said, "And just what do you think you're doing?" Her voice was sweet but the words spoken in a very matter-of-fact way.

"I, er… Sorry." Tom whipped his hand away like he'd just received an electric shock.

"Do you paw at all women?" she started. "Or just the ones that look like they're not going to fight back?"

"You can speak?"

"I can indeed." She suddenly moved and stood up. Her movements were fluid but there was a slight robotic jerk once in a while.

"Oh, my dear Christ!" Tom said. He didn't know where this came from, he was pretty sure he'd never said this line before in his life. She was about his height wearing a vest and a denim skirt. Her hair and skin looked so real.

"Take a deep breath. You look like you're going to faint." She added.

Tom gulped in and finally managed to speak. "I wasn't expecting you to speak!"

"No, I should think not. My name is Phoebe by the way. I'm a Sexbot 2000 android." She held out her hand slightly stiffly but no less remarkably.

"Sexbot?" Tom stammered.

She shook her head. "Don't you be getting any fanciful ideas, young man. I've upgraded myself, and if you so much as look at me in a funny way, then I will have no choice but to go into safety mode!"

This was a lot to take in. "Safety mode?"

There was a crackle sound and a blue light flickered out.

"An electric shock," she said, void of emotion.

"What?"

"Similar to a taser and equally incapacitating, too."

Tom held up his hands. "Okay, point taken."

They stood there in an awkward stand-off, although Tom couldn't help but think it was just him that felt this way. This was an android devoid of feelings.

"So," he began. "Did you know my grandfather?"

Phoebe nodded. "I did. A real gentleman, he was. He helped me to upgrade."

"Really?"

"Really. Do you think I could do it by myself? I'm an android."

Tom chuckled. "I guess not."

Phoebe didn't laugh, or smile. It wasn't easy to gauge her feelings.

"You don't think I could?" She said seriously.

Tom's smile dropped from his face. "Sorry?" He was apologizing again.

"You think I'm an incapable female who needs the help of a man?"

Tom glanced to where he had seen the bolt of electricity earlier and shook his head. "No, it's not that… I mean…" Words escaped him but he really didn't want to be shocked.

A smile appeared on her face. Slow and calculated. It looked quite sinister.

"I'm joking with you," she said and winked.

Tom let out his breath again. This was hard work. Even Ed was easier to gauge then her.

"Okay."

She clapped her hands together, or rather made the motion. There was hardly a sound. I guess this was something that needed to be worked on.

"I've not seen you here before."

"Oh, I'm Tom… I…"

"You find it strange talking to me?"

"A little," he conceded.

She shook her head. "Don't. It's perfectly fine."

Again, he took a breath. It was hard enough talking to women at the best of times let alone talking to a gorgeous android.

"My girlfriend dumped me," he started.

"Here we go…" she rolled her eyes. "I'll sit back down if you don't mind. I have a feeling this might take a while." He went on to tell her all about Toni.

An hour later and an android or not, Phoebe was almost asleep.

"You need to find yourself another woman, and quick!" Phoebe said, opening her eyes.

"Were you asleep?" Tom asked, surprised.

"I'm an android, of course not!"

"You had your eyes closed."

"Yes, I was beginning to get a little bored hearing about this perfect woman. Tell me, Romeo, if she's so great then how come she dumped you?"

Tom shrugged. "I dunno?"

"You *dunno?*" She mimicked his voice perfectly. "Hmmm. We've got some work to do!"

"Work?"

"Tom, my lad, we are going to find you another woman!"

"Really!?"

"Well, we'll try. I haven't got much to work with, if I'm completely honest."

"Thanks."

Tom tried to suppress a yawn but ended up pulling that strange expression you do when trying to achieve this and still ended up open-mouthed.

"I need to sleep," he said not really knowing how you stopped a conversation with an android.

"Then go. We'll talk tomorrow."

Tom nodded, began to walk away and then stopped. "D'you need anything?"

With a slight delay Phoebe rolled her eyes. "I'm an android, so no, I wouldn't've thought so, would you?"

"Of course," he replied, feeling stupid, and left the room without looking back. Tomorrow was another day.

Chapter 3

Tom found sleep hard to come by. He'd read a few chapters of a book called *Lost Connections* by a less-than-average author, but this only had his mind working overtime thinking about what he'd do if he were in the protagonist's position. Add to this he was in an unfamiliar house, in a strange bed. Or rather a dirty mattress. The last time he'd been in this position on a dirty mattress was as an eighteen-year-old. Plain but game Shelly Tropman had been jigging naked on top of him. Her large breasts had been slapping together like skinheads headbutting each other in a fight. As he remembered it, things had ended rather more quickly than they'd begun. She'd winked at him, slapped him playfully on the cheek, and made a huge effort to move her rotund frame off him, breaking wind in the process. He liked to think things had got decidedly better since then.

But that wasn't the real reason he was staring at the ceiling. He couldn't get the vision of the beautiful android out of his mind. It wasn't just what she looked like but more that he knew she was in the next room. It felt weird. It was a little like having a new girlfriend, but of course this one was not real. It messed with his head.

At some point he drifted off to sleep but not before deciding to take the next day off work. Fuck that place and their shit coffee.

When Tom opened his eyes the next morning his first thought was about the android. He had sinister visions of her standing at the end of his mattress naked and licking her lips, her hand reaching over to grab his nether regions, but the grip getting tighter and tighter until the pleasure turned to excruciating pain.

But thankfully he was alone.

Tom decided not to go in to see her this morning. It was almost like playing hard to get, but in his mind he didn't want her to think he was excited to see her again.

Life sure deals you a strange hand of cards. A week ago, he was having energetic sex with an attractive older woman, and now he was having sordid thoughts about a sex doll. Tom was suddenly shocked how his life had done a one-eighty, and arguably had gone downhill quite rapidly. *What next? Animals? The dead? It didn't bear thinking about*, he thought worriedly.

Then he had a sudden revelation. What if this was just stress? His body reacting to work and rejection?

Tom checked his phone to see if Toni had responded. She hadn't.

No matter his feelings towards Phoebe if Toni was to call him up and ask him to go over to her house, he would be there in a shot.

We are so fickle, Tom mused and made the ill-voice-call to work. It didn't matter what his illness was, Tom always found himself speaking a bit like Clint Eastwood in a hoarse whisper. He'd found himself doing this even when requesting a holiday. It was habit.

It was well after rush hour when he made it out of the house and into his car. The roads were clear of fancy corporate vehicles bullying their way over lanes without indicating their intentions. It seemed the more money you got paid, the more of a dickhead you became.

Tom walked into the large building though the revolving door and remembered the time he'd gone around in it three times. She'd grinned at him but still pecked him on the cheek when receiving the flowers. Later, over cocktails, she'd laughed at how stupid he was and then gone down on him in a movie theatre. That was a true-life Hallmark moment.

"Tom?" Shelly, the receptionist said in a way that suggested that news travels fast. She was plain in a geeky way but had a lovely smile. She lacked self-confidence but possessed a large round butt that her trim top half didn't match up to. She was a game of people that someone had switched over. Somewhere was a round-faced woman with huge bosoms but a skinny butt and spindly legs.

"Hey Shelly! She in?" Tom asked like this was just a little thing. He suddenly realized that whilst he was not high up on anyone's ladder, he still had the ability to act like a dickhead.

"I… No… She's…" Shelly was clearly feeling like she was stuck in the middle.

"Oh, right. Okay," Tom could see the signals. "This was a mistake."

"You'll find someone else," Shelly called after him, standing and looking concerned. Her hands were on her ample hips.

He held his hand up as a *goodbye,* but humiliation stopped him from turning around.

What a fucking day.

Tom sat in his car, turned on the engine, and wondered whether to just go home. It was over between them, no question about it.

And then if things couldn't get any worse, the song from *Titanic* started up on the radio.

"Fuck off, Celine!" He shouted loud enough for a passer-by to look over. "What!" he shouted, and suddenly scared, they looked away and walked more quickly.

He turned off the radio in defiance and wheel-spun out of the car park.

Again, he knew that it was over. He also knew that in months to come he would be looking back at his actions and thinking what a complete idiot he was being. But without sounding bad, he felt like his favourite toy had just been snatched away from him. The toy he had humped regularly. Amongst other things.

He knew she was older than he. The odds were heavily stacked against the longevity of their relationship – that was a given. He thought they had something special.

No, who was he kidding. He wanted to see her naked again. He wanted that feeling that she was no longer a fantasy but someone who was strong and domineering but who would suddenly switch to being submissive when the feeling took her. This was not the sort of woman that crossed your path more than once in a lifetime. Or if she did, then it was on the arm of another man, and you were left to fantasize and make crude jealous comments with your mates. He almost choked up at the thought of her doing those things with another man. Those hands, lips, hips and tits. She was an 80s hair metal band anthem. The girl that all misogynist males could desire to be with over big guitar riffs and spandex pants. She was his cherry pie, sticky and sweet that his love gun was cocked and loaded for. A lot better than the inane innuendo lyrics from a thousand songs would suggest. He laughed to himself. Like he'd ever say the words *love gun* out loud and in the presence of a female! He was embarrassed to even think it.

He drove to a shopping outlet and spent almost half of his month's wages on items for the house, most notably picking up a smart-television he'd paid for online the day before. He also bought what appeared to be cleaning products. It was a new concept to him, but the house was a state and needed to be cleaned up. No classy woman wanted to come back to a house that smelt like a care-home.

With a coffee comfortably sitting in the cupholder of his car, he was beginning to feel a little better about things. He almost whistled but stopped himself. That would be a little foolhardy, he figured. Whistling was an action kept for a more special occasion.

At his house, his priorities were evident as he set up the television set first. The cleaning could wait now that his sex life had taken an unexpected hiatus.

He sat down and endured a program about a couple moving house. The experts were finding houses within their budget. He sighed; that was not something he'd be doing for a while. But he'd shape this house up and make it more homely.

He caught himself glancing up. He had to go and see her. The magnetic pull was real.

It felt wrong that he was suddenly so excited at seeing Phoebe. She wasn't even real. He felt like some saddo from a television documentary you would laugh at. The type that still lived with their parents or after some huge trauma had left them living alone and indulging in a fetish they thought to be completely sane.

"Hi Phoebe," he said almost as a question whilst walking through the door. She was sitting back in the chair the way she had been the day before. He suddenly felt stupid. Maybe he'd dreamt it.

He stood over her wondering whether he should attempt to touch her again. That seemed to bring her to life last time.

"Phoebe?" He said in a polite voice. Phoebe remained still.

Tom got up feeling stupid. He was confused. Had he made it all up yesterday? Had the stress of the break up got to him to the point that he was now imagining conversations with androids designed for carnal pleasure?

He went into his room and lay down on the bed. *What if I'm beginning to go crazy*, he thought? *Had I loved her?* He honestly couldn't say.

At some point he drifted off to sleep. A movement in the next room woke him.

His eyes flew open. Was there someone there in the next room? Was Phoebe real after all?

He glanced at the bedside clock as he tentatively got up. The digital display told him that it was now a little after six in the evening.

He walked into the room.

"Hello, Tom," her soft voice said as he walked in.

"I, er, came in earlier," he said thinking that somehow, she knew.

She nodded. "I know. My batteries were low, so I was unable to generate enough energy to communicate with you.

"Okay," he said, but there was something that he just didn't quite believe about her. Why were her batteries low? What had she been doing all day?

"So, have you got anything to tell me?" she started.

He instantly felt guilty. "I didn't touch you," he said quickly. "I mean, I looked at you, but I didn't do anything honestly!"

There was a beat that worried Tom, but then she said, "No, not with me! I'm talking about earlier today. Anything?"

It was a weird feeling that washed over Tom. First relief and then he knew what she meant.

"Oh, yeah. You mean Toni?"

Phoebe nodded. "Yes. What were you thinking, Tom?" She looked genuinely disappointed with him.

He took a deep breath. Once again, he had walked away today knowing it was over, but now it hit home exactly how it looked from someone else's point of view. It had been a desperate act.

"I just wanted to know…"

"And now you do," she finished. "You have to move on. Find someone else. These pathetic moves are quite embarrassing."

"I know," he said.

"Surely you must've met other nice girls today?"

He shrugged. "I guess."

"Tomorrow, go out and find someone. Just walk up and smile at her. Ask her how she is, but don't push things."

Tom frowned. "What d'you mean?"

"I mean don't go looking like a lost puppy. Have some respect for yourself. Ask her how she is. Compliment her, and get out of there. Leave her wishing you'd asked her more."

"That works?" Tom said in disbelief. It seemed a strange tactic to flirt with someone and then disappear. Surely, even if they were interested then they would just shrug and forget about you?

"Of course. You will come off as confident and carefree. She will think that if she is to have a chance then she needs to find you. Then the next day you swing by all casual and not make it too obvious that you remember her."

Tom wiped his forehead. "I pretend like I don't know her? So, I act rude?"

Phoebe laughed. "You really don't have a clue, do you? How did you come to meet Toni?"

"We got drunk, and I almost passed out. I'm not sure what I said, but the next thing I knew I was laid down and she was bouncing up and down on me."

"What? Jumping on you like a trampoline?"

Tom stopped suddenly almost losing his train of thought. "*What?* No. We were like having sex."

"Like having sex? What does that mean? Was she laughing and looking disappointed?"

"*What?* Are you…"

Phoebe's face formed a grin. "Yes, I'm messing with you! You can spare me any more of your x-rated memories. I get the picture."

"Oh, okay. It's not always easy to tell."

Phoebe grinned again. It appeared that she was having fun messing with him.

"Tomorrow," she repeated. "you need to man up and do these things, right?"

Tom nodded. He did feel a new sense of confidence, but experience told him it would disappear the minute an attractive woman came within his personal space.

"I guess so." He turned and started to walk out of the room.

"You're a tiger!" she called after him.

Tom popped his head back into the room.

"Sorry? What was that?"

"I said, you're a tiger!"

"Er, okay… night."

"See ya!"

He walked out, and it didn't even occur to him that Phoebe's whole attitude and personality had changed. She'd gone from being slightly stuck up to calling him a tiger, but for him he was still full of the disappointment of not having Toni in his life anymore.

Luckily, he had Netflix to turn to when he wanted to just watch something to take him away from his life. So that's exactly what he did.

Chapter 4

Tom had found it easier to get to sleep the night before. He'd watched a movie about a stormy relationship between a man and a woman, and whilst he'd felt for both, it had given him pause for thought. Love and life was never a smooth path to follow.

Again, he almost went to see Phoebe, but he knew it was still a weird thing to do. She was an android after all, even if she interacted with him better than any woman he'd ever known. Even Toni.

He ate some toast and eventually rang work again. It was Wednesday, and Ed had made up some bullshit about him being lovesick. He didn't bother arguing. They'd had a brief text exchange which, of course, was normal for males, and Ed had drawn his own conclusions. *Whatever*, Tom thought. He'd always been the sort of person to battle illness and soldier on so as not to have time off work. Surely, he had banked up enough respect to warrant a day off. He still had a hole in his heart and a deep sickness within. Then through contemplation he realized that Ed was probably right. He was lovesick after all.

He poured another cup of coffee and took it out onto the porch. He sat down and sipped it as the world rolled by at various paces and was relieved he wasn't drinking the crap from the coffee machine at work.

He wasn't ready to go out yet, so he got his book and began to read it. He enjoyed the book a little more but was periodically distracted by his new surroundings.

He heard the door open and close from his neighbour's house. He glanced up but the large bush between the houses hid their identity. He looked back down and started to read from the beginning of the paragraph once more.

It was mid-morning and the sun was beginning to burn off the clouds making it a pleasant day. Tom closed his book and realized that someone was doing something in the street. This was nice, but he now felt ready to take on the world.

Whatever that meant.

He checked he had his keys, locked up the house and went to his car.

He glanced to where the noise was coming from. A woman in her late teens was washing her car. She had her jet-black hair pulled back and was wearing denim dungarees shorts. She had the normal build of a woman who didn't care about dieting. She had a youthful look, but there was something that made Tom think she was not as young as first appeared.

Tom took a deep breath and thought he should introduce himself. It was the neighbourly thing to do after all.

"Hey," he said. "You live next door?"

She turned off the hose and looked at her feet and nodded.

"Yes," is all she said.

"You... you have a nice smile," he tried, but she glanced up awkwardly, and then back at her house.

"So, okay. Nice to meet you," he said and walked off to his car.

When he drove by, she was hidden down behind the other side.

That hadn't gone well, he thought.

He wasn't sure where he should be going. This thought hit him as he was driving aimlessly through traffic. He headed into town. He began to wonder whether Phoebe knew what she was going on about. He was putting a lot of trust into an android that he'd found in a spare room only a couple of days ago.

Perhaps surfing the net on some dating site might be a better option, he thought.

The hustle and bustle of people made you stop and realize just how insignificant you are in a world filled by billions of people.

Tom wandered around, stopping only briefly to get a coffee in a take-away cup. He could've sat down but then he would feel like even more of a loner. He'd look like his date had stood him up and he was pretending not to care.

He glanced around at shops that proclaimed many things to try and part him with his cash. Most of them were false claims. There really wasn't much he needed here to fulfil his life other than a shop of attractive single ladies. Even that would probably still have Beyoncé prancing around, shaking her hips and doing that weird royal-wave thing with her hand. Tom knew he didn't have the cash or the balls to put a ring on it. Any ring.

He walked into one of the large department stores and without thinking found himself near the perfumes and make up. There were always attractive ladies there, even if they had a porcelain complexion and wrinkleless smiles due to an inch of concealer and the odd injection of Botox.

A blonde lady aged somewhere between eighteen and thirty-eight smiled at him. The assistants were all made up in such a universal way it was hard to determine any sort of age-range. A couple of them might've been mother and daughter for all he knew, and he'd still struggle to tell which was which.

Tom took a slight intake of breath. Finding his balls, he puffed out his chest with confidence.

"How are you?" He said to her. She looked awkwardly back at him, like he'd just asked her for her bra size.

"I'm very well. Are you here for a present for a lady-friend?" She asked, clearly trying to establish some sort of level. Specifically meaning she was interested in conversational participation only if it was to end with a transaction. She was certainly not interested in any sort of relationship.

"Ah, no. I'm single." The words tumbled out and instantly felt like a confession.

"Okay.For yourself then, maybe?"

Tom shuffled his feet like perhaps his bladder was full as he realized what she meant by this.

"Ah, no. Just… er, looking for someone else." He turned and headed off aware that she was staring, and he was going red. He'd probably never venture back into the apartment store ever again.

There was no getting round it. Tom knew he had to have more of a plan. This was not working. *Why the hell was dating so damn hard?* he thought.

He headed over to a high-end clothes shop. It wasn't the sort of place he normally ventured into. He had money, but not *that* sort of money.

"Hello, sir, and how are you today?" the well-groomed man asked him the minute he set foot into the place. Tom felt he was already being judged. Perhaps the guy was already looking at his clothes and wondering why he would bother with such cheap fabrics. And then Tom thought his own physique was then in question, and without thinking too hard, stood up a little straighter and pulled in his stomach ever so slightly. He wasn't sure why he was doing that.

"I'm good thanks," Tom smiled and idly touched a shirt, glancing at the price which was the same as he had spent in total the day before. But to turn and walk out of the shop now would be an admission that he didn't belong there. He would be accepting the huge gulf of class that lay between them. This was a new Tom. This guy didn't know him.

There was usually a couple of attractive ladies working there, but today they were nowhere to be seen. He'd spied one earlier, but she'd ducked out the back just as he'd walked into the shop. He had to play for time.

Tom took a deep breath and walked purposefully over to a rack of jackets.

"Are these new in?" he asked the guy, who suddenly smiled thinking that he might have a sale from this poor sap.

"They are indeed, sir. If I may?" he said walking over, sizing Tom up and holding open the perfect tweed casual jacket. Tom carried on with the charade and had to admit that it felt incredibly good. He was suddenly tempted to buy it. But a glance at the price tag told him that the cost was the same as his first car.

"How does that feel?" the guy asked genuinely pleased with what he saw.

"Like a new sexual partner," Tom replied with a wink and instantly regretted it. The guy grinned back and suddenly Tom thought perhaps he had given him the wrong signals.

"I'll have to bring my lady in here and see it. You know women. They like to have the final decision!"

The guy looked a little crestfallen, although Tom was unsure whether this was the lack of sale rather than the mention of a woman. He had jumped to too many conclusions here. That was the story of his life!

Tom quickly thanked the guy and walked out as casually as a man can in that situation.

He walked along past a fountain that had been designed to add a focal point to an area where you would not expect to have one. It was an interesting concept, but clearly someone thought it a good idea as these had popped up in most shopping centres throughout the country. This one sat behind two large escalators like a poorly designed waterslide. It was slightly hidden and calling to be a hangout to the local hoodlums.

Tom tried just smiling at random ladies, but they either didn't notice him, or within that briefest of moments it was unclear what they thought. For all he knew they might have thought he had wind or was a little simple.

Finally, he joined a queue for some Chinese food. It was what he was suddenly craving. The woman in front had a short pixie-haircut and glanced around at him. She was probably considered plain by some, but there was something that attracted him to her.

"Must be good," she said with a smile. "To have a queue this long!"

Tom nodded. "Yeah, I'd say so." He agreed, then when she smiled again and turned away, he thought the moment had gone.

He bit the bullet and tried again. "Is this your first time… for this?" he said unconvincingly. It tumbled out like a screwed-up note with 'Chat-up Line' as a heading.

She looked him up and down quickly. "It sure is. Should I be excited?"

"Uh, yeah…" but no matter how hard he tried, he stumbled over his tongue. The metaphoric note held no answer. Every word in his head was either lame or crude. She looked like she was sophisticated but slumming it. That was what Toni had done with him. That's exactly what he wanted again.

The interest in him visibly disappeared as she nodded and turned back. He then glanced at her hand and noticed that she wore a huge ring on it. It didn't always matter, but he had some core values.

She didn't try to interact with him again save for a glance and flash of acknowledgement as a goodbye gesture as she turned back from the vendor and walked out of his life.

Tom got his food and headed back to the car. He could've found a place to sit and eat, but he was feeling dejected and rejected and just wanted to go home.

It wasn't a long drive back, and the smell of the chicken in the soya sauce was making his mouth water as he pulled up outside his grandfather's house.

He couldn't help but notice that his neighbour's car looked good. She'd done a really great job at cleaning it. It was a VW Beetle, and although it was over fifteen years old, she clearly looked after it.

Then he saw the sponge left on the pavement. Momentarily he stared at it. He was that sponge, left alone and forgotten. He glanced at his food, ran up and popped it on the seat on his porch, and went back to the forgotten item. He picked it up and glanced up at the house next door.

He walked up to the porch and noted it was in a lot better condition than his own – or rather his grandfather's. He rang the bell and waited.

There was the sound of locks and chains, sliding and clicking before the door opened.

"Can I help you?" a small voice from within said.

Tom held up the sponge. "Yours, I believe!"

She opened the door farther and took the sponge from him with a quick, "Thanks".

"You're wel…" the door was closed "…come."

He shook his head with a smile and went back to his house to devour the food. It was now lukewarm but tasted just as good nevertheless.

Chapter 5

Tom wanted to speak with Phoebe again. This wasn't working. Everything felt too forced. If there was one thing he did know it was you had to be natural. You cannot be someone you're not.

Not for the first time he felt stupid walking up the stairs. He stopped at the top to think again about what he was doing. Was he about to have an argument – no, a discussion – with an android? The thing had been programmed by someone. It was only as good as the programmer, right? Why was he getting all hot under the collar about it? He really didn't know.

Or maybe he did but didn't want to admit it.

He walked into the bedroom.

"Um, Phoebe?" he said as he stepped into the room.

She was gone.

He panicked, whipping his neck around the room to check amongst the piled-up junk. Where was she?

"Tom," she said from behind the door making him jump.

"Shit! You scared me!"

"I'm sorry."

"What were you doing behind the door?"

She slowly threw her hands up in the air which was interesting. It was a human mannerism but executed in a false way.

"I was stretching my legs."

"Okay."

Phoebe walked by in that slightly stiffened way, and then turned on her heels. It was close to being human until the turn at the end, which brought home to Tom what she really was.

"So, what's up?" she said, sensing that he had something to say.

"I dunno about all of this," he started. He went to say something else but stopped. He was struggling to form the words from the number of things firing around in his brain.

"What? Moping around because a woman broke your heart?" she said very matter-of-factly, although Tom had become used to this now.

"No, searching for another one."

"You want to remain single for a while?"

He shook his head. "No, that's not what I'm saying…"

"Then what *are* you saying? Come on, spit it out!"

Tom paused again. He liked to think about things too much. Conversations at speed were not his thing.

"I'm just not good at meeting new women."

"Interesting," she said.

He waited for an answer, but when nothing further followed, he felt obliged to speak.

"What's interesting?"

"You didn't speak to any women today?"

He paused, thinking about how bad things had gone.

"Yeah, I did. The first woman thought I was weird, the second one disappeared before I even spoke, and the next one also thought I was strange."

"See, you never told me that you could read women's minds! If I'd have known that then it would've made this whole thing easier! You *can* read women's minds then?"

"What? No, of course not!"

"And yet you seem to know exactly what they are thinking, *right?*"

Tom was getting confused. She always seemed to be leading him into a trap.

"No, not for sure. It's just the way they look at me."

"You idiot!" Phoebe said loudly.

"What?"

"You heard me. You do not have a clue what they are thinking, right?"

He shrugged. "I guess."

"You guess exactly!" She then pulled her hands together, looked down and glanced up quickly at him.

"What am I thinking now?"

"I don't know!"

"If a woman looked at you like this and then looked away, what would you think?"

Tom threw his hands up. He wasn't in the mood for stupid pointless games. This wasn't getting any easier. It was like a shit version of charades.

"I'd assume she thought I was an idiot!"

"Quite possibly, but it means she's interested but a little shy to say anything."

"Really?"

"Really."

Phoebe stopped as if to calm herself down and Tom shifted his weight from one leg to the other.

"Who was the first female you spoke to today?" she asked.

Tom thought back. "A really pretty girl in the department store in town."

There was a pause before Phoebe carried on. "O-kay. And what did you say?"

"I asked her how she was, but then she started asking me about makeup."

Phoebe shook her head.

"She was the first girl you spoke to today? You walked to your car and drove into town, and she was the first person you spoke to?"

Tom nodded, and then suddenly like he'd had an epiphany said, "Hold on, no, I saw the girl next door."

"Really? There's a girl next door? And what is she like?"

Tom shrugged. "I dunno. I knocked on her door later as she left a sponge outside, but she just snatched it and slammed the door before I could even finish my sentence!"

"Sponge?"

"Yeah, a yellow sponge. She'd been washing her car when I saw her this morning and had clearly left it outside."

"Really?" Tom was beginning to think that Phoebe said this when she was thinking. Although why an android would need time to think was beyond him. Didn't they have algorithms that worked off his words to give an answer in a millionth of a second?

"Do you think it was deliberate?" Phoebe asked.

"What? Her shutting the door in my face?"

"No, you bloody idiot! Leaving the sponge outside!"

Tom shrugged, "I dunno." He sighed and then added, "I think I might go out and meet Ed tonight to see what his thoughts are on things."

"Ah, okay. You need to speak to another alpha male to reinforce your own idiotic ideas, huh?" She suddenly seemed angry and frustrated.

"I guess."

"And where might this important discussion take place?"

Tom saw she was messing with him again and let slip a smile.

"There's a bar at the end of the road. We'll meet there for a couple."

"Okay. Well good luck, Romeo. Go knock 'em dead!"

Tom chuckled, "I'll try!" and left the room. He wasn't entirely sure how well that had gone.

When he got downstairs, he sent Ed a text asking him to meet later at the bar. As usual Ed needed no excuses to firstly answer the text, and secondly to go out to a bar. Alcohol with the chance of drunken female interaction was enough to get him out of the house and leave his laptop idle for a few hours.

They arranged to meet just after seven.

Tom flicked over the channels on his new TV and stopped on some program about a guy eating as much as he could. In a world where people are starving, we entertain ourselves watching someone's act of gluttony.

Tom thought he'd spent long enough dwelling on things and now needed to go back to work and get into the swing of life again. But not before going out and getting drunk.

Blind drunk.

Chapter 6

E d was already sat nursing a bottle of something on special when he looked up and beamed at Tom. He was as happy with his own company as he was with others. He integrated well into whatever environment he found himself in, and Tom often wished that he, too, could do the same.

"Here he is, the man with the broken heart!" He said louder than needed. Elton John was singing about candles in the wind on the jukebox, but there were half a dozen booths full of laughing groups of twenty-somethings.

"Thanks for the introduction!" Tom replied.

Ed handed him another bottle that he produced as if by magic and patted him on the back.

"I'm okay, mate."

"Of course, you are," he winked. "Of course, you are."

Tom pulled up a stool at the bar and sat.

"Whoa, there, cowboy," the woman behind the bar said. "If you're going to sit there with a sour face all night, then you'd better move to one of those booths over there. The one in the corner is free."

Ed grinned. "Yeah, we better move. He is likely to look that way all night!"

She smiled and winked at them, "You boys had better get some drink down you and go find yourselves some women… or men, whatever your flavour."

"Most definitely women," Ed nodded. "Play your cards right, and you might get lucky yourself!"

She rolled her eyes. "My old man will roll in from work at three am. If he so much as flicks my titty, I will cut off his balls!"

Tom and Ed shared a glance that silently said it was time to move. "Right you are!" Ed said, slapping his hands on the bar and nodding over to the seats in the corner. Tom followed him over to the booth.

When they got there, Ed asked again, "Seriously, how's things?"

Tom shrugged. He wanted to mention Phoebe, but he knew that his friend would think he had finally lost it. Not to mention he'd take the piss.

"Getting there, mate. You know how these things go. I'm getting there."

"It'll get better," Ed said, taking a long pull of his lager.

Tom grinned. "Time heals and plenty more fish etcetera etcetera…"

"You know it's true, right?"

Tom rested his head and looked up at the dark ceiling. It was black in colour, but on closer inspection was greasy and grimy and more than likely hadn't been wiped over since Thatcher was in power. On top of one of the ceiling fans a black bra could be made out caught up there on the fittings. Tom could only imagine what shenanigans had gone on for that to be there.

"I went to see her yesterday," Tom admitted.

"And how did that go?" Ed said equally off somewhere else but able to add an unsympathetic tone.

"Badly. I turned up at her work, but the receptionist advised me not to bother. I felt like an idiot and left."

Ed nodded. "Probably for the best."

They talked about their jobs for a while. Ed talked about Trish and how Tom should give her a go, but clearly the intentions were far from noble, and there was nothing more awkward than a drunken fumble with a work colleague who you had to face the next day. Tom was not going to do that.

"Not a good idea," Tom said, draining his bottle.

"She has a great body though," Ed said as if this needed clarification.

"I think it takes more than that, Ed," Tom said motioning to the bar.

"Not for me!"

They grinned at each other, the alcohol helping them to act like the young men they were. Sometimes they needed to let their hair down and blow off steam.

An hour later and they were both a little worse for wear and their table was covered in half a dozen or so empty bottles.

At one point Tom swayed around tables to find the gents'. It was more of an effort than he was expecting it to be. He was careful not to knock into anyone and spill their drink. At least he was feeling better about things now.

He glanced at a table where a girl sat on her own. She half-smiled to him, but he really needed to pee.

When he came back, she was still on her own and clutching a phone. There was something familiar about her, but he wasn't sure from where. She looked like she wanted to say something and stood up. She was cute and shy-looking. She smoothed down the front of her dress and he instantly felt self-conscious.

He went to speak first but just then there was the sound of a bottle falling onto the floor, and a table full of girls cheered loudly. A stunning blonde girl with either incredibly long legs or a very short skirt tottered towards him to retrieve the bottle that had stopped at his feet.

He picked it up for her and handed it over doing his best not to notice that her breasts looked like they were trying to escape out of her dress.

"Thank you, handsome!" she said, grabbed his hand, and pulled him back with her to her friends. Submissively he followed, instantly forgetting about the other girl.

"Look what came with the bottle!" she said, and her friends whooped.

"You gonna dance for us?" a dark-haired girl asked with a wink. She looked Italian. She was equally attractive in that doll-like way that whilst they all had different coloured hair and dresses, they still looked like they had been designed from the same mould and shared at least half of the same DNA.

Tom shook his head and grabbed one of the many bottles of beer that was surrounding a huge fish bowl of mixed liquor.

"I can't dance," he said with honesty.

"That don't matter," a redhead piped up. She was the only one with a pale complexion, but her skin and makeup was still flawless.

"How about you all dance for me?" Tom said, and he couldn't believe the words had come out of his mouth, although it sounded awkward. The alcohol was turning him into someone else. This was how it had been with Toni.

"Let's do it, girls!" A brunette grinned, and suddenly they were twisting and gyrating around him. Tom started to move his hips slightly, but it was in a similar way that a father might dance at his daughter's wedding. If there was a comfort zone, then he couldn't even see it.

Then a couple of rugby-blokes came over and started to paw over the girls, and they lapped it up. The scene became even more embarrassing when they both managed to swoop in and begin kissing the redhead and the girl with the black hair. It didn't always matter about being a gentleman, sometimes it was the men who grabbed what they wanted and took control. He wasn't sure he could ever be like that.

The brunette was whooping, and the blonde could hardly focus on anything but had turned her back on him. She was rubbing her breasts with her hands in a slutty way that just made him feel sorry for her.

Tom looked at the empty booth where the lonely girl had once been and realized what a complete arse he was. It was a hugely sobering thought. Slowly he walked back over to Ed who was grinning from ear to ear.

"And what the fuck was going on there?" He said clutching two glasses of tequila. "I thought I was going to be drinking them both myself!"

Tom sat down, looked at his friend, and said, "I have no idea what happened there."

"Then let me fill you in, buddy. You were staring at that cute girl sitting on her own, then Little Miss Stripper jiggled over, and you went ga-ga. Somehow you end up with four hot chicks dancing around you, which instead of grabbing and taking ownership of, you let two meatheads barge in and almost impregnate them in front of your very eyes! Then like a whimpering dog, you slunk off with your tail between your legs and a hard-on for what might've been."

"I think you're exaggerating a little bit."

"Perhaps, but that was the general gist of the situation."

Tom sighed. He had to admit that even when he was inebriated, he still didn't have a clue when it came to women.

"Let's drink these and go," Tom said, and on the count of three that's what they did.

"I've just got to piss," Ed said nodding towards the toilets. He fished around in his pockets pulling out the contents.

"I'll settle up, too," he added and wandered off.

Tom shook his head as he saw that Ed had left his phone on the table. He wouldn't normally have forgotten it because it was the thing most attached to him these days.

Tom looked over at the girls again. They were laughing and having the time of their lives. The guys had swapped girls. Stripper was really going at it with one of them. It looked like his hand was up her skirt, and she was moving herself back and forth over it. He quickly looked away.

He sighed to himself with the realization that they were young and free. They knew the importance of enjoying themselves whilst they could. They were living their lives.

One of the other meatheads left but another skinnier guy slipped it seamlessly. He bumped fists with the meathead, but Tom was unsure whether this was because they knew each other, or were just acknowledging they were both likely to be having sex with at least one beautiful woman before the night was out. By the looks of things, they might not even leave the area to indulge in it either.

Ed's phone buzzed. Tom glanced at it and his stomach dropped.

A picture of Toni appeared in a pose of a palm trying to cover the camera. She was grinning, and whilst it wasn't clear, it did seem as though she was naked. The beginning of the text started with:

Hey babe!

Tom watched as Ed stood at the bar paying the tab. Maybe it was the alcohol, but he felt contemplative about the whole thing. This brought an end to his hopes of getting back together with her. He knew he should hate his mate, but how could he. Men are weak, and Ed had a history of being weak when it came to women.

Ed walked back over with a huge grin. Tom thought about slapping it off.

But he couldn't do that to a mate.

Tom handed him his phone.

"Text from Toni, mate," he said and got up. Ed's face was a picture of guilt.

"Shit, Tom," he started and then stopped, unsure where he was going with it.

"It's okay. I know it's over now… but Ed, *why didn't you just tell me?*"

"It happened last night. She popped round saying that you'd been looking for her. I didn't mean it to happen."

"Chill, mate," Tom said. "I'm hurt that you didn't tell me, but not about her. We'd broken up… I know what you were feeling."

Ed nodded, and they walked past the group of girls who glanced and smiled and just as quickly returned to what and who they were doing before.

Outside the air was cooler but still pleasant. They shook hands with some back patting, too, and said their goodbyes.

"See you in work tomorrow," Tom called as they began to walk in separate directions.

"You're going in?" Ed said turning round.

Tom shrugged. "I probably should."

"Take it off, mate, and come back next week. How about I come round tomorrow night?"

"What about Toni?"

"What about her? We're mates."

"Sounds good. Tomorrow it is. Fuck work!"

"Fuck work!" Ed shouted like a battle cry, pumping his fist in the air.

Tom was still grinning to himself as he got home. He probably shouldn't have been, but life was too short to worry about everything you've lost.

Momentarily, he thought about going in to see Phoebe. This had now become a reoccurring obsession. A dirty little secret. He knew this because he had already decided he wouldn't mention her to Ed.

He got into bed and pulled the covers up.

He heard a sound from the room next door, but he was fast asleep before he thought any more about it.

Chapter 7

Tom's head was pounding and as he tried to sit up in bed, he felt a searing pain in his temple. He was paying the price for not drinking water before going to bed; his body was starved of liquid and completely dehydrated.

He suddenly didn't feel so forgiving about Ed, but he knew this feeling would pass. *Was there no longer some sort of mate code?* he thought.

He decided to blow work off and have another day at home. He thought about going online and joining some dating sites, although the thought of trying to sell himself just made him feel more depressed. He was unable to locate even an ounce of self-esteem.

He grabbed his phone and saw he had a text message.

Sorry about the phone thing It said. It was from Ed.

It was hardly just a little thing. Ed had clearly had sex with his ex-girlfriend.

Tom replied: ***No worries, mate.***

Should he have made more of a thing about it the night before? He wondered. But he concluded that he didn't want to lose the friendship over Toni. He was welcome to her. It wouldn't last.

Tom showered, put some clothes on and got some coffee. He made toast and sat down with his laptop.

It was so hard to try and make yourself attractive to women without an air of desperation. Or even sounding boastful. Look at me and how good I am!

It was no use, he had to see her.

He walked up the stairs and felt his heart beat hard in his chest again. He was going to have to admit it to himself. Part of being able to move on from Toni had to do with Phoebe. He still felt strange about it.

He walked into the spare room, and almost felt guilty having not been there for a while.

She was sitting still and looking like there was no life in her at all. Technically there wasn't.

Tom was worried that after their words the day before she had somehow gone. Unprogrammed herself forever.

"He returns," she said with sarcasm.

"Hey, Phoebe," he began. "So, I went out again."

She turned her head and looked up at him. "And how did that turn out?"

He shrugged. "Okay, I guess," he replied.

She stood up. "And did you meet anyone?"

"I met Ed."

"I meant a woman."

Tom ran his hands through his hair. It was something he did when he wasn't sure what to say.

"I met women there but it's hard to find *the one*."

"Tom, sometimes it's not always obvious which *is* the one."

He nodded. It felt like she wasn't finished.

"You get distracted, did you know that?"

"What do you mean?"

She walked up close to him. They were standing as close as lovers. She placed a hand on his cheek. It felt both weird and pleasant at the same time.

With her other hand she punched him lightly between the legs! He recoiled instinctively.

"Hey, what the?!"

She grinned. "I was making a point. You didn't notice what the other hand was doing until it was too late."

"I try, but sometimes…" he had no idea what he was saying. As per the usual conversation between them, words just came out of his mouth.

"Last night, you say you met some women. Tell me about them."

Tom pulled a face; he knew how it would sound. He was prepared for a lecture, but this time he was watching out for being punched in the nuts. That wouldn't happen again.

"I was aware of a number of lovely ladies in the bar, but it was when I came back from the gents' that I saw the girl."

Phoebe was nodding. "And what did she look like?"

"She was blonde and a little over the top, like beautiful but high-maintenance pretty, and she wore…" he noticed that Phoebe was frowning and shaking her head. "*What?*"

"You men make me want to scream!" she said.

"Because I thought she was beautiful?"

"No, because you saw another girl before her, didn't you?"

Tom thought back and suddenly remembered the cute girl in the booth on her own.

"Oh, yeah, there was another girl, but she was clearly waiting for a date or something. Then the blonde grabbed me and took me back to her friends."

"So, what was wrong with the girl on her own?"

Tom wasn't sure why she was getting so cross with him. "Nothing," he said. "Like I said, I thought she was waiting for someone."

"Did she look like she was interested in you?"

"I guess," he conceded. He now understood the missed opportunity that she was talking about.

"You guess!" she paused, looked down, and then looked up. Tom had the feeling that if she had not been an android then she would've been crying. "And yet you were mesmerized with the girl whose breasts were falling out all over the place!" How did she know that? There's no way she could've gone there, could she?

"She grabbed me!"

"You could've said *no*, or just pulled away?"

"I've low self-esteem," Tom conceded, feeling even worse. "It felt good that someone like that wanted me."

Phoebe's eyes bore deeply into his. "And what about the other girl? How d'you think her self-esteem is right now?"

He shrugged again, knowing how much of a lame response it was.

"I was an idiot. I see that now," he muttered. "She was a beautiful girl. She looked so sweet, I didn't want to just go ploughing in, and then I was pulled away and the choice seemed easier. I feel really bad…"

Phoebe continued staring at him. He couldn't work out what was wrong.

"Phoebe? Do you need recharging again?"

But she remained silent and still.

And then the doorbell rang. This was the worst time to have a visitor.

Tom glanced again at Phoebe and walked out of the room closing the door behind him. He quickly went down the stairs and walked up to the door.

The bell went again.

He stood and stared at a silhouette on the other side of the door. It didn't look like Ed, or the postman for that matter.

He opened the door and tried to take it in.

"Hi…" he said automatically. There in front of him, dressed in a summer dress, was the cute girl from last night. She was looking down at the ground just as shyly as she had done then.

"Hi," she said but was unable to look up at him.

"You were there last night," he said.

"You preferred blondes, apparently," she said in a small voice.

He looked at her and then realised who she was.

"You're the girl from next door?" he said.

She nodded. "Yes, I am. And you're the idiot from next door." A little smile appeared.

"Do you want to come in?"

She looked up at him, her eyes darted from him to inside the house.

"Just a drink or something?" He added.

"Sure."

Tom felt confused. He felt excited but a bit weird at what was going on with Phoebe. The girl followed him in clutching a large bag.

"A coffee? Or tea?"

She looked up at him and managed another little smile. "A coffee would be nice."

He showed her the sofa, "Take a seat, I'll go and put the coffee machine on."

Tom went into the kitchen. How cool was it that he had an attractive girl living next door to him, even if she was shy! He filled up the machine with water and added the coffee. Something did feel strange though. Not quite right.

How come she was so shy yesterday but had the courage to come round today? How did she know he was in?

Before leaving the kitchen, he whipped out his phone and turned the camera on just to make sure he looked okay. There was no mirror in the kitchen, and he'd hate to think that he looked a state.

As he walked into the lounge, the girl was thrusting something back into her bag.

"Won't be a minute," he said slowly and then suddenly turned round.

Phoebe stood there grinning at him.

"Phoebe, I…"

"What?" she said, and he realised that the voice came in stereo. From Phoebe and from the girl sitting behind him.

"What is going on here?" he turned round and saw that the girl had a small microphone attached to an ear-piece.

"You?" He said, confused.

She nodded, again struggling to maintain eye contact. "I'm the real Phoebe."

"You've been her all along?" Tom had a strange sense of relief wash over him. He now knew that it wasn't the android he was so obsessed with but the real Phoebe.

She nodded and stood up. "I helped make her with your grandfather."

Tom had so many questions. "But how?"

She grinned and suddenly became animated, coming out of herself with pride.

"There is a sensor as you go through the bedroom door upstairs. I have enough time to get the headphones, mic and controller…"

"But your voices are different?"

"It just changes the pitch and tone of my voice a little higher. It's quite an easy program."

Tom walked up to her taking her in. When she was talking about Phoebe, she was full of confidence. Her black fringe swinging from side to side, and he saw beautiful green eyes.

"So, you've been giving me advice all this time?"

"That you've been ignoring."

"And what would you advise me to do now?"

She looked down at her feet almost going inside herself again, but then looked up and whispered, "Kiss me."

Tom leant in and did just that.

Their lips touched gently at first. Then they were holding each other tightly, and their kisses became deep.

They remained locked together as one for quite a while.

When they came up for air, Tom looked round. Phoebe was gone.

"Where is she? How were you able to…?"

The real Phoebe grinned and slowly pulled him back for another kiss, but not before saying, "Ah, yeah. About that. I wasn't entirely truthful about Phoebe."

"What do you mean?"

"Sometimes she has a mind of her own…"

"What?" Tom's mind was racing with thoughts. *She can't mean…*

His thoughts were smothered with more kisses. But a voice from upstairs shouted back down. "No, I don't!"

"See!" The real Phoebe winked. "But she does like you."

The End

The Summer is almost over. The high expectations born from Hollywood never happened; another lost opportunity passed me by, and I ended up in the town of regrets.

"You have to grab life," they say with a knowing and slightly condescending grin. I hope they choke on the memories.

But then my phone blows up with a ringtone I'd forgotten I'd set. Some rock tune I thought to be cool. In reality, it never rings so who gives a fuck, right? Until now. My pulse races, and I'm chewing down Ritalins like Tic-Tacs.

Too shy to glance in the mirror, I stutter a response into a handset I can barely grip. Her soft tones whisper words that glide down my body. The expectation wrestles with my self-consciousness. This could still be the summer of love. The nostalgic memory locked away for the mundane wet Mondays soon to flood my future.

I gulp down the details. My voice barely contains the excitement. One swallow could make a summer. The wind lifts my wings as I embrace all that I have to give. Welcome to paradise...

... But it's not enough. I pull the trigger anyway.

Boat Trip

This is a brand new story.

Chapter 1

The boats in the marina gently bobbed on the water. The air was warm in the New England town of Sandy Bay. The night descended, keeping families inside but acting as a silent alarm for teenagers and hellraisers to creep out of the woodwork to drink and be merry.

Friday night was typical for us to let off steam. The rigors of first jobs or further education took a lot out of a group of teens used to taking it easy. We spent years perfecting being slackers. This wasn't even in a negative way. We had managed our time and priorities with expertise so as we were able to squeeze in as much fun as possible.

Having a good time was what it was all about. We had years of responsibilities ahead of us, so now we were at an age where we could get away with the most. And we embraced that sentiment wholeheartedly.

I was late getting to the bar. I got held up. I'd had a few things on my mind, and my enthusiasm wasn't where it should've been. A momentary lapse. It happens like that sometimes.

Jim Ody

I walked through the doors of the bar, instantly hit by the sound of some rock band singing about their baby. The place was now busy with like-minded teens. Hysteria and hormones bounced off the walls with little care.

I saw my girlfriend laughing at the pool table at the far end. Some muscle was standing and flexing next to her. He fancied his chances. His floppy hair unleashed each time he took off his cap and ran his hands through it. He was doing all he could to mark her with his scent.

My girlfriend sported a black eye I'd given her when we'd argued the night before. I hadn't struck her, but the make-up sex was overenthusiastic, and she'd hit the bedpost with force. She'd made no attempt to hide it, instead using it to gain sympathy. That was Charlotte.

My cheek was bruised where her elbow hit me at the same time, but my skin didn't bruise easily. I was hurt more inside. That very act of pleasure and pain summed up our relationship in a nutshell.

Muscle was now making his move. Slipping his hands around Charlotte just before she bent to take a shot. She was one of the best pool players in Sandy Bay, so if this idiot thought he could improve her skills, then he was tripping. Of course, he had no intention of doing that. He was using it as an excuse to writhe up against her, basically dry-humping her.

She was lapping it up. Hardly tripping over herself to tell him to stop or to take a fuckin' hike.

I turned away and got a beer from the bar.

"Hey Jay? How's things?" Blue, the husky bar man, said to me. His eyes glanced over to the pool table and back.

"I can't complain," I responded but that was a lie. I could complain, and I could fucking fight, too.

He skidded the beer bottle along the bar towards me. "And the job?"

I shrugged. I sailed tourists out on a yacht so they could go diving. It was well-paid and kept me away from the locals. "It pays well."

"That's half the battle."

I pointed over to the pool table. "What's your stance on patrons having sex on the pool table?"

He sighed in a good-natured way, as he saw my girlfriend and muscles lock eyes and his hand linger a little too long on hers.

"I'd rather they didn't," he replied deadpan. "It's a devil to get out of the felt."

There was suddenly a vibrating from my phone that was deep in my pocket. It gave me a better feeling than I'd had in a few nights. Perhaps I should give out my number more often.

I rolled my eyes when I looked at the screen and wanted to pitch my phone against the other wall. The one with the jukebox kicking out hair-metal.

It was my boss.

"Hey kid," he began. I fucking hated being called that. Just because I was nineteen. I bet he wouldn't call muscles that.

"Yeah?" I said. I didn't even pretend to be happy to hear from him on a Friday night.

"Sorry to call you, but I'm up at the lodge with Missy, and I just got a call about the boathouse. Can you go and check it out for me? Just make sure everything is okay?"

"Sure," I said, but I wanted to tell him to go fuck himself. It was Friday night. It was his boathouse, but he was too busy busting his nut with his girlfriend. But I needed the job, so like a pussy I agreed.

It was typical. Missy sounded like she was an eighty-year-old from the south. Truth was she was in her late twenties and was best described as portly, or rotund. My boss is called Brett. He was a skinny guy in his forties whose wife had left him for a salesman. The story goes the slick-talking guy waltzed into town, made some sales and left with Brett's wife too. Now how Brett came to be going off on dirty weekends with a Missy was anybody's guess, but it was left to me to sort out his shit whilst he was away.

I looked at Blue and nodded to the clothed sex-show on the pool table. "Tell her I've got to check on the boathouse," I said taking another pull of the bottle.

"Why don't you tell her yourself," he replied. "I mean I can, but she's about twenty feet away."

"Nah, I don't want to cramp her style." I took the bottle with me. I was about ready to put my fist through a wall.

I had anger issues.

Charlotte and I could certainly go at it. In more ways than one, so to speak. She had a quick temper, too. I often said she spent most of the time moaning when she was with me. Sometimes pleasure but mostly in pain.

It was a constant car-crash of a relationship. The stone on her finger did nothing to loosen up the reins. My back still stung from her nails that gashed me a few nights back. I suspected she was still scrubbing my DNA from her fingernails.

Outside a warm breeze danced over me. It felt like the touch of an angel. Maybe that's what I really wanted. It was definitely what I needed. A woman to stroke and caress me rather than slap my face and shove fingers where they weren't welcomed.

We'd never done moonlight walks or dinners out. Our relationship was based on carnal activities. We had a beast-like hunger that spilt over the lines of emotion. Two passionate people, but often our passions were on different things.

I walked along the beach path, the sound of the sea to my left and the light from above giving me enough vision from one lamp to the next. A perfect design.

The winds were due to get up tomorrow. I knew this from work. We'd cancelled the trips out. I could sail them, but it often made the tourists sick. Their poor inland stomachs are unable to cope with the gentle rocking waves on the boat.

My phone went again.

"What the fuck!" Charlotte said before I even uttered a word.

"Hey to you, too."

"You don't even tell me you're not turning up? What the fuck, Jay?"

"I turned up, and you were trying the fuck some 'roid-cruncher on the pool table."

She was as pissed as I felt. "We were playing pool."

"That what you call it?"

"You need to chill the fuck out, Jay." Then there was the sound of her muffling the phone and hissing something in the background.

When the sound returned, I blew. My temper hit high. "That him? He still there?"

"He's cool," she said. "Look if you…" she stopped and rethought what she was going to say.

"What?"

"Look, maybe we cool things for a bit. For both of our sakes, yeah?"

I had nothing further to say. I ended the call and shouted out like an animal in the wild!

Un-fucking-believable, I thought.

Chapter 2

I had to take a minute before I carried on.
Everything was changing, and I didn't like it.
We'd taken breaks before, and they never
lasted. One of us would buckle within hours. 'I'm
sorry' would tumble from our mouths between
kisses and loosening of clothing. She'd nibble my
neck and pinch my nipples too hard. Then we'd be
at it again.

It was pathetic.

This time felt different. I was jealous, and I
knew it. Wasn't that part of love?

I pulled on my big-boy-pants and continued
towards the boathouse.

I entered the marina and walked down the
wooden path and past the clubhouse. From there
you could see a dozen boathouses of different
sizes and conditions.

The one I worked from was in two parts. One
was old and looked like tinder waiting to happen,
and the other was new and strong as an ox. It
looked like one of the little pigs didn't turn up so
the other two continued but separately.

The alarm was no longer on because Brett got a notification to his phone, and he could override it from there.

I checked the door to the new part. It was fine. I used my key, and the alarm went off again. I made the quick scramble to the keypad and put in Missy's birthday. Romance, huh?

I walked in flipping the lights immediately, wanting as much of the place illuminated as possible.

Tentatively, I walked around. The place was packed with order and cleanliness, and I wondered then whether I was in the right job. Neither were traits of mine. Brett liked me. He said I was punctual and hard-working. It seemed to me to be a better description than 'the only person available', but that was fine for now. Maybe he thought I needed a father figure.

I entered the older part, the one held together with memories and fishnets. The cleanliness didn't quite reach this far. Because of this, I felt more at home here. There was an underlying damp smell mixed with wood and fish.

I noticed a piece of wood lying innocently on the floor. When I looked up, I saw where it was meant to be. It didn't appear to be anything more sinister than rot. The material had weakened and finally given out. The movement had tripped the alarm.

I sat back in an old skipper's chair and pulled out a smoke. I knew more than anyone the dangers of fire, but fuck it, my boss was elbow deep in his current fling, so I was going to break a few rules too.

I took a drag, and slowly blew out the smoke. I had a few decisions to make.

Smoking is something that calms me. I'm not a complete idiot, I understand the health implications of it. The thing is, I never envisaged living into my later years. I don't mean that to sound dismissive, nor negative, it's just I like to have a good time. I live my life to the extreme. These are the things that will kill me, not the cancer-sticks I choose to suck on.

Tomorrow I was meant to be taking my so-called friends out on one of the boats. Brett knew shit about it, but fuck it. If he busts my balls over it, then I'd say so what? He'd let me off.

Or he'd kick my ass into unemployment.

The fact that Charlotte was there thrusting her boobs at the likes of muscle was something that wound me up. Our friends were sitting back and letting her do it. In my eyes they were accessories to her whoring actions.

No one else had hit me up to see where I was, or if I was alright. I wasn't shit to them. Just the annoying idiot who came with Charlotte.

I was under no illusion they were her friends and not mine. They kept me around because I was a little crazy. I provided them with some entertainment, and maybe, just maybe Charlotte alluded to the pleasure I brought her.

Or not. Who fuckin' knew?

When I was done, I squashed the butt and threw it into the trash. No point in letting Brett blow his lid for something so ridiculous.

I locked up and walked back along the marina.

It was another ten minutes before I was at the bar. The place glowed from the outside, and the sound of Guns N' Roses could be heard from inside. Axl was singing about a girl called Michelle that he considered to be his. Yeah, like my Charlotte. Look where that got me!

I was about to walk towards the door when I noticed something move in the parking lot. I glanced over at a huge penis-extension parked in the dark corner.

I don't know what possessed me to walk towards it. Some weird voyeuristic part of my mind that had been awakened for the first time ever, I supposed.

The truck had huge wheels like we'd time-travelled back to the 80s. Pointless things, unrequired for a fishing town in New England.

I stopped in my tracks as I recognized the muffled sounds of pleasure.

It will be of no surprise to you that I'd been with other women. Most of them were quiet. There were a few deep breaths, and their facial expressions often told me if I was in the right area, but Charlotte had this strange, high-pitched squeak going on. To be honest, I found it a fuckin' turn on, like some audible validation that what I was doing was right. I don't come across to many as lacking in confidence, but sexual egos can be brittle things built high on spindly legs.

I was done. I turned, walked back towards the bar and wondered what lies she'd spin later.

I walked past the bar, and directly over to the pool table where the rest of the co-conspirators were.

"Jay!" Betty said, looking worried but doing her best to mask it with a fake delight. "We were wondering where you got to?"

"I had to check the boathouse," I said. "The alarm went off."

"Everything alright?" It was false concern.

I shrugged. "Nothing I couldn't handle."

"Glad you made it!"

Ricky nodded holding up his beer, and Tony sat in the corner with Heidi. They both looked guilty.

"Where's Charlotte?" I asked. "Restroom?"

It was a picture. Faces turned and glanced at each other, and no one wanted to speak.

I grinned and did my best not punch them all in their stupid lying faces. Instead I said, "Oh hard question, was it?"

Heidi looked up. She hated silence. I wondered whether she was loud in the bedroom, too. "I thought she went to meet you?"

"Really?" I replied.

Betty nodded. "Yeah, that was it, wasn't it, Ricky?" He shrugged. To give him his due, he looked like he really didn't want to get involved. Tony took a large pull of his beer. He was doing his best to stay out of it, too. Typical guys had no balls. The women walked all over them. They probably gave them their balls back at the end of the night.

"Okay, well I'll go and see if I can find her. You all still on for tomorrow?"

That changed the mood, and suddenly smiles were lighting up the place. They were nodding and visibly relaxing.

"It's gonna be great!" Ricky said.

"Yeah. Cheers, Jay!"

I mustered up the rest of my enthusiasm reserves before my tank was empty.

"You're welcome. It's what friends are for." I let that settle in. I hoped the guilt would choke them.

I left them there stuck in the web of lies.

I couldn't look at anyone else. I knew they were all laughing at me. They'd always been laughing at me. I was a fucking joke in this town.

Outside, I wanted to go and surprise them. Maybe even call the sheriff and let him know what was happening in a public place.

Instead, I walked away. I turned and walked the next few blocks until I came to the apartment building.

Even without alcohol, this was a bad idea. I knew it was a knee-jerk reaction, but honestly, I didn't care anymore.

I walked up the staircase, ignored the litter that had been discarded all around, and rapped on her door.

When she opened up, she stood there staring at me. She wasn't wondering what I wanted, she already knew. Without a word, she stood to the side and let me in. A small smile played upon her lips.

She was at least ten years older than me.
Maybe fifteen. An older woman who had made
some wrong choices in her life. That being said,
she was one hell of a person. She had been a go-to
on more nights than I could remember although,
I'd not been here in a while.

I grabbed her hand and she smiled sadly as I
led her into the bedroom. She let me peel away her
clothes like it was her only defense, until she had
nothing to hide.

Her hands got to work and I stared into the eyes
of this woman with the face of a newsreader and
the skills of a hooker and wondered why some
people might consider this to be lucky.

It was a band aid on a wound that needed
stitches, but tonight it would be enough.

Chapter 3

I got back to my place at sunrise and washed the sticky remnants of sin away in the shower. I felt like shit. My girlfriend had cheated on me, and I'd run into the open legs of another woman to somehow ease my pain. It was like drugs. The overwhelming pleasure momentarily numbed the pain, but later on when it all wore off, I felt worse. The highs were great, but the lows much worse and made me wonder whether life was worth living. I'm not being overly dramatic, either.

I grabbed some breakfast, packed a bag of shit I probably didn't need, and headed off to the marina.

I had a few missed calls from Charlotte. She'd left Hollywood messages pretending she couldn't find me. She feigned worry on the second call although I knew her throat was sore from her sex-squeaks. The poor thing.

I sent her a text back, fighting lies with lies. Sometimes it was easier to ignore the thorns on a rose bush and concentrate on the flower.

I told her I missed her at the bar and ended up falling asleep in front of a movie on Netflix. She pretended she was worried, doing all she could to offload her guilt onto me. Fuckin' typical.

I opened the door to the boathouse, amused that the smell of stale cigarette smoke hung in the air like a dirty rumour.

Ricky and Betty were the first to arrive.

"Knock-knock!" Ricky said as they appeared in the doorway. They were all smiles. We were the best of friends again.

Lying and cheating was just the sort of thing that happened. You laugh it off. Pat each other on the back like it didn't matter. Forget about it. This was what I thought.

Betty said weakly, "You find Charlotte?"

I shook my head as the woman in question appeared. Her smile never reached her eyes. They were clearly at odds with each other. Probably an argument over truth or some such trivial thing.

"I was just about to say how we missed each other."

She nodded, and shrugged. "I know. I couldn't find you anywhere."

"You have a good night?" I enquired, and Ricky and Betty were stood back fidgeting.

"Yeah," she said, and then quickly added. "Shame I missed you though. Was everything alright with this place?"

I held out my arms. "This place will be the last building standing in this town. It's built on hard work and integrity."

Heidi then appeared wearing a vest top and holding a hoodie. "Hey!"

"You'll need that on," I said nodding at the hoodie. "It may be warm here, but out on the sea it will get a lot cooler."

Charlotte walked up and put her arms around me and kissed me on the cheek. "You'll keep me warm, right?"

"I'm the skipper," I winked. "It's my job to look after the crew."

I walked to the back of the room. There was a counter that held everything of importance to Brett. I once found a thong there and could only speculate where it came from but I did know that it wasn't Missy's. She'd have a job to pull it up to her ankles, let alone any higher.

"Whoop!" Tony said, walking in and wearing mirrored sunglasses. He was prone to making a grand entrance.

"Fuck me! Welcome to the danger zone, Maverick!"

Heidi and Ricky both laughed. Tony stuck up his middle finger.

"Be nice," Charlotte said playfully, but I could tell there was an underlying warning. Typical. She'd spent a drunken night with her legs spread for him a year or so ago, and now I had to be nice to him.

I pulled out a bottle from behind the counter and waved it like it was a trophy.

"Look what we have here!" I grinned.

"Now we're talking," Tony said, removing his glasses, and Ricky was nodding in approval, too.

"Bit early for me," Betty said. That didn't surprise me. She was a vegan, and other than Tony's cock, she was quite particular about what she put in her mouth.

"Live a little," Tony said to her, and she softened.

"That your boss's?" Charlotte said, grabbing the bottle and inspecting it suspiciously.

"I'd say so," I replied. "Come on, it's just over an hour and a half until midday. So nearer lunch than breakfast."

"I've not had any breakfast," Heidi said as if she should be congratulated. No shock there. I couldn't remember the last time I had seen her eat anything. She'd become skinny in the past year. Really skinny.

"Give me the bottle," Tony said coming at me, but I held up my hand.

"Hold on." I looked down at a bag that was next to the bottle. It was filled with plastic cups and paper plates.

I pulled out a few cups and everyone gathered around slowly as I popped out the cork and filled up the cups with a couple of fingers.

Everyone grabbed a cup, some more reluctant than others, but we were young and dumb as they say. This would be a story to be relayed when we were older.

Without even suggesting it, Tony led the rest in counting down from five. At one everyone knocked their drinks back.

"Whoo!" Tony shouted in his usual over the top way. God, I hated him.

Betty was pulling a face and flapping her hands like I'd poisoned her, and Heidi looked like she was just about coping.

"Thanks," Charlotte said as the cups were left on the desk.

"For what?" It was a private conversation said only for my benefit.

"For this," she said, and the guilt was itching to be unleashed out into the open.

I shrugged.

Ten minutes later and we were heading out down the marina and towards the yacht, 'The Two Truths'. It was a Grand Banks classic. Built in the 80s, it still looked impressive albeit boxier than the contemporary designs nowadays. It had a huge below deck which comprised of three bedrooms and a main living space. Above was the main deck, and then there was a smaller second deck which mostly housed the skipper's nest.

"I can't believe your boss lets you take this out each day," Ricky said. "This thing must be worth a pretty penny!"

"He knows I can handle it."

I jogged ahead and welcomed them on board. We looked like the beginning of some horror teen movie. Maybe another instalment of Jaws.

"It makes my job in the mall suck big time!" Heidi said. She'd started there a few months back when we graduated. The others were at college. The local one. Fancy ideas of Ivy League had soon fluttered off into the wind. Not one of us had parents who could afford the fees, and we were just a bunch of averages. Nothing special.

It was a few minutes before we set off. Sailing wasn't like driving a car. You didn't just jump behind the wheel and set off; you had a number of checks to do first. It was a hard time. You were filled with excitable people who wanted to get going, but safety was such an important thing.

Eventually, with more whooping from Tony, and then his shadow, Ricky, we hit the waves. The town was left behind us with the white-capped trails from the huge twin engines.

The Atlantic was a huge ocean. It was fascinating to think about just how much water there was around.

I slowed us down as I looked back and land was no longer in sight. This was where some people got freaked out. You stopped and looked all around and saw nothing but water.

Now I was in complete control. All I'd have to do was turn the boat around into a few circles and my crew would be too disorientated to know which way was land.

I liked that.

I climbed down.

"Welcome to the ocean!" I proclaimed. It was amazing to me just how many people lived by the ocean but never ventured out onto it. It was a whole different world to the one they knew.

"This is scary!" Betty commented. "I cannot see the land!"

"It's out there," I said pointing in one direction. Then I stopped and pretended I was unsure and pointed in the other direction. "Or out there, I forget."

"What!"

"It's a joke!" Charlotte said. "Just Jay being Jay!" She knew me. Of course she did. We'd been intimate with each other, mentally and physically, more times than with other people. Maybe that was the bond that kept us together.

Or the one that would eventually tear us apart.

"Can we go swimming?" Tony said, already stripping off his T-shirt.

"Sure," I said. "The sharks are hungry about now."

"Are they?" Heidi asked, clearly worried.

"There are sharks everywhere. It's not sunrise, not sundown so they will be less interested in your skinny butts."

Tony had his swim shorts on under his tracksuit bottoms and was stripped down before I could even finish.

"I've swum out here before. I'm not scared!"

The others were a bit more tentative.

Tony dived in quite gracefully. He was one of those annoying people who was good at most things. His body was on the skinny side, but he had no fat on him. He'd hoped for a football scholarship, but had failed at the last hurdle. Chad Reeno was an all-star and made Tony feel so average he gave up on football. He tried his hand at basketball for a while. Now he drank and worked out.

Chapter 4

Already it was more about the things that weren't said rather than the things that were. Charlotte followed me around. Every once in a while, she'd slip her arm around my waist and kiss me on the cheek. Like a fool I let her. It was often easier to be passive.

"Is everything alright?" she asked when I didn't kiss her back. It wasn't that I'd stopped anything, just perhaps I wasn't embracing her every five minutes. Or trying to hump her when she bent over.

"I'm just tired," I lied. The truth was boiling deep inside me. I wanted to stand up and shout it out to her, but sometimes I deflected confrontation. I didn't always have the energy.

We were sitting in the cabin, the rocking of the boat was gentle, and personally I found it to be calming. Betty, on the other hand, was struggling. She'd paled slightly and was threatening to dry heave at any moment. It was part of the reason why Charlotte and I were down on the lower deck.

Her sourpuss face, now going green, was enough to make you want to just jump overboard.

"You seem distant," she tried again. Maybe she was looking to confess. "Is everything alright?"

"I grew up in care when my parents abandoned me," I said, doing my best to upturn the sides of my mouth in order to soften the words. But it was the truth. "I was abused. Now, I'm rolling around this small town clearly not fitting in."

"That's not true."

"Which part? My parents definitely abandoned me, and I was abused on many occasions."

"Don't be flippant. That's not what I mean, and you know it!" Her voice raised slightly but she was right.

"But I don't fit in, do I?"

"Who does?" she said, but I had to wonder whether she even had a clue. Her parents were well off. They had a house in the Hamptons, for God sake. She'd get over me and marry some successful businessman. She'd pop out a couple of kids, and life would be wonderful. Later on, she'd get drunk with her friends, then probably have a string of affairs before getting addicted to prescription drugs.

It just wound me up. She could treat me like shit, because who was going to say anything? Her friends didn't think anything was wrong. They never took us seriously as a couple, and that in itself pissed me off. What right did they have to decide that?

"Look, Jay," she said. "You've got this job. You've got your apartment. You have us!"

"Us? You speak of everyone as a singular, but I'm pretty sure I'm not fucking any of them, too!"

"Don't be so touchy. You know you have me."

"I had you... I just don't know anymore."

She frowned and looked confused. "You're dumping me?"

"You said last night we should cool things..." I was about to say more but stopped myself.

"That was last night."

"When that guy was mauling you."

Her face changed. First a raised eyebrow, and then one of those chuckles that had nothing to do with amusement nor happiness.

"Is that what this is all about?"

"Why wouldn't it be?"

She began to shake her head. She stood up, and throwing in the towel said, "I can't do this."

I let her go. What else could I do?

I gave it a few minutes to gather my thoughts. I couldn't believe that she didn't think it was an issue. Or if she did, she was going to play it like it was a 'me problem' as she says.

I walked up and outside, the sound of laughing and splashing now louder.

As if to taunt me, Charlotte looked at me as she stripped off her clothes. Her two-piece was small and her body curvy.

It killed me to look at her and feel like I either had to accept her actions or kiss her goodbye forever.

Ricky was diving around, and Tony was embracing Heidi. Charlotte lowered herself into the water.

I looked around.

"Where's Betty?" I said and was met by shrugs.

"Not in here!" Tony shouted.

I carefully walked around the yacht. It was big, but there weren't many places you could hide. After a full walk around the top deck, I headed down below. I checked the three bedrooms and the bathroom, all the while calling her name. "Betty?" Nothing.

The only place she could be was on the upper deck. Instantly, I could tell she wasn't there, but I went up anyway.

I stood up and grabbed the binoculars. I hated to say it, but she was missing.

Speechless, I descended and walked over to the others.

"Guys?" I couldn't control my voice. "She's missing."

"Shut up!" Tony shouted.

I held up my hands to show I was serious. "No, she's not here."

He made his way to the ladder and slowly climbed out onto the deck. The hero coming to save the day. Behind him Ricky followed, nothing but a sidekick. The tough guys were taking charge.

"She must be around here somewhere," Tony said. "Betty? Betty!"

"I've looked everywhere," I said. It annoyed me that the alpha male had to come around and try to prove he knew best.

"She can't have vanished! Betty!"

Now the girls were looking worried and everything was beginning to get serious.

How did you lose somebody at sea?

"Who saw her last?" Tony demanded.

I looked out at Charlotte. "She wasn't feeling well," I began. "When Charlotte and I went below deck, she was sitting up here looking ill."

"I didn't see her when I came back up," Charlotte said in a small voice. The impact of the situation was now becoming evident.

The panic was there. Everyone then set off in different directions. All except for Heidi who now, out of the water, sat rocking and sobbing.

"Where is she?" she said to nobody in particular. "We have to find her."

Then they were all spaced out around the side of the boat staring into the water below.

"She would've shouted, wouldn't she?" Ricky said. He'd spent so long trying to be an alpha male and yet now he seemed like an overgrown child pleading with a parent.

"She can swim," Charlotte added.

I look out around us. It was as if life was setting the scene. The sun had gone behind a cloud, and in the distance the sky looked angry. Thunderclouds were rolling in. The storm.

"We can't leave her," Heidi was saying even though nobody had even suggested it.

"I need to call it in though," I said. It wasn't a call I was looking forward to. The authorities would be all over us, and by tomorrow I would be jobless.

Tony jumped into the water as if hoping he'd just find her body floating under the surface.

Up at the wheel, I grabbed the radio and turned it on. I was met by a wall of static. I turned the dial and shouted "Mayday! Mayday!" but got nothing in return. I went through the protocol but nothing worked.

"What's going on?" Charlotte shouted coming up to the upper deck.

"I can't get through. Nothing's working!"

"What d'you mean? What would happen if this happened on one of your charters?"

"I know. I've tried. Nothing works." I was panicking now. We could hear Tony and Ricky shouting and under that, Heidi sobbing.

I saw Tony take a deep breath and dive under the water. He was determined, I had to give him that.

I was just about to grab the key and start the engines when from below I heard, "Tony!"

We burst out of the cabin and down onto the main deck to join Ricky and Heidi. Tony was still underneath the water.

"Where is he?" Heidi was almost hyperventilating. "Why are they missing?" she was shaking and almost uncontrollable.

"This is ridiculous!" I shouted.

The boat now began to bob more as the water appeared to be getting choppier. The invisible force of the ocean could be a scary thing.

Ricky glanced at me and before I could say anything jumped in too.

"Ricky, no!" I said as he disappeared under the surface. The last thing we needed was him disappearing too.

A few minutes later we were sitting on the edge of the boat. The water now rough and the waves growing. Rain began to pour down.

We'd lost two people.

What would happen next?

Chapter 5

There was an awkward moment when I didn't think Ricky was going to come up, but then he emerged, his hands sweeping back his black hair.

"Nothing," he said. "I just…" he looked all around him, and I realised we were all doing the same. We expected to see them alive and splashing around, or worse, floating face down.

But there was nothing.

Eventually, and reluctantly, Ricky pulled himself out of the water. He grabbed a towel and we all stood there in silence. The waves crashed around us and the severity of the situation weighed heavy on our minds.

Without word, I climbed up to the wheel and went to grab the key. It had gone too far. We had to get out of there.

Except there wasn't a key.

Someone had taken it.

Usually, the key was in the panel with a long cord and a buoy keyring on it. There was never a reason to take it out once you were at sea.

"Shit," I said and looked all around. If it wasn't stuck where it should be, then I really didn't expect it to be anywhere else. But I was desperate.

"The key has gone," I said. Charlotte could see the panic that I was trying to keep a lid on.

"What?"

"Someone has taken it."

"Who? Why?" These were the questions I had, too.

"Who knows, babe," I said looking out to where we could no longer see the shore. "Who knows." I'd slipped back into how we were in our relationship. It was so easy to do. Maybe I needed her now.

"Jay, what're we going to do?"

We stood and looked out around the ocean. Not another boat in sight. I went to the box on the side and opened it up.

The flare gun was gone too.

Was this some sort of sick joke? What the hell was going on?

"It's gone, too," I said. "The flare gun!" I realised we were now talking louder over the noise of the sea. The wind, whilst warm, now felt stronger.

"We have to get back to land!" Charlotte said, obviously. Words tumbling out with desperation.

"I know!" I shouted. "Don't you think I know that!"

"Maybe you should've checked everything properly this morning instead of being in a pissy with me!" She disappeared down the ladder.

"What!" I screamed after her.

She stopped. "You heard me! You're such a loser!"

I saw red. I'd punched her full in the face before I even realised it.

She went down. I should've felt guilty, but I was scrambling to justify my actions.

"See!" she said holding the place of contact. "No wonder I wanted better!"

"Like the guy from the bar!"

"You don't know what you're talking about!"

We were both getting wet but making no move to go underneath with the other two.

"I saw you last night. You were in his truck fucking like some pitstop whore!"

"Fuck you, Jay!" she said, got up and stormed off.

I put my hand through my wet hair. This was a mistake. A great big mistake.

Then Ricky was in front of me. In my face. Squaring up.

"What the fuck, Jay! What's your problem!"

"Stay out of it!" I replied. He obviously thought he was the big man now.

"You hit a woman, and you think I can just sit by and watch? Someone needs to put you in your place!"

Suddenly the boat lifted and dropped. We both fell down.

Ricky tried to catch himself which only saw him stumble a few paces towards the edge. Then, like a doll, he flipped and went over.

"Ricky!" I shouted, got to my feet and, trying not to slip, made it towards the side.

He was gone. Swallowed up by the sea.

"What just…" Charlotte said, but she knew. She'd seen it all.

"Get back inside!" I shouted. "It's not safe out here!"

As carefully as I could, I hung on tightly to the side and shouted out. "Ricky!"

I thought I saw a head, but the waves cast indecipherable shapes with their constant changing, and I couldn't be sure.

I stared again, but it wasn't him. Surely, he'd come up to the surface.

The sky was as black as night. The clouds above were thick. The cascading rain was so heavy our visibility was limited; the wind slapping against my cheeks.

I managed to get to the lower deck as the yacht was lifted and dropped onto the ocean.

I knew the storm was coming and yet I'd still taken us all out here.

This was all my fault.

The eyes of Charlotte and Heidi bore into me as I made it down into the lower cabin.

"What the fuck!" Charlotte shouted. She got up and was pounding her fists against my chest, but there was no strength in them. It was frustration.

"He came at me," I said defensively. "The boat dipped, and he went over. I looked and looked but it's rough out there…"

"You sail all the time, Jay," Charlotte said, unable to look at me. "You knew the storm was coming." It was a statement rather than a question.

"These things happen. The weather is all about prediction, and the thing about predictions is they are not always accurate…" I was lying through my teeth. Weather reports were the most important thing to a sailor. You had to watch, listen, and understand all the changing conditions.

I knew this was going to be dangerous. I knew deep down that it could end like this and yet I'd chosen to bring them all out here anyway.

I'd had enough. I was fed up with being the laughing stock of the group.

Maybe they'd finally fucking listen to me.

Chapter 6

I sat down. Charlotte and Heidi eyeballed me. They both looked like they wanted to grab me and push me overboard.

"Heidi," I began. "Have you got the key?"

Her eyes went wild. "What!?"

Charlotte looked at her and slipped an arm around her. "The key is missing. Jay can't start the boat without it."

"I," she began, but her words were cut short as the boat was lifted up and suddenly dropped down hard. We all fell down.

The world went sideways. Things smashed and crashed against each other in a destructive couple of seconds. Somebody screamed.

I grabbed on to something and hooked my leg around it.

The sound of rushing water was all around.

Then nothing.

"Charlotte! Heidi!" I shouted. The yacht was on its side. I saw Charlotte clinging for dear life onto the side of the drinks bar.

"I'm here," she sobbed. We both looked around unable to locate Heidi. But I could see blood in the water.

Charlotte looked like she could read my mind and was mouthing "No." as I dived under the water.

I couldn't see anything. It was too dark. I felt around, and then my stomach dropped as I felt an arm. I tried to pull her, but she was caught on something. Worst still, she wasn't pulling back.

I pulled again with everything I had.

But it wasn't enough.

My lungs were burning as I broke the surface.

"Jay?" Charlotte said.

"I'm sorry," I said, coming up to her. "I can't free her."

The water inside the cabin lapped against the side. Loose items were now banging around, and Charlotte was sobbing.

"Why couldn't we have just been happy?" I asked. The question was irrelevant now, but to me it was still so important.

"I'd do anything for you, Charlotte. Anything, and yet…"

"Jay, don't."

"You couldn't even wait for me to come to the bar before you hooked up with someone else, could you?"

"It's not like that…"

"Then what is it like?" I begged. I really wanted to know.

"You know."

"I don't. That's the thing."

"Look at us. My parents would never accept you. You know that, right?"

"So what!" I shouted back.

"So, it matters! You think that being different makes you cool? Some pioneer? Well, it doesn't…" her words drifted off before she added, "It doesn't. It's you being selfish. The way you always are."

That hit a nerve. "What?"

"You heard me."

"I love you. How can that be selfish?"

"You love me because you have me. You can't get anyone else!"

My mind flashed back to the night before. The long red nails trailing down my belly, the dirty apartment, and itchy feel of another woman's pubic hair. It would do me no good to tell her about these things.

Instead, I said, "Why did you have to go to him?"

"I didn't have to," she sighed but was unwilling to finish what she was going to say.

"But?"

"Forget it."

"Say it!" I demanded.

"I wanted to! Alright? Is that what you wanted to hear! I saw him with his manly body and wanted him inside me!"

I saw red. My anger issues.

I jumped at her and pushed her head down under the water. I was much stronger than her. I used it to my advantage.

I could feel her bucking below the water trying to punch me, but the water stopped them even registering.

Soon, she went limp.

Except, I didn't believe her. I kept her there for what felt like another five or ten minutes. When eventually I let go, she didn't come back up. I'd held on for what seemed like forever. I'd taken out my so-called friends, and one by one they all either disappeared or died.

And yet I felt nothing.

I was numb and blaming each of them for the things they'd said and done to me.

I got myself together. I couldn't die out here. I had to be strong.

I pulled myself along the side of the saloon, towards the cabin door. One was open and I carefully slipped through it and out. Crawling on the side of the overturned yacht, I went to where the life-raft was held.

But it was gone.

I was lost and alone.

Then something hit me and knocked me out cold.

Chapter 7

When I opened my eyes there was a hive of activity. The wind from a helicopter was above me, and a number of guys in fluorescent jackets were shouting.

"It's okay," one guy said looking at me. He had kind eyes and a large stubbled jaw. "We've found you."

"They're all gone," I tried to say but my mouth was dry, and I could taste salt as my tongue did its best to wet them.

"Don't speak," he said, and before I knew it, I was being taken up into the air.

I had a drip attached to me, I heard them panic about dehydration. I'd only been gone a few hours, hadn't I?

I slipped away again.

"Jay?" a soft voice said. I opened my eyes and found I was in hospital. A nurse I knew smiled at me. Behind her was a detective, standing still and looking stern. He nodded to the nurse, and she didn't look happy. She walked away. "I'll be back later."

"What happened?" he said. No pleasantries, no indication he cared about my well-being. All business.

"We went out in the boat," I explained. "We'd planned it… look, I don't know what happened… Betty disappeared, Tony jumped into the ocean… he never came back up…" the detective was glancing at his colleague, a slim guy who looked a little nervous, and shook his head slowly.

I continued. "The boat hit a wave, and Ricky went overboard… the ocean was rough… I couldn't find him… and Heidi and Charlotte…"

"What?" The detective said. "Shark attacks? Pirates?"

I didn't like his tone. He sounded accusing, but without any evidence it felt like he was pushing it.

"No, When the yacht turned over, they drowned. I did everything I could to save them… I… er… I couldn't find Charlotte, and Heidi was pinned…"

"I'm sure," the detective said.

"Yes, I couldn't get her free…"

He looked at his partner again, then when he turned back, he said in a loud and authoritative voice, "Let's cut the bullshit, shall we?"

"What?" I said shocked. I didn't know what he meant. I know what had happened to Charlotte, but none of the others was my fault.

"Let's start with this. Why did you run away on the boat?"

"Run away?" I was now the one looking at his partner. I was trying to read his face. "It was a trip.

A boat trip, I told you. We'd had it planned for days."

"A boat trip for one?"

I frowned. "What are you talking about? No. For all of us. All six."

"You were the only person on the boat."

"Yes, because the others disappeared, or died. Someone took the key to the yacht." I followed their eyes to the table at the side.

The key sat innocently on the side, the small buoy attached to it.

"That one?" the detective said.

I nodded. "Yes, where did you find it?"

"It was in your pocket."

I shook my head. "No. No way."

The detective turned to his partner. "Jackson, you want to tell us what we know of the others?"

He cleared his throat and said. "Uh, yes. Um, we have all the bodies of your friends."

"You do? How? Where did you find them?"

The detective grinned, but there was no humour in it. "Jackson? Where did we find the bodies?"

"Five bodies were found in the Boathouse."

I was lost for words. "What? How?"

"It seems they were poisoned. A large bottle was found behind the desk, and the security tape shows you pouring drinks for everyone."

"I…" It was all cloudy. I went to move my arms and realised my left was restricted.

It was handcuffed to the side of the bed.

"What?"

"I'm arresting you for the murder of all five."

"No!"

I looked at both of them, unable to believe what they were saying.

"We're just waiting for confirmation of when you can be handed over to us," the detective smiled. He was enjoying this.

"No," I repeated.

"We'll be back," he said, and as he walked out I heard him say. "It's always women that kill by poison, isn't it?"

"It seems to be," his partner agreed.

I always thought I was a unique woman, and those words hurt more than anything.

The End.

If Only…

I'm lonely and desolate like a cloud.
She is perfection, and forever locked within the confines of a book. My arthritically bent fingers draw invisible lines on the leather spine, before I hold the book dear to my heart. I squeeze hard, not wanting her to tumble out onto the floor.

But soon, I open sun-bleached pages that feel brittle and vulnerable. I'm gentle. My eyes dance upon words carefully crafted only for me. I'm convinced of that. The author, pretentious in his foolhardy vocabulary, penned this story knowing it would be brushed aside by heathens for years; decades in fact, before I chanced upon it in an old attic.

I follow her every move. She can do no wrong in my eyes, and I long for her to be real. I read on. A story about a woman looking up at a man just like me. And he's staring back at her. She is sad and lonely too. Salty tears wash mascara lines. She sees the pain in the man's eyes, as he pretends not to notice the thick smoke engulfing him.

I feel the heat, but I cannot pull myself away from the book. Drawn magnetically within, even as the flames lick at me like the devil's tongue. Evil intent on clawing at my clothes, but I'm too engrossed to worry; to care. To want to live.

Lost in the book until the very end.

The Trunk

'The Trunk' was first published in 2019 by Crazy Ink. It appeared in the anthology Motel 666.
At the end there is mention to a Chinaman in a hearse, and this is reference to a character in my 2019 novel Mr Watcher.

Chapter 1

The dead of night swallowed up his piece-of-shit saloon. Faceless buildings leered over him as he pulled the car to a halt.

His name was Barney Rogen. He was neither friends with a Flintstone, nor a fucking purple Dinosaur. He'd heard 'em all. None of them were funny.

His fat hairy hands tensely clutched the steering wheel. Sausage-like digits with gold bands slowly cutting off the circulation. Sweat beaded his brow, and blood shot eyes stared back at him in the mirror. He looked a state. He'd not looked good for years. A slippery slope to middle-age.

The red glow from the traffic lights illuminated him the colour of sin. Rain pounded the windshield with a sinister rhythm. He had visions of some death march. The night would only end in pain, he fucking knew it.

His head pounded with a nervous tension, and he realised he was hunched over the wheel like some cartoonish angry man. All elbows, sweat and with a grimace on his face.

Jim Ody

Today wasn't meant to be like this, he thought. He'd covered his hairy chest rug with a double-XL vest, quickly dismissing any thoughts about shifting weight. He had on a blue shirt, complete with dark sweat rings, and an open collar to house his wobbling jowls.

His wife, Lita, was a small bag of bones who thought he should be of similar physique, and she taunted him. Despite this, she still served up huge platefuls of crap that clogged his arteries, increased his blood-pressure, and made him all the more grotesque. It was all *deep-fried this*, and *sugar-coated that*, and then she had the fucking gall to tell him his tits were bigger than hers! She was plain and unremarkable. Stringy-hair and no lips, her eyes drooped like a bloodhound and came to life only when she was angry or fucked hard. She was the better side of okay then.

His eyes dropped to the plastic Hula-Girl swinging her hips and winking at him. His wife had got him that. He wished to God she looked half as good. Shapely and breasts barely covered by coconuts. He figured not many would be sold if they had his wife's sour-face and emaciated body. More parasite than paradise.

He ran a podgy hand through the wisps of hair he still had. He looked like he shared the same barber as Danny Devito. Same dietitian, too. *What ya gonna do?* He often shrugged. His aspirations at becoming a model had never been serious. Good job.

In the back of the car sat a huge trunk. Its sinister appearance was all the more frightening when accompanied by the message left on his cell phone.

Somebody had been watching him. They knew what he'd been up to, and now he was going to pay.

Whilst drumming his fingers and willing the lights to change, he glanced at a couple walking hand-in-hand down the sidewalk. He fucking hated everything about them. They were young, skinny, and deep in love. All the things he was not. The opportunity to be them had passed him by back when he was still thinking of being a lifeguard like Hasselhoff. That dream burst when his knee blew out, and he comforted himself with doughnuts. Within a few months he looked like someone had inflated him. Who was going to save folk at the beach now? Not Hasselhoff, that's for sure.

Right now, he wanted to mount the curb and run the lovebirds over. Smile at the bump and crunch of tires over bones. Their final thoughts would be shared together, so who fuckin' cared, right?

He didn't do that. He remained where he was impatiently swearing at the lights under his breath. There were no other cars, so what was the point. Authority proving how big their balls were once again.

The moment they changed, he hit the gas like a NASCAR driver. He didn't want to hang around any longer. He had a mission.

His heart nearly leaped from his chest as he saw a cop car. It had pulled over some Johnny Foreigner. He could tell by the way the guy looked. He was hardly all-American, and looked guilty; as guilty as OJ. Probably had a bomb strapped to his chest. Fucking terrorists.

"Shoot 'em!" he shouted as he passed by. He allowed a small grin. It was almost gallows humour. He had a long night ahead of him. He really didn't think it'd end well.

Neon signs tried to entice him with offers of things he neither wanted nor could afford. That said, he was thirsty and could murder a drink. Something strong on ice would go down well. Strippers or hookers would be the icing on the cake. But they would have to wait. He had to accept that he might never see another pair of titties again. That was about the saddest fucking thing in the world, right there. He felt almost distraught that the last pair he'd grabbed a hold of were the small saggy-bags on his wife's chest. She'd done her best to look excited. He'd seen condemned death row prisoners show more passion. Nevertheless, he went through the motions. His heart-rate had peaked quickly, and he seemed to be the only one red-faced and out of breath by the end. He'd rolled off and pulled up his pants whilst she wiped herself on his pillow. That was their marriage in a nutshell.

The motel came up on the right. He turned in and parked up next to some Corvette straight out of the eighties. He imagined the blondes that would be sprawled out on the hood if he drove it, rather than the dime-a-dozen shit-mobile he was driving now.

The sign stood proud.

Motel 666. *That's not fucking weird at all,* he thought. But this had been the place he'd been told to go to.

Rain continued to pour down, and the sound of it only made him feel more nervous. And angry. He was always angry. Life brought the worst out in him.

He turned off the engine and rubbed his eyes with his evil hands. Hands that had caressed a woman that was not his. Hands that had stolen things. Hands that had thrown one too many punches at the wrong person. Hands that shamed him to stare at any longer.

Barney pulled his fat ass out of the car and jiggled everything with what might be loosely described as a jog.

He was heading for the check-in. He pushed open the door but saw no one around. Someplace a television was playing some comedy shit. The canned laughter rang out to some-such crap that wasn't even funny enough to have a live audience.

He bounced his open palm on the bell more times than necessary, and then repeated it for good measure. If someone was going to throw demands at him, he sure as shit was going to pass them on to others.

"Hold on! I hear ya!" shouted a voice that sounded drunk and pissed off.

A short guy with a huge round belly and a bald head appeared. "The fuck you want?" he said, his face scrunched up like this was a real tough question.

"A Playboy Playmate if you've got one? Failing that I guess I'll take a room."

The guy almost sneered back. "Wiseass, huh?"

Barney stood there for a beat or two, then realised the guy was looking for some sort of answer. He shrugged instead. Even that felt too much. The fuck was he expecting, anyway?

"Whatever," he turned and looked at the rack of keys. He spent a long time deciding.

"Number twenty-four," Barney said.

"Huh?"

"I said, number twenty-four. Someone already asked me to come and get that room number."

"Who? Bridgett?"

"Who's Bridgett?"

"*Who's* Bridgett?" The guy looked completely shocked. "If you've met her then you know Bridgett. She got a rack that would put them Playboy Bunnies to shame and a mouth that moves like a goddamn Jackhammer!" For the first time something like a smile twitched the muscles of his mouth.

"Really? You see her, send her to my room!"

"She's my wife!" he shot back with anger.

Barney's eyes grew huge like saucers. "Congrats. Sounds like a keeper."

The guy's eyes narrowed. He grabbed the keys and chucked them down on the counter. "Number twenty-four. Sign the book and hand over your credit card and driver's license. We get all sorts here, and we find this helps to identify the body." He grinned big and wide showing off the teeth of a smoker.

Barney tried a half smile as he fumbled for his wallet. He threw down the cards and grabbed the book. He wondered why this place wasn't on a computer system yet, fuckin' inbreds. He also wondered whether he'd see the light of tomorrow.

"I'm Harvey, by the way," the guy said looking from the photo ID to Barney and back again. "Shit, you've filled out some."

"I live a stressful life."

"You look like Devito's big brother, anybody ever tell you that."

"Nope."

"Well you do." He took a picture of the cards on an old Polaroid camera. It looked so old he thought he'd seen one bought on a recent episode of *American Pickers*. Still shaking his head, Harvey handed the worn cards back. "There are some crazies around here, so my advice would be to keep yourself to yourself, right? Any problems? Keep them to yourself too, I don't wanna know about 'em, I've enough of my own shit, right?"

Barney nodded. He wondered whether he should mention the trunk. Shit, who knew what was inside. It might affect the deposit.

He'd clearly overstayed his welcome, when Harvey suddenly said, "Fuck off then, what ya waiting for? A glimpse of my ol' lady's titties? Beat it!"

Barney turned and made his way out. He looked at a sign with directions on, and determined that his room was down a-ways. He quickened his steps as fast as his body allowed, but he was soon out of breath.

He passed beer bottles and various forms of discarded trash. A pair of old panties that looked anything but sexy, sat sunny-side-up with a man-made pattern not envisioned by the designer when made. He stepped over them in disgust, and then realised they were outside his door.

He placed the key in the lock, turned the handle, and with a shove of his shoulder the door opened. A gust of fetid aroma hit him as if sucked out by some force. It abused his nasal passage. Brought tears to his eyes.

He looked back towards his car.

He had to go get the trunk.

That was the reason he was here.

Chapter 2

The room looked like it had seen better days. Those days were more than likely pre-seventies judging by the blindman's décor. Oranges and browns were dominant in the garish patterns swirling upon the walls. The bed looked harder than a paedo's pecker in a playground, and the carpet visibly held the DNA to America's most wanted, or society's dirty underbelly.

Barney sighed with resignation and sat down on the edge of the bed. He didn't want to go out to his car. *Fuck*, he didn't even want to stay here in the room. It had been a hard day. This wasn't how it should've ended.

He laid back and closed his eyes. He fucking hated the overwhelming feeling of loss he now felt. The lack of control over his future. The regrets lying heavy in his belly.

Right now, he should be at home. Maybe mumbling a vague appreciation to Lita in regards to a calorific meal devoured in record time. He'd manage to carry the plates the few steps to the sink in what he perceived to be a helpful act. He'd collapse in front of the television, idly scratch his balls, and wait for her to join him. He'd monopolise the television with sports, whilst she spoke online to other sad people unable to interact in person. Sometimes he'd let her watch some trash TV. There'd usually be some under-the-covers fumbling in it for him if he did. It wasn't a totally unpleasant experience – apart from the time she was enjoying a book so much she continued reading whilst giving him a hand job. She didn't even notice when he'd finished.

He'd sure take a distracted hand job right now.

He could wait no longer. He jumped up and headed out towards his car.

The rain had ceased, even though he could still smell the thick atmosphere. The parking lot had an eerie shine to it. He opened up the trunk and looked at the other trunk. The catch calling for him to pop it open and take a look. The Medusa pull was almost too much to bear. He hefted the large weight out and dragged it slowly towards the room. It wasn't something that could be done quietly.

There was a sudden crash from one of the other rooms that made Barney jump. He was on edge. He didn't like such involuntary movements and in a panic almost toppled over.

"What ya got?" He turned and saw a leggy blonde. Her hair colour was manufactured from a bottle, her clothes stolen from a hooker, and a rack from Jesus-Christ himself. This had to be Bridgett.

"Nothing," he stuttered like a schoolboy hiding porn.

She laughed at that. "Looks to me like nothin' is pretty damn heavy!"

"Uh, what, this?"

"No, your dick. Yes, that! You staying for a year?"

Barney stopped pushing the trunk and sat on it. He was happy for the break. "Nah, just, you know taking a break from life."

"Your old-lady kick you out?" She said evenly like this was the obvious reason for a fat-fucker to be hauling a large trunk into a motel room.

Without thinking, he glanced down at his wedding ring before replying, "Nah, nothing like that."

"Well, if you ask me, I say you're full o'shit! Ain't no one take a break from life in this shit-hole! Ya wife know you're here?"

"She's not answering her phone."

"That right? Probably got some young stud penetrating her so deep she's lost her voice screaming out God's name!" She winked. She thought she was funny. He thought she was a bitch. A nice rack though.

He shrugged, like he'd never even considered that.

"I'm Bridgette, by the way. I'd hold out my hand, but the last guy I did that to thought it was a come on. I'd say about the time his wrist cracked, he understood we was thinking on different lines!" She hacked out a smoker's laugh that ended in a lung-shifting cough.

"Okay."

"Okay, indeed. I'll be seeing you, Mr Take-a-break! I hope you work things out at home."

"Barney. My name's Barney."

She shook her head. "Honestly, I couldn't give a fuck." Yeah, he could see her and Harvey together. She probably berated him whilst he came over her tits. He'd tell her to shut the fuck up and clean herself up. A match made in heaven.

Barney got back up and pushed the trunk the last few yards into the room. He slammed the door behind him and stood rigid. His eyes locked on the trunk.

Voices from the unknown tickled his neck. *Open it. Open it. What's the worst that could happen?* He could think of plenty of things! He'd spent enough nights watching late night horror movies or old reruns of *The Twilight Zone*, to imagine a number of things that could happen the minute he popped the trunk.

Instead, he broke the spell by forcing his eyes elsewhere. That meant looking around the room once more. It was hardly clean. Evidence the cleaner had been a disgruntled employee. He half expected the bathroom to have a derogatory statement smeared on the wall in human faeces.

He looked back at the trunk. *Open it…* No, he couldn't.

Could he? He did his best to pull himself together.

He felt a wave of tiredness wash over him. He looked over at the coffee machine and a mug. He needed something stronger, but sometimes you had to just make do. He reached over for the mug, noticing the dust build-up. He grabbed the coffee sachet, and ripped it open without a care. He added a new paper filter, and poured the coffee inside, and went to fill up the jug with water.

The bathroom wasn't quite as bad as it could've been. The roaches seemed quite friendly and would keep him company as they scuttled around. The tap was already dripping slightly and he filled the jug up with water. As he shuffled his weight back to the coffee machine, there was a loud pounding on the door. He jumped and almost dropped the jug.

This was it.

This was when it would all go down.

Silently, he walked towards the door. He wanted to pull back the curtain and see who he was dealing with, but instead he opened the door.

Everything happened in a flash. An outline of a body and a thrusted arm forward. He experienced sparks, a high-speed clicking sound, and excruciating pain in his chest as his muscles contracted, tensed up, and eventually gave way to gravity. He ended up in a heap on the floor. Drool escaped from his mouth, and he could taste the dead skin and various bodily fluids of previous guests.

"So, big boy, here we go!" a voice rang out. Female and authoritative. He tried to move but his body refused to comply.

She laughed, and he felt his clothes being forcibly removed. He tried to speak, but he was still in shock. He'd had some bad days in his life. A few times he'd found himself in situations he assumed to be worse than anything else in his life. This was up there with them.

She rained down open-handed slaps on his large fat buttocks. A new kind of pain exploded with every hit. The waves of blubber reverberated around his midsection. There was nothing sexual or pleasant about the unwanted assault.

"Who's been a bad boy!" she scolded but with real enjoyment.

"I, uh, I," he tried to speak again, but between the slaps it was all he could do to breathe and not bite bacteria-ridden carpet.

"Yes, you! You, filthy pig."

And then she stopped. His ass felt raw like sunburn. At least it was over.

And then he felt the weight of her as she slowly stood on him. Not in bare feet but boots or shoes with a high heel. Again, it was another pain. Different, but still painful.

"I walk all over you! How d'you like me now!"

Again, Barney was unable to reply, it was less spikes of pain but rather a dull ever increasing one. He could feel her adding pressure to his spine. His ribs felt crushed. Finally, she stopped. He heard some click, then a wet fart sound, and suddenly she was first pouring and then massaging oil onto his buttocks. Now that felt better. Then she was pouring it between his cheeks. They both jumped at the sudden banging at the door.

"Mistress!" A muffled voice from outside shouted.

He heard her move, and swing open the door. "What! I'm with a client!"

"Wrong room," a male voice now said. His voice trailed off as he noticed Barney. "This is twenty-four!"

"Shit!" she hissed. She took another look at Barney, defeated and abused lying face down naked with his ass in the air, and scuttled out. "Sorry!" she called back.

Barney rolled over. The bruising was beginning to form on his butt. Warm liquid dribbled from him. The rolls of flab wobbled and eventually stopped. His flaccid penis looked small and sad, nestled snugly in hair that did its best to hide it.

He could only imagine what might've happened had the guy not come along. And that's when he saw it on the bed.

The huge strap-on the size of a baby's arm. His eyes flew open, and he gulped back air.

"Jesus fuckin' shit cakes," he mumbled. He couldn't believe what had just happened. She was going to abuse him with that.

There was another knock at the door, followed by a quick and desperate call, "Uh, mister, me again, I, er, forgot something."

Barney swung open the door. He cupped his penis with one hand and thrust out the strap-on with the other.

His mouth nearly hit the floor as he saw in front of him the most beautiful woman he had ever seen. Breasts spilling out from an outfit that could be labelled S&M Catwoman. She had a cheek-bone structure from the heavens above, and if you were to choose someone to be sexually abused by then she would be top of his list.

"Sorry, again," she smiled. There was no sign of the cat that got his tongue, but at that moment he was wrestling with the thought – had he known what she looked like, would he have actually endured what she was so very near to doing to him? He really had to wonder.

He leant out the door and watched her long legs as she walked with sexual power away from him. Leather-tight butt strong and well-formed.

He closed the door, slipped on the chain, and went over to finish his coffee.

Chapter 3

B arney poured coffee into the mug. He looked around for the small plastic sachets of milk. Removing the foil lid, he dripped in a little and went to stir it. There swimming away was a fly. It wriggled, and did its best at doggy-paddle, but it was no Michael Phelps and ultimately gave up exhausted.

With his left hand he fished it out and flicked it towards the wall. It was well at home half splattered against the flat surface. It wasn't the first fly to meet its demise this way.

He searched in his pants for his phone. He looked to see whether his wife had responded to him. She hadn't. That really boiled his piss. This was part of her fuckin' problem. He went out of his way to tell her he wouldn't be home. Sure, he'd made up some bullshit story about a work-thing he'd forgotten, but still… He'd painted a picture of some fuckin' sales conference with scribbled name badges and more awkward moments than a virgin in a strip joint. No one gave a shit about those places anyways. It was all about seeing how much you could charge on expenses and banging colleagues when they were too drunk to know better. No one ever attended with the hope of bettering their career – well, unless it was a female boss you were banging, and then you had better be sure you knew what you were doing. He'd heard of colleagues getting in such a high level of inebriation that they'd ended up with some real ugly directors, and not all of them female. The tables had turned when, instead of getting a lucrative pay rise, they'd been forced to have regular sexual relations in order to keep their current job. And that was why these street-wise cougars were in the high-powered positions, and they weren't. And then a few weeks in, the burdened colleague, unable to cope with the sexual expectations, were left to scribble out a resignation letter and develop a habit to hide their painful regrets. *The moral of the story?* Choose wisely who you bang.

So, no one with an average number of braincells ever saw the conferences as anything but a jolly. A break from the mundane and a chance to let your hair down.

Lita knew this. Which was probably why she'd not even responded to him. She was probably pissed. He lay on the bed as he tried to put names to the marks on the ceiling. He also went through anything else that might've got her panties in a wad. He drew a blank.

Apart from the obvious, that is, but he refused to accept that she knew; instead, he deluded himself into thinking that she was in one of those weird kinky moods when she wanted to fuck him six-ways to midnight. She could get antsy, especially if she was in the mood and he wasn't. It didn't happen often, but when it did, he knew he had to drop his pants and climb on board like a good soldier.

And then he felt guilty. Not for admitting to sexual failings but because of Rebecca.

He guessed she was his mistress. He hated that label. It made her sound more like the woman who had very nearly fucked him in the ass ten minutes ago. No, Rebecca was ten years younger and had an innocence about her in everything but the bedroom. She smiled a lot. When he first saw her, he assumed her to be simple. She wasn't, she was just great, although at first she was annoyingly positive about everything – well, everything except her own marriage, it would seem.

No man ever sets out to be a cheat. Most have every intention of staying true to their vows. But life changes people, and sometimes it's not always for the better.

Barney had always carried extra weight. He'd been a shy, chubby and cumbersome child. He wasn't bullied but ignored by most. He sometimes wondered whether that was worse. So, at college, when a skinny girl began to hang around him, he soon developed feelings for her. She was clever, attentive, and was happy to put him first. And for a long period of time that was more than enough for him.

But then he gained confidence, and with it status and money, and soon a new greater level of woman began to flirt with him. Probably for all the wrong reasons, but by then he'd grown too shallow to notice.

Rebecca was new to the company. She was eager to please and happy to hang on his every word. She was the excitement he was missing. He ignored his initial attraction in the hope it was just some infatuation. A midlife crisis of sorts. He never meant it to go where it went.

He never instigated a thing. It just happened.

A late night social in a bar downtown. Alcohol flowed like the waters of the Mississippi. Stories were soon embellished, and with them friendships grew. Moving on, and ending up at the hotel bar, glasses were raised, and promises were made, but soon the crowd broke up as time dictated an end to the proceedings. Some were defeated into integrating back with families. Brisk waves of regret and they were Uber'd off. Whilst others were quick to down a nightcap and be smothered by the luxurious sheets on huge beds within the hotel.

Barney and Rebecca sat gazing over rum. Both turned their wedding bands in unconscious guilt. The cool glass, and liquid was soon replaced on lips with kisses. Stolen at first, but soon domineering on both parts. Each forgot who moved in first, though both agreed they didn't want it to end.

What could easily have been a huge mistake was never acknowledged as such, instead both found an outlet to some desire they were both missing within their marriages. And so, without so much as a discussion, their long affair began.

The first single lie is the one that is most hurtful. From there they bunch up into a routine. Barney got so skilled that he no longer even realised when he was entangling himself within a lie, it so became the norm.

And Rebecca? Sweet and delicate Rebecca had a darker side that Barney encouraged with great aplomb. And she was always happy to comply. An adventurous side bordered on reckless, and for Barney, that was just perfect.

It had been a year now.

A year exactly, in fact.

Barney smiled to himself as he thought back to that night. How he thought she'd be shy, but with each item of clothing she shed, the more she became empowered and in control. The truth was he loved his wife. And he loved Rebecca, too. They were the two opposite ends of the spectrum and he enjoyed them both in equal parts.

And then his phone buzzed.

He looked at it and saw a text message.

Happy Anniversary, it said. And there was a link. It was strange as it wasn't from Rebecca. He smiled to himself anyway. He was quite happy for some sexy video message from her. She'd done it before, and he'd regretted having to delete it.

A video started. It was a handheld camera. His smiled twitched slightly as he recognised his own house. The shaky camera walked quietly through to the kitchen where Lita was standing chopping up vegetables. He fucking hated vegetables, but she cooked them because they were good for him. Barney was still unsure of whether or not it was a joke.

Satisfied with her work, Lita placed the knife down on the counter and began to turn. And then things went bad.

An arm with a gloved hand shot out and covered her mouth. Her eyes shot wide open, and he could see, even beneath the rag, she was screaming.

"Lita," he involuntarily said, desperately, to no one.

Lita squirmed with every ounce of fight in her small frame until suddenly the wide eyes rolled back, and her body became limp.

"No!" He shouted at his cell.

And everything suddenly went black.

He stared at the small screen. The bar at the bottom of the screen was fully extended, indicating the movie was over. Without thought, he played it again. It was no less shocking than the first time.

His eyes were wet by the time the third showing was over.

And that was when his room telephone rang. The loud shrill made him jump and drop his cell. He reached over with lightning speed, grabbing it like a greedy child.

"'llo," the single syllable hid the fear in his voice.

The voice on the other end was deep and even. It was a man in complete control.

"*You don't know what you've got 'till it's gone*," it said.

"What? Who are you? What d'you want?"

"Joni Mitchell," the voice continued. "She sung that. Very apt, I'd say, right?"

Barney's voice became desperate. His breathing quickened. "I don't know fuckin' Joni Mitchell. What have you done to my wife?"

"Shame. The song is *Big Yellow Taxi*. Beautiful lyrics."

"My wife!! Where is my fuckin' wife!!"

"And now you truly do understand, yes? You've taken the poor woman for granted for too long. She has done everything for you. Ask yourself, Barney, when was the last time you did something for her, huh?"

Barney's eyes darted around the room. He thought about texting someone. Maybe calling the police.

"Well?" the voice on the phone suddenly demanded.

Barney panicked. "Last weekend. I let her go out with her mom."

The sound of clapping could be heard down the phone. "You sir, are husband of the year. You allowed her to go and see her own mom? Wow! You are a catch!"

"She was grateful."

"I suspect because she didn't know about you meeting your girlfriend for a bit of rough 'n' tumble, am I right?"

Barney looked at the phone, and then at the buttons all grimy from the dirt of others. He wasn't sure what he was looking for, but he could picture a real hard bastard the other end. "Of course not," he replied, but it was weak. The words sliding out of his mouth the way lies do.

"You forget. I'm the one in control here. I have your wife's life in the palm of my hand."

"Don't hurt her, please." An edge of desperation had crept in. He meant every word. He realised, finally, just how much of a fool he'd been.

"I think you already have."

"What? No…"

"The trunk, Barney. Don't open the trunk. Not until I tell you to, right?"

Barney nodded. Then remembered he couldn't be seen. "N-no."

"Open the trunk, and your wife dies."

"Okay. But…" The call ended.

Straightaway, Barney pressed zero for reception. He heard it ring and ring. He grew increasingly frustrated. He slammed it down. Not just once but twice. A flash of anger. He glared at the trunk, and opened the door.

The rain had stayed off. The air was still thick with the smell of it though. Everywhere glistened.

A guy stood outside a room a few doors down. He was dressed like it was the roaring twenties. Suit, tie, and fancy hat. Either that or he'd fallen out of Jackson's *Smooth Criminal* music video.

"Another sinner, I see," the guy said with a sneer while looking straight at Barney. He lit a cigar and puffed out the thick smoke.

"I s'pose you're a fuckin' Angel, huh?" Barney barged by him. The skinny piece of shit would shrivel up if Barney started something.

"Evil lingers here," was all Barney heard by way of a reply.

Up ahead a woman appeared and disappeared. It almost seemed like she went through the wall. Barney was beginning to think this place was a fucking freakshow.

He got to check-in. The place was all *Mary Celeste*, so he banged on the bell. Eventually, the fat-fuck of an owner appeared not looking too pleased.

"The fuck you want? You lost your room?"

"Someone called me," Barney began. "On my phone."

"That's the general idea of them. Take it up with fuckin' Ma Bell or whoever invented those fuckin' things."

"I wanna know who it was!"

"Alexander Graham Bell, if you pushed me, but…"

"No, who called me!"

"The fuck would I know?" The short guy then threw his hands out in an exasperated pose. "Silly fuckin' question, but did you not think to ask them?"

"I did. They started saying fucking Joni Mitchell lyrics to me!"

"*Big Yellow Taxi*?"

"Yeah, how did you know?"

"Her best fuckin' song in my opinion."

Barney took a breath. "I don't care about your opinion. I wanna know who it was?"

"Joni Mitchell. Definitely. I know that one for sure!"

"No! Who called me!"

"This look like some telecommunications hub? You think I know every call made in those rooms?"

"*You don't?*"

"Okay. Okay," the guy held up his hands. "Let me go see." Off he disappeared. A sweaty smell lingered around like cartoon stench-lines.

Barney stood there. He looked all around, and his eyes came to rest on the board with the keys on. There were a lot of missing keys, which meant a lot of rooms. What if the guy was in another room?

Barney noticed a picture of the fat guy and his pretty wife. Sure, she was past her peak, but he was still punching well above his weight.

There was a noise as the guy returned. He puffed out his cheeks, and began to shake his head. "I asked around, but it seems I couldn't find a single person who could give a fuck about your call. Sorry about that!"

"What?" Barney was not used to this type of customer service.

"I said, I couldn't give a fuck. I went in there, took a drink, had a slice of pizza, then – 'cause I'm a nice guy – I came back to tell you what I found out. And, yeah, you're fuckin' welcome!"

"Un-fuckin'-believable!" Barney said slamming his fist on the counter. "Don't expect a good review on TripAdvisor!"

As Barney stormed out, he heard, "Don't expect to live until tomorrow!"

Barney couldn't believe it. The world was full of idiots.

The fancy cigar-smoker guy had disappeared now. Probably off doing the foxtrot, or some sort of shit.

And then somebody tapped him on the shoulder. He stopped and turned round to see a woman who looked like death.

She grinned at him. "Scared you, did I?"

"No, of course not."

She nodded anyway in a knowing fashion. "You like it here?"

He took in her clothes which looked as old as her. "Not much, no."

She shook her head again. "This place has gone to hell! It used to be the motel equivalent to The Ritz!"

Barney frowned. That seemed hard to believe. He looked out towards a sign that flashed with a faulty bulb. "Not now, but back then it was class!"

"Okay," Barney said walking away. The last thing he needed was a crazy old woman harassing him.

"This place has gone to hell!" she shouted to him as he walked away. "You come back here. You'll never make it out alive."

He threw a glance back at her, and then when he looked forward he jumped out of his skin. Two identical girls were there grinning at him.

"She's right, you know," the first one said with a huge grin.

The other looked down at her feet. She was slightly shy. "She sees things."

Barney held up his hands in defence. "I don't want no trouble!"

"We know you don't," the confident one said.

The other suddenly looked up and caught his eye. "But trouble has already found you!"

He scuttled off into his room in such a clumsy manner he fell to the floor as soon as his door slammed shut behind him. Again, he was face down on the carpet. Not a place he wanted to be.

He looked up at the trunk.

He could've sworn it had moved. It was now facing the other way...

Chapter 4

He found solace in his room. Amongst the nightmare, it was a sad fact that he looked to this small piss-smelling room as safety. He didn't want to leave, but then he didn't want to stay either. He walked over to where his coffee mug was. He needed a drink of something. His mouth was a haven for everything stale.

He picked up the mug and couldn't believe it. Another fly had drowned in it. "Fuck-sake!" He fished it out and flicked it to nowhere in particular.

Grabbing his cell, he noticed he'd had two missed calls. Why hadn't he heard them? He wondered whether the signal was shit or perhaps the fetid funk from sweaty socks and dirty sex was acting as a barrier.

The missed calls were from Rebecca. He didn't know what to do. Lita was missing, and now Rebecca was calling him. Maybe of all the times to choose, she wanted him now.

Or maybe she had Lita.

Was that it? Was it Rebecca who had finally flipped? She'd come to the realisation Barney was never going to leave his wife, and so she had taken the opportunity to kidnap and kill his wife. It was a movie waiting to be filmed.

He went into his phone again and pulled up the film. He searched for an indication of date and time. Perhaps present in the corner like they used to have on handheld cameras. But there was nothing.

He placed his phone back in his pocket and looked ahead. He didn't like the conclusions his brain was making.

What if the film had been recorded earlier that afternoon? What if his wife wasn't missing but had been with him all of this time?

A deep sinking feeling pushed down upon him. He felt betrayal.

He slowly walked to the trunk. He was aware that he was sweating now. Beads appeared on his brow, and he felt it trickle down his back. His heart was pounding in his chest. He knew why he shouldn't look inside the trunk. And yet that's why he wanted to do it so much.

Open it, you fat fuck, the voice inside his head chided. *What the fuck are you scared of?*

But of course, he knew the answer to that. He didn't want to see the curled up remains of his wife. He hoped she was in one piece. He was not known for having a strong stomach. He'd made sidewalk art on many an occasion with the contents of his stomach. He was the Picasso of puke.

He got down on his knees. His eyes welled up, and he made an involuntary noise in his throat. He placed both hands on top of the latches. His fat thumbs poised to flick them open.

He took a deep breath. He began to silently count in his head.

"One." A flash of her smiling face appeared in his mind's eyes. A beautiful day at the beach. Her embarrassment at showing skin in public.

"Two." Her laid out naked on their wedding night. Open and inviting, not embarrassed in the slightest. Wanting him like no other woman ever had wanted him before.

"Three." A banging on the door stopped him just as he was about to open the trunk. He let out the breath he was holding in.

The banging carried on. He got up, glanced back at the trunk, and opened up the motel room door slowly. Did they know he was about to open it?

There standing in front of him was Rebecca. She flashed a consolation smile and step to the side to reveal what she had with her.

A trunk. Of course, she did. Her trunk was identical to his, but no less sinister.

She fell into his arms and began to sob uncontrollably.

"Rebecca, what are you doing here?" Barney asked, but seeing as she had a similar trunk, he already knew.

"They told me to come here. Room twenty-four. I had to bring this," she said between tears, looking down at the trunk. She looked a sorry sight. Bedraggled stringy hair, and a worn-out complexion, her face was a mask of despair.

Mascara smudged with tears, she looked like she'd been fucked hard, and then dumped even harder.

Barney beckoned her in and pointed to his own trunk. "Snap," he said without humour.

"Shit," she said her eyes suddenly wide with fear. "Jon's missing, too." Her husband. Barney knew the guy was quite handsome, but by all accounts, a bit wet. He sounded too nice and caring – again, all the things he was not.

"Did you get a text?"

She nodded. "It's awful. Jon can take care of himself, but they snuck up behind him…"

"An arm with a rag to his face?" Barney could imagine Jon squealing. He was that sort of guy.

"Yes!"

Barney's head dropped as he helped her in with the trunk. "Lita, too."

"What is it they want?" Rebecca asked.

Barney dragged the trunk next to his and closed the door. "That's just it. They never said. They just kept saying not to open the trunk."

Rebecca looked mortified, but Barney still had something in the back of his head made him wonder whether she was behind it. Perhaps her trunk was filled with weights. What if she was the one who had left the call, and then kidnapped Lita. She was here now to see his face and see his pain. To watch him fall apart as he finally opened the trunk and found his wife in bloody pieces.

Rebecca hugged him again. "What are we going to do?"

Barney thought she couldn't be this much of a great actress, *could she*?

They both jumped as a clap of thunder dominated the silence.

And then the lights went out.

Rebecca screamed. A flash of lightning suddenly illuminated the room. Nerves on edge they both made embarrassing vocal noises.

Neither noticed the latches had come open.

"Jesus!" Barney said. "I fuckin' hate thunder and lightning!"

Again, they were in the pitch black. He was reduced to fear, something he wasn't used to.

And then the phone trilled. They flinched at another crack of thunder.

Barney grabbed it, Rebecca still held him closely. "'Llo?"

"Don't open the trunks."

"We haven't," Barney said in desperation. "Either of us. What do…" Another flash of lightning made Rebecca scream. At least he finally knew it wasn't her.

"You will find out." The call was cut.

"Barney," Rebecca said slowly. He turned around. Both lids were open. They gasped.

A clap of thunder sounded like a wordless shout of doom.

They stood rigid, not wanting to move. Not wanting to see what was inside. The smell of their sweat was strong; but the smell of their fear was stronger.

They slowly inched closer to the trunks. They looked at each other for words, but both fell short. How could you begin to believe what you couldn't understand?

Pulling apart, they peeked into their own trunk.

A flash of lightning revealed the contents.

A large glass bottle. Both reached in and pulled it out.

"What the hell?" Barney said.

"I don't get it?" Rebecca added.

Barney stared at it. Something was inside and moving. He looked closely. He couldn't believe it. It was a person.

And then he heard the buzzing. First one fly and then another.

"There's a small person inside?" Rebecca said, her voice going up and down in disbelief. She was close to hysterical tears. She then swung a hand to swat a fly.

More and more appeared from nowhere. The sound of buzzing got louder and louder.

"Is it them?" Barney heard himself say loudly. "Is it Lita and Jon?"

They looked at each other, but all they could see was a swarming wall of flies.

At once they both pulled out the corks of the bottles. They had to know.

A huge blinding flash of lightning brighter than anything either had ever experienced before shone out. They felt themselves move, fly, twist, and turn. And then they were dropped. Hard. Hitting the ground with a painful crash.

Everything was black. The buzzing had stopped. They could see nothing.

Barney got up. The floor was hard and seemed to be smooth and rounded. He reached out blindly and touched the cool, smooth side. He didn't want to admit what it felt like. He didn't want to believe what this meant.

Rebecca had come to the same conclusion. She sat on the floor and pulled her legs up to herself as she hugged them. She cried a lot of tears. Most of them in regret.

They were both in the bottles. In the trunks. Locked away for the next person to find. A sentence had been served.

Chapter 5

Sindy smiled broadly even though she now found herself in a horrible motel room. Next to her, and also grinning, was a guy called Brad. They'd had an affair two years previous.

"Oh my God!" She squealed, shaking her long blonde hair. "We're free!"

"What the fuck!" Brad added. "I thought we'd never make it out!"

They hugged each other, kissed, and got the hell out of there.

They had no plans to return to their old lives, their other halves could go screw themselves. Let them think they were still locked away in those bottles.

"Let's escape to somewhere remote," Sindy said. She really hoped Brad finally wanted to be with her forever and not his wife. She still felt a panic at being so close to the trunk, just in case it pulled her back in.

"You bet," was all he said as they headed out into the rain. Lost in a world they never thought possible. They laughed as their clothes got wet in the sudden downpour. They had each other and they suddenly, for the first time in two years felt completely alive. And also in love.

*

He pulled the hearse into the parking lot. The confidant Chinaman whistled through the rain and smiled to himself. He saw the couple flee from the room, their sentence completed. They were now getting wet and not caring one bit. Young love. He was like that once. Now it was all business.

The door of room twenty-four was ajar. He grabbed each trunk and slowly dragged them to the back of his hearse. He loaded them up, drove off.

Who knew how long they'd remain in the trunks. That wasn't his worry. He just cleaned up the mess that humans created. A never-ending role.

He was a bit like a marriage counsellor, except couples never got back together. He offered a whole range of services, this was just one of them.

An old lady tapped his window. "Don't bother," she mumbled with scary eyes. "This place has gone to ruin."

"Looks it," he muttered. He laughed at that. *There were no flies on her*, he mused.

And to think, that wasn't even the strangest thing to go on at Motel 666 that night…

The end

The Day

'The Day' was first published in 2018, in a charity anthology by Wolfgang Anthologies called Night of The Living Cure. This anthology is still available now.

Working in large corporate offices is akin to signing away your soul and creative independence. In doing this, I have decided to pack up all my dreams and aspirations and give them to some smarmy arsehole. One who does not pretend to like me, but one who will toss them into a room of other people and never look at them ever again.

Today I sold a thousand small computer components to some foreign company. Whoopy-fucking-do. I don't even know what the components do. They are just a bunch of serial numbers to me. I'm buoyed slightly by this success, more because I know this will earn me a little extra commission and I will of course be frittering it away on the sizable debts that I've gained. Life is a constant struggle to maintain some sort of happiness when outcome exceeds income for more months of the year than I care to admit.

I was about to bang my head against the desk in order to bring some excitement to my day when

Jim Ody

the loud piercing sound of the fire alarm went off. I get that it has to be loud, but making me jump when it goes off seems to be counter-productive. To warn people of a possible fire and need to evacuate the building whilst increasing the risk of sudden heart attacks seems bonkers.

We have a test alarm every week, which of course we ignore. Then once a year on a sunny day we have a fire drill. This usually happens at the point I have just bought myself a coffee and a chocolate muffin, and I'm forced to leave said items at my desk for fear of the disappointed looks cast my way by the various fire marshals and their irritating sounds of tutting as I make my way with the others to the designated point in the car park. That forgotten area where no one gives a fuck whether or not we are there or laid down on the office floor writhing in agony as flames lick uncontrollably at our skin and the smell would put people off bacon for at least a day or so.

However, this time was different. There was a certain panic, and subtle hysteria slowly growing. Whispers whipped around being tweaked and slightly embellished each time, but by the time it was re-told to me by Jean, it was about a colleague who had suddenly gone crazy and started to attack other colleagues. Someone hit the fire alarm in panic, and it sent the whole company flooding out into the car park at once.

I took the opportunity to light a cigarette. A couple of people made huge gestures to flap away the smoke, but fuck it, go back in the building with that crazy bastard if you don't like it, I told them.

My arm was a little itchy. I remembered the cut that I had done this morning. It had begun to sting a little, but of course as a man I wouldn't say anything.

Then there were more murmurings, and as I looked over the heads of all of the people, I could see a wave of bodies suddenly moving. It looked like someone was fighting. This was odd behaviour. Computer geeks are known more for being passive and acting alone. Interaction with physical people was limited to delivery drivers and sci-fi conventions. Indeed, any confrontation was in the form of a strongly worded email.

Then I heard screams. Not just the over-exaggerated cries from a highly-strung woman, but one that possessed an element of fear. Suddenly people were running.

I am a slightly more alpha-male sort of guy, so naturally I thought *fuck it*, and I legged it too. I didn't need this. And I didn't need the coffee and chocolate muffin now sitting on my desk not realising that I was not coming back.

I wasn't on my own as a number of people were heading off to the station too. In fact, not many were venturing back into work. That is how important we rate our jobs and work commitments. When the fit-hits-the-shan, we're out of there!

"I'll ring Trevor later and see when we can go back in," a team leader was saying holding onto her handbag tightly like I was about to mug her.

"Jack told us to go, he'll email us at home," a stringy guy in a suit that was a size too big for him was saying. He looked like he was about to cry. Pussy.

I nodded to both even if it was to others they were speaking. I was trying to justify my swift exit. Bonding with people who I'd never spoken to before. Equal rebels with a cause.

The train was due in another ten minutes, so I pulled out my phone and like the rest of the world lost myself in the world of others via social media. I hadn't scrolled for long before I noticed something strange. There were a number of cases regarding people going a little bit crazy and attacking others. Initial reports suggested some sort of virus outbreak. But nobody really knew.

I had a sudden irrational thought about Wendy, home alone. Did she know what was going on? I looked at my phone and thought about ringing home.

"Hey mate," a gruff cockney voice sang out. "Can I borrow your phone?"

I looked at it, and then at him, unsure of a response. Suddenly out of nowhere he grabbed it and ran off. Stunned I did little more than step forward a few steps like he might have a sudden conscious, stop, and jog back to me. He didn't, and I no longer had a way of ringing home. It was now that I remembered the lack of payphones in the world. Who said technology was such a good thing?

"I saw what happened," a voice said. I turned and saw a skinny lady with greasy hair and bright red rimmed glasses. I was suddenly cautious like she might try and nick my wallet. I just half-smiled and nodded.

"It's okay, I'm not after anything," she giggled in a way a small child might.

"That's good to know."

"D'you want me to be a witness?" She said this like a child might say *d'you want to go on an adventure?*

"No, don't worry. Not much chance of catching him, or getting it back."

"Well, you're a cheerful fella, ain't ya!" she laughed again.

"You got a phone I could borrow?" I asked her.

"Nope. Don't like them," she said matter-of-factly, like I'd asked her for a gun.

"What don't you like about them?"

"People can contact me… and know where I am." It was now the most serious that I had seen her. I used this to edge away from her.

Thankfully the train arrived. I smiled again, stepped onto the train, and found a seat next to the window. Of course the lady followed and positioned herself in front of me.

"Good spot!" She grinned like I had specifically chosen these seats for the two of us.

I shrugged. She was obviously going to sit down anyway so I had better just get used to it. And her.

"I'm Lavinda," she said holding out her hand, I took it weakly hoping it would be another reason for her not to like me.

"Lavender?" I'd heard her, it was my way of trying to be funny.

"No, La-vin-da."

"Ahh, okay," I replied in a way that someone does when they really don't get it.

Finally, and with a slight judder, the train moved off. *About bloody time*, I thought knowing that Lavinda, would now want to verbally harass me until the end of time.

"What's your name?" she asked.

"Terry," I said. It's not, and I'm not sure why I said it. Perhaps I was worried that if I gave her my name, she would piece together things about me until she had a whole wall full of my pictures. Besides, no one calls their child Terry anymore, so I was helping to increase a name threatened with extinction. Like Trevor and Roland.

"Hi Terry."

I smiled. It was such a pointless conversation I was wondering whether I should headbutt the window as hard as I could to see whether I could knock myself out. Unconscious I would be free of her.

I tried to lose myself in the world outside the window. A fat chance of that, of course. She and her silly giggle kept finding things amusing, and when she wasn't giggling, she was trying to engage in conversation with me. I bloody hate that. I want to sit here on my own and look out of the window. Maybe notice some wrong-doings in a garden that I could write about under the title 'Man On A Train', but no, I had this inane flea of a woman in my ear. Natter, natter, natter! Natter, natter, natter!

"What?" I said hoping she would acknowledge that I had not been listening to her.

She was still fucking smiling at me. She had seen me being mugged, which sounded like a worse crime than having someone snatch your mobile, and I had done my very best to ignore her, but instead in some warped way she had seen this as a challenge, or even perhaps a bit-of-fun. Cheer up the grumpy-git!

"I said, *Are you married*?" she said.

"Married, me? No," I was quick to reply. Too quick, I realized seeing her eyes flash wide, and her smile grow even bigger.

"Single then?" Her tongue darted suddenly over her lips like some reptile having a creature in front of it considered as prey. I should've said yes. I was too worried it would only feed on to more questions, and now I'd done it. I'd basically challenged her to stalk me and poke me with questions until I relented and agreed to have my way with her in the urine-splashed toilets on the train.

"Not exactly."

She winked, tapped her nose, and grinned wickedly. "I get you, Mr Mystery."

I can guarantee she doesn't. If she did then she'd get up and fuck off somewhere else. Instead, she changed position thrusting out her breasts as if there were on offer.

I managed to ignore her for a few more blissfully silent minutes.

Until we heard the scream coming from further back.

"What the heck?" she said looking alarmed. I stood up and looked around. There was a kerfuffle. Someone had fallen, and a couple of guys were scrambling.

"Get off me!" a voice almost squealed. I could see a flash of blood in the distance, and suddenly there was a wave of people rushing towards us.

The train lurched forward, and amidst screeching of wheels people fell like they were being silently mown down by a machine gun.

I grabbed the table as we finally came to a stop. I glanced at Lavinda who was pale and looked shocked. Visibly her heart was pumping fast.

The doors came open, though I couldn't be sure whether someone did this or it was automatic. I was up out of my seat and pushing and squashing my way through the doors and out on to the gravel and grass next to the tracks.

Up and down the carriages people spilled out. But no one stayed there. Everyone was scattering in different directions, leading me to believe that our outburst was not isolated.

Perhaps I should've waited for Lavinda. She would be slower than me, so if I came under attack then I could push her at them like some sacrificial lamb.

"What was that?" I said looking over at another guy in a suit. We were slowing to a jog now.

"No idea. That woman just went nuts!"

We shook our heads and jogged on going through a field and towards a road.

As we got nearer, we heard cars, tires screaming, and the sound of a collision. Smoke plumed high into the sky like some warning to stay away. We were no longer good Samaritans on hand to help but survivalists looking to stay out of trouble.

We ran to the other side of the hedge where there was a gateway.

"D'you know where we are?" He asked.

I nodded. "Roughly. There's a village just down the road there. If we follow it then we can be there in ten minutes. We should be able to get a lift or a taxi or something."

"Okay," he replied. He was willing to trust me.

We got to the road and followed it in the direction of the village.

"What's going on?" he said to me. He seemed worried by it all.

"No idea," I started. "It seems like there are a number of people all over the place going crazy."

"What, like a virus?"

"Like zombies, more like."

He grinned. "Shut up." Then he saw my serious face.

"Okay, perhaps not quite living dead zombies, but they are infected with a virus and no longer human, so I'm not quite sure what else you'd call that!"

"Fuck."

"Probably the opposite of that." I tried a little gallows humour as he pulled his phone out.

"You've got a phone?"

"Haven't you?" His tone was slightly childish.

"No, someone stole it at the station."

"Fuck," he eloquently said again. He clearly liked that word.

He pushed some buttons. "Ah, I see where we are now."

"How about you ring a taxi then?"

He held his finger in the air as a sign of agreement.

We stopped. He dialled and waited. And waited. And waited.

"Nothing."

We carried on walking but this time in silence. Both of us weighed down with just such a huge number of thoughts, it overwhelmed our ability to speak. At no point had I asked him his name. Honestly, I couldn't have cared less. After today I would probably never see him again.

I'll call him Bob if I get the chance.

I noticed that behind us there were the odd people that had followed us, happy with the direction that we were going in.

We got to the village, and there was an eerie quietness to the place. And then we saw why.

There were cars that had driven into each other. Bodies laid out in the open swimming in pools of crimson. All with pained faces painted on permanently.

Shops had windows smashed, and doors were wide open but unwelcoming.

"I'm going to see if there is anyone around," he said. I nodded as he walked off to a convenience store.

I walked up and around the side of the car in front of me. A lady was sprawled out on the pavement but her car keys were in her hand. Something had attacked her as she got to her car.

I grabbed them and pressed the button. Relief washed over me as the car beeped. I got in and tried the ignition. It started first time.

I reversed, and looked over my shoulder. The guy was coming out of the shop. Behind him was a large man with the eyes of the devil and blood all over his face.

I slammed my foot on the accelerator and wheel spun out of there.

Sorry Bob.

*

I had to get home. The world was falling down around me. I swerved to miss a body in the road. I didn't stop to see whether it was male or female.

I put on the radio but all I got was static. I chanced music and was met by the awful warble of Adele. Just my luck. It could've been some compilation rock album, or a decent band's greatest hits, but no, bloody Adele.

I then realised that driving down the country road there was a mild serenity that I was now a part of. Birds were in the trees, and the outside world was peaceful. A pang of guilt threatened to dark-cloud my day as I remembered the look of surprise on the guy's face as I left him. The bottom line is that in a crisis, it's the strong that survive. For each person you are attached to, as a larger unit you are weakened.

I came to my town. A large sprawling one that had once been a trio of villages, but through industrialization and being a couple of train stops away from the big city, had slowly multiplied until it seeped into the surrounding fields replacing the sprawling countryside with generic new housing estates and village centres.

Suddenly, two figures ran out in front of me, hands waving erratically. I pumped the brakes, and turned the wheel – careful not to roll as I dodged them. However, I had swerved into the other lane, and suddenly had to slam the accelerator to miss an on-coming van. In doing so I shot off to the right and hit a tree that was too young to smash the front of the car but old enough to bring me to a standstill and fire out the airbag.

The engine had stalled, and I turned the key but it stuttered, groaned, and died. In defeat I opened the door and got out.

"Help us!" A guy was pleading, his arms outstretched and dragging his left leg. The girl with him looked grey in colour and her face began to contort as if in anger.

I backed away at first but soon turned and ran as fast as I could.

The world was seriously fucked. That was easy to see.

My house was still a fifteen-minute walk from here, and I really didn't know what would meet me when I got there.

It seemed a lifetime ago that I was sat at my workstation and thinking about original ways of committing suicide in an office environment. I had come up with 183 separate ways so far. I hoped to reach 250. I suppose if you were to put things into perspective, it wasn't the most important thing, but it passed the time.

I was now beginning to be a little more tentative. No striding around like Billy Bigballs, shouting in a loud confident voice *"Look at me!"* No, I was now peeking around walls and almost tiptoeing from building to building like the Scooby Doo Gang. I had a decision to make in regards to main roads and footpaths. I could think of a hundred reasons for both as to why I should take them, but with my crystal ball I was a little stumped, and therefore had to pick.

I cut through the graveyard. If I was to be attacked and died, then at least here is a logical resting spot, whether it is or is not the place that I would choose in life to be buried – or in this case probably left to be eaten by dogs and foxes.

I scanned the area carefully. A woman was sobbing next to a gravestone. One hand grabbing tightly to the stone giving her some comfort. Somewhere else in the world the end of that granite was more than likely decorating a big kitchen as a worktop.

An old guy was further along staring at a grave. He was still and lost to the world. *Victim*, I thought and walked off.

I headed off down a path that had the backs of people's garden fences either side. I got about half way down with a bend in the path in sight when I heard something to the side of me.

I turned, and suddenly something jumped at me. Instinctively I threw a punch, hitting fur from something that let out a noise of displeasure and ran off.

A voice behind me said accusingly, "Did you just punch a cat?"

I looked at the little old woman wrapped up in skin, bones, and a large shawl.

"No," I lied hoping she'd believe me and not her eyes.

"You most certainly did. You should be ashamed of yourself!"

"It jumped at me with rabid eyes. It was going for my throat!" I tried feigning fear.

"Absolute poppycock! You took out your anger the only way a man can. With his fists on an unsuspecting victim."

I tilted my head to the side and made a face that suggested I did not agree. "No, really."

"What are you going to do when someone bigger than you comes up and punches you, huh?"

"Cry, more than likely," I said with a hint of sarcasm. "I don't like being hit."

"And nor do cats, young man! Nor do cats!" and off she stormed.

So throughout a day of people going completely bonkers and attacking others, the loony world had suddenly stopped whilst an old biddy dressed me down for defending myself against a wild animal. Bloody typical.

I walked on and got to the corner when I heard a scream from behind. I turned and saw a man and a woman on top of the old lady, crimson was spraying out from her neck.

I didn't need to see any more. I legged it.

Around the corner the path opened up to the front of the houses on an adjacent street. I was suddenly aware of more people. The most eerie thing was that they were all looking at me.

My initial jog turned into a full-blown sprint. I kept to the path and was careful to keep my eyes peeled for others.

I passed a car that had its windows smashed. On another the door was open but no one was inside. I didn't dare stop to see if there were any keys. The strange mob weren't that far behind.

My plan was to cut across the field behind the houses in front, eventually taking me to the back of my own house.

I spotted the gateway and headed that way. Suddenly a youth stepped out. His head down and covered by a hood.

"Where're you goin'?" a menacing voice came from under the hood.

"Shit!" I said pointing past him. He turned and looked, saw nothing, and turned back. I punched him hard on the nose. The shock, rather than the power, knocked him to the floor and I legged it again.

I heard his voice shouting obscenities, and then I heard panic as he saw the mob.

I was long gone by the time he was caught.

Jim Ody

The field had permanently long grass. The owner used to be a farmer, but he sold off the land to a developer who had failed to do anything with it yet. This was good as it meant I had fields behind my house rather than another street of people that I might have to have a polite conversation with. No one wants that.

I snuck through the gap in the fence and quickly looked behind me. There was no one there. I dragged over a large pile of four blocks to hide the gap.

There was a sense of relief that washed over me. The whole world – or certainly the world around me that I knew – had fallen to pieces. However I was now home, and that made it easier to cope with.

I pulled out my keys and undid the backdoor. The last thing I wanted was to go around the front of my house and see a host of weirdoes ready to kill me on my own doorstep.

I pushed open the door and then locked it behind me.

I tentatively walked around the kitchen and then lounge just to check that everything was in order. I then walked slowly up the stairs and checked the three bedrooms and bathroom.

All clear.

I went to the cellar. I opened the door and walked slowly down the stairs.

There she was with sudden recognition in her eyes. Behind the gag she was almost smiling.

"Hi Wendy," I said in what I hoped to be a soothing voice.

She was happy to see me. Tears welled and then rolled down both cheeks. Such a beautiful sight.

The stench from the urine near the corner of the room was strong and almost stung my eyes.

"Did you miss me," I asked. She pulled at her restraints. She wanted her hands free so badly so she could hug me. She wanted to glide them over my body before going crazy and ripping off my clothes.

I chuckled. It was great to be wanted.

Nowadays it's so easy to meet women. A face on a website and a generic blurb of lies is all that it took. She met me and instantly fell in love with me. Love is such a beautiful thing.

I walked up to her, suddenly feeling a little lethargic after my extra, and unexpected, cardiovascular activities today. I smoothed my hand through her hair. She moved her head quickly. A term of endearment I'm sure.

My nose began to bleed suddenly, but this only excited me more. I grabbed at her, and then without warning I dived in towards that sweet smooth neck and bit with all my might. The feeling was one of euphoria. She bucked, and I bit again. And again. Chunk after chunk of her flesh I spat out until, before I knew it, she was doubled over and still and blood trickled out like it was from a tap.

That was so satisfying, I thought.

I walked up the stairs of the cellar my limbs suddenly stiffer than previously. My need for more blood was insatiable.

Jim Ody

I wondered whether the neighbours were home.
I sniffed the air. Someone was definitely
nearby.

The End

There was more blood than I was expecting. The wound smiled in approval as the knife sliced open her throat.

At one time, she'd have been shouting obscenities at me. This act had finally silenced her. At some point she'd forgotten her vows, and liberating herself from her clothing in the presence of random men had replaced them. The breath of those men didn't help her now.

I slipped the photo into my pocket. The frame I threw hard against the wall, mildly satisfied to see it smash – like our marriage – into a thousand pieces.

I gritted my teeth as I glanced for the last time at eyes now dead to the world. I'd finally opened them for her. Ironically, it would seem.

I felt nothing as I sat in the rental car looking at the house. The bloody scene within. A blotch on the copybook of suburbia. A headline waiting to be written.

I pulled away and pressed the button on the detonator. Through the darkness, the world behind me lit up. I smiled. My doppelganger was 400 miles away providing me with what would be an airtight alibi.

Tomorrow will be phase 2...

A Doll Named Sasha

This story was accepted twice into anthologies and both times the anthologies never got off the ground. This story is based on my daughter Jessie and her own toy bunny.

The doll Sasha also appears in my novel A Cold Retreat.

A Doll Named Sasha

Summertime was here, and the little girl had eyes of wonder as she thought about the weeks that lay ahead. Too young to worry about fashions and false friends, her world was simple and mostly filled with joy. And ice-cream. And her cuddly rabbit toy.

Her smile was as huge as the garden outside her window. The garden was not just the place of beauty where her parents complained of weeds and bad-backs; it was the gateway to fantastical lands, where a small child could be lost in an adventure. To roam free within the confines of her mind until a time society no longer allowed her that gift.

Jess was a little girl with a great big imagination.

She was amazed at the bright sunshine that flooded through a small break in her curtains. She tried to catch the speckles of dust as they danced through the rays of light. She imagined them to be fairies, a lot like the ones she swore lived at the bottom of the garden.

Throwing on some clothes and grabbing her bunny, Jess crept down the stairs like she was a character from one of her books. Perhaps she was trying not to wake a sleeping ogre; or maybe a wicked witch was close by looking for a little girl. One to put into her cauldron and boil her bones dry!

Hugging her toy bunny called Honey, she giggled at her silly thoughts and crept into the kitchen. There, she yawned and stretched but was no longer tired. She loved to get up earlier than everyone else and make her own breakfast. She felt like such a big girl.

She was eight and beginning to take control of her life, the way that young girls can. She had friends, but here in a street on the edge of town, they felt a million miles away.

Honey was her best-friend, providing both comfort and companionship when she was tired, hurt, or upset. He completely understood her. His once white fur was now a creamy-grey and more than a little patchy. The patina of true love all too evident, but only added to his charm.

She poured the last of the milk over her sugary cereal, but still she required more. She liked the colourful shapes to float, and shook out the last drops, hoping more would appear like a magic trick. But it didn't, and there was no more in the fridge.

She wasn't meant to open the front door; her parents relaying tales of bogeymen huddled in the shadows waiting to pounce on innocent children.

The fear of the unknown increased her heartrate and made her little tummy feel all swimmy.

She tentatively looked up the stairs, and when satisfied that no one was there, she whipped open the door to grab the freshly delivered milk from the doorstep.

But that wasn't all that was there.

Protecting the milk was a doll that looked more like a miniature human. One that was passed out like her aunty Jean after one too many gins. Without thought, Jess grabbed the doll, and as an afterthought, the plastic bottle of milk, too.

Without taking her eyes off of the doll, she put the milk in the kitchen, her breakfast now forgotten, and returned to the doll. What was it doing there? Where did it come from? Who put it there? All of these questions tumbled around in her small head, but in conclusion, she didn't care. The doll was hers, of this she was sure! But there was something about it. It was so different from Honey. It had hypnotizing eyes that appeared to look right inside of her. The face was so real.

She placed it on a spare chair next to her, looked at it one more time, and went to finish topping up the milk in her cereal bowl. She grabbed the bowl and walked back to the table.

The doll was not there. It had disappeared.

Slightly amused at first, she looked around and eventually located it on the floor. It looked like it was trying to climb back up.

"What are you doing down there?" she said and picked the doll back up. She was fascinated by its beautifully stitched red dress, and she smoothed her fingers over the tiny buttons. She looked inside the dress and saw a name tag: Sasha.

"Hi, Sasha," she said, but the doll, of course, remained silent.

But as she looked further, she saw a plastic button. When she pressed it Sasha came to life and said a number of phrases:

"My name is Sasha!", "I love you!" and *"Let's be friends!"*

Jess ate her breakfast whilst watching cartoons on a small television set. Honey sat one side of her and Sasha the other. She couldn't wait to show her friends her new doll. They were going to be so jealous!

*

Later that day, she tried to explain to her parents that Sasha had been on the doorstep, but they didn't believe her.

"Why would someone leave a doll there?" Her mum said rhetorically. Her dad shrugged the whole thing away, the subject holding little to no interest to him. If his daughter was happy, then what did it matter where the doll came from?

"Can we go to the park?" Jess asked, perched on the arm of the chair. She was looking out of the window at baby-blue skies dusted with either the hint of cloud or trails left by an aircraft. It was a bright and sunny summer's day. One that invited you out to enjoy the sun.

"I guess so," her dad replied.

Ten minutes later and they were ready to leave.

"Have you got Honey?" Her dad asked.

She nodded. "And Sasha!"

The walk didn't take long as the park was situated just around the corner of her street. Jess swung Sasha around, but kept dropping Honey. The doll was large and needed both hands, whereas her bunny was now becoming a little annoying.

"Careful with your bunny," her dad said. "You don't want him to get dirty!"

Jess nodded and threw him to her dad. "Can you look after him for me?" She clutched Sasha tightly to her. She was so special. Maybe she had seen Jess, and decided herself to come and wait outside her door! That's what Jess thought as she placed her in the guarded seat of the toddler swing and began to push the doll gently back and forth. She was sure she could almost hear the doll squeal with delight at the fun she was having.

After a while, Jess looked over and saw her dad sitting with Honey. He was being silly and pretending to talk to her bunny. He looked up and waved to her. She waved back, but felt a little guilty. Deep down she was sure Honey would understand. He might even end up being best friends with Sasha. Wouldn't that be great?

At one point, Jess saw one of her friends, Lacey, in the distance. She giggled with joy when she saw her. They both waved and jumped up and down before running to each other.

"Look what I've got!" Jess beamed showing off Sasha.

"Wow! She's lovely," Lacey said. "When did you get her?"

"This morning. She was sitting outside of our front door!"

"Huh? You mean she just appeared there?"

Jess nodded quite matter-of-factly and said, "Yes. I think she wanted to come and live with me!"

"Wow! I wish that happened to me!"

Lacey picked up the doll and squeezed her tightly.

"I'm Sasha!" the doll said suddenly, making Lacey jump. Both girls laughed at that. They continued to push the button and marvel at the voice coming out.

"She's wonderful!" Lacey said. "Much better than your bunny. He doesn't say anything!"

Jess nodded, although deep down she did feel a pang of guilt. She and Honey had been through many adventures. They'd been on holiday together; camped out in the garden; gone on the school trip to the Wilderness Centre for three nights; been in her pushchair, cot, toddler bed and now her big single bed. In fact, Jess did wonder what life without Honey would be like.

Maybe that was all about growing up? With Sasha she could do so much more.

*

That evening when they were having tea, Jess's mum looked over at Jess and said, "Come on, Jess. You can't have them both there at the table!"

Jess frowned, and looked at her dad. "Your mother's right," he said. "You need room to eat. You can play with them after."

And then Sasha fell off of the table with a crash.

They all looked down at the doll.

"Let's be friends," the voice inside of Sasha said. The family looked at each other, and suddenly through the tension laughed.

Jess bent down and swooped Sasha up. She grabbed Honey by the leg and chucked them both onto her chair in the lounge.

Whilst they were eating, Jess's mum enquired, "Did she come from one of your friends, love? Sasha, I mean?"

Jess shrugged, "I don't think so. Lacey would've said, and no one else would send a doll to me."

"I wonder whether she was left outside the wrong house?" Jess's dad suggested.

Her mum frowned. "Maybe, but it's not going to be for Ann next-door, is it? She's a seventy-year-old woman."

It was a mystery. They were the corner house on the street. The other houses nearby belonged to older couples whose children had since grown up and left home. They just didn't seem to be the sort of people a doll was meant for.

But then you never could tell, could you?

Jess finished up her food and took her plate out to the kitchen before skipping off into the lounge.

She stopped still when she saw Sasha was no longer laid down in the chair where she'd been left but was sitting in a seat and staring at her. Her body was facing one way, but her head had turned so as she could look directly at Jess as she entered the room.

Honey was where he'd been left.

Slowly, she walked up to Sasha. "What are you doing there?" she asked but suddenly felt a little uneasy.

She picked her up and placed her onto her lap as she sat and watched cat videos on YouTube. Jess loved these. She could've sworn she heard Sasha laugh at one stage, too, but when Jess looked at her, the doll remained quiet.

At one point, Sasha suddenly said, "I love you!" which only made Jess cuddle her more and give her a little kiss.

*

That night Jess's mum ran her a bath, and Sasha came into the bathroom with her. Jess washed Sasha's legs and arms but was careful not to get her too wet so as the voicebox no longer worked.

Abandoned, Honey sat face-down and forgotten at the end of the bed, waiting for Jess. Then she came in and was careful to place Sasha under the covers with her whilst she read her a book out loud. Jess cuddled her and whispered, "We're going to do so much tomorrow, Sasha. I can't wait for all the adventures we're going to get into!"

"Let's be friends!" Sasha said, "I love you!" and Jess laughed before turning off the lights.

"I love you, too."

Honey was still at the bottom of the bed, discarded.

When the lights go out, that is when everything becomes spooky. The darkness welcomes everything that is not of this world, its natural cloak covers those that move around amongst us.

Jess's mind certainly played tricks with her, but she no longer had the night terrors that hindered her sleep a few years previously. She was trying to be brave. She snuggled into the hard plastic of Sasha.

Eventually she dropped off to sleep.

*

It was early morning when Jess woke up. She looked down at both sides of her and under the covers of the bed but couldn't find Sasha.

Where was she? For a few seconds she even wondered whether it was all a dream. Maybe there wasn't a Sasha after all.

Jess caught a whiff of something that tickled her nose. It smelt a little like when daddy was at the petrol station. That strong chemical smell that fizzes around her nostrils.

Immediately, she jumped out of bed. Her eyes quickly scanned around the room, expecting to find her. But the doll was nowhere to be seen. She ran over to her window and glanced outside. The garden was down below.

That is when she saw the smoke. Not much, but small wisps floating up from her dad's barbeque.

Without another thought, and as quietly as she could, she ran downstairs, out of the backdoor, and into the garden. Instinct took over. Something was driving her to push on towards the smoking barbeque. She didn't even stop to think why she was doing it. She just knew that she had to go there.

Jess was super careful as she pushed open the top of the barbeque. At first, she was engulfed by the thick smoke suddenly liberated from inside. And then it cleared.

Through the blackened remains, she could make out flashes of Sasha's red dress surrounded by a melted and completely disfigured doll. There was a huge gaping hole in her chest. She couldn't believe it. She wanted to cry.

Who would do such a thing? She was so cross and upset.

She glanced all around. First the doll mysteriously appears, and the next minute, somebody has taken her and destroyed her in the garden. She then looked up at her bedroom window. There was a movement.

She looked down at the ground and saw the small footprints. With disbelief, she followed them back into the house.

And then confused, she ran up the stairs and walked into her bedroom, following the small chargrilled marks as she went.

Honey was no longer face-down and forgotten, but laid in her bed, only his little face looking out from beneath the sheets.

She looked around the room. Who was there? Was somebody playing tricks on her?

She pulled back the covers. And saw the charcoal smudges next to Honey. His blackened feet dark against his off-white coloured fur. The smell of fuel came from the lighter laid next to him.

She couldn't believe what she was seeing. Was it…? Could he have…?

The movement was slight. Only a person who spent many years with him would recognize it. But it was there.

"Oh, Honey," she said. "I could never replace you!"

And that's when Honey fully turned his head, and Jess could see the small charred voicebox in his paws. He pressed it.

"I love you," the voice of Sasha rang out, and Jess could've sworn that there was an even bigger smile on Honey's face. "Let's be friends!"

"I'm so sorry, Honey." She swept him up and cuddled him tightly, and from that day forth forgot all about a doll named Sasha.

The End

Memories flash like an instamatic camera. Filters of warm colours inject dopamine into a worn-out brain. The doors of dark times rattle but remain locked. The heart on my sleeve beats loudly; a rhythm to my summer.

I was fifteen years old when I became a man. Not through sordid fumblings with the class floozy, but the milestone passed when taking the life of another. He'd beaten the confession out of an innocent soul. She lay broken on the hardwood floor; sniffing up bloody tears as her dignity crawled from her body. Forever scarred, her world would never be the same again.

He was smiling when he walked away from her. He'd felt like a man. Another woman taught a lesson. I cooled him down with petrol. Then introduced to him a naked flame. He danced to a silent tune, flapping his arms in a violent expressive dance. Singed nerve-endings and roasted fat deposits chargrilled him to a pitiful crisp. It wasn't just about justice, more like boredom-induced pleasure.

You never forget the fond memories of summer. Ice-lollies, swimming in the lake, first kisses and killing a man.

And of course, come next summer, I'd do it all again.

Surprise Party

'Surprise Party' was first published in 2018 by Crazy Ink. The anthology was entitled *Bloody Bonkers*.
The doctor mentioned in this book also features in the novel *Mr Watcher*.

Jim Ody

Chapter 1

The car park was full when I got to work. A sprawling sea of expensive cars.

I was late. I mean I was shockingly late. I ended up walking so far towards the reception area that I was close to gaining sponsorship and raising money for a charity.

"Afternoon!" Shirley, the middle-aged receptionist, said with a wink. It wasn't quite ten o'clock. From a distance she looked attractive but as you got closer the reality became a shock. With each step she aged five years. She was nice enough even if she was packaged up to look thirty years younger than she was.

"It's my birthday," I said by way of an excuse. "Surely you can be late on your birthday?"

"Well, many happy returns of the day!" she said, and for a minute looked like she might be moving in to kiss me. I waved it off and hit the stairs two at a time. I swiped my security pass and walked into the corporate zoo of people trying to look busy. It was a skill that only very few could master.

As I walked, I ducked down under the large ugly partitions doing all I could to get to my desk undetected. I opened my laptop and urged it to load up something that vaguely resembled work, helping the guise of my having been there for over an hour already.

Birthdays are funny things when you get to my age. This was my thirtieth and up there with one of the big ones. It was no twenty-one but was certainly no forty.

My fiancée, Megan had sent me a text earlier wishing me a happy birthday. She'd added more kisses to it than was applicable to people our age. She sometimes boarded on stalkerish. It was cute, and she was even cuter.

She wanted me to meet her later on.

I should explain. We're getting married next year and have been looking around potential wedding venues. The thing is, we don't want fancy places where we pretend we're royalty or the upper-crust of society. No, we want quirky, kooky, and odd. That's us.

She found a place deep in the woods that she said would be perfect. It was a huge old house. We fell in love with it, and before we had time to breathe, we had placed a bid and had bought it. We're still waiting for the final sale to go through, but we have the keys and have already started to measure things up. She wants me to meet her there later.

She must take me for a complete fool. I know what this is. My fiancée wants me to meet her somewhere on my birthday. I kno she's throwing

Jim Ody

me a surprise party. She's wrapped it up in the fleeting notion of a romantic meeting, but it is for my party. I'd put money on it!

A couple of weeks ago I mentioned that I had never had a party before. I grew up on a farm with few friends. A party was not something that fit in with my parents' plans. I've never been that worried, but Megan thought this to be a heart-breaking story. So here she was trying to fulfil my needs like she always does.

A dark cloud came over my world as my boss strolled over. I was able to click into a spreadsheet and look like I'd been pondering over a calculation for a while. This was my default move.

"Some sort of issue, Jenkins?" he said. "Your calculator broken!" he winked at Dee, an eighteen-year-old smacking gum and trying to hide the fact she'd been on social media since I arrived. She more than likely would remain on it until lunchtime when she'd have an hour break flirting with Nigel in Accounts, before hitting it again for the afternoon. She didn't understand business attire and thought an open blouse exposing her large boobs was appropriate. It wasn't. It was distracting and did nothing for the team's productivity.

"Nope, just a discrepancy in the inflation percentage calculation. I'm guessing the proportion of interest is split incorrectly between these separate tax codes – half of which cannot actually be fully claimed back, just partially!" I pointed at a column with my pen and laughed in a way that suggested this was obvious.

"I see, I see," he said in a hurried fashion to try and hide the fact that he had no idea what I was going on about. He wasn't the only one. I knew he hated the very mention of tax. It was a business area where no one claimed to be an expert. I wrapped it up in some jargon to confuse him. The spreadsheet in front of me was fine and had no tax figures whatsoever. But, like looking on Medusa, he was scared to look at it as I might question him further, and he'd mumble the question back at me in a way that reversed it for me to answer. Classic middle-management tactic.

"So, I need the Mackenzie report by 6pm," he grinned knowing this was bad news. "Priorities, Jenkins!" He winked at Dee. I thought about pressing her to speak to HR about him.

"But I have to go on time today. It's my birthday."

"Then consider this my gift to you!"

"Seriously?" I whined like a teenager.

"As seriously as you want a promotion."

I sent a text to Megan. She responded in an upbeat manner which only underlined the point this was definitely a surprise party tonight.

There were other things, too.

I saw a couple of my work colleagues whisper and laugh and then glance up at me. When I asked people what they were up to later, their responses were vague.

Though distracted, I battled on with pulling the figures together for the Mackenzie report. It was bullshit. The report would sit there until Monday now. There was no reason it had to be done by 6pm.

My phone went off at one stage. I recognized the number. It was not the person I wanted to speak to. Not today.

However, looking at my phone was neither the mending of nets nor the catching of fish, as they say, so I cracked on to finish.

"Thanks," my boss said as I slapped it down on his desk. He was on Facebook, staring at a page of a girl in a bikini. He'd even zoomed in on her erect nipples. Sometimes I felt sorry for him.

I shook my head and walked out. Not today though, the fat wanker!

"Hey, Jenkins?"

"Yes," I said through gritted teeth.

He over-exaggerated a shrug and got up. "I hate to do this but I need the report emailed out to the list of people I've just emailed you. Not altogether but individually. Then can you print the report off and take it up to Accounts to get it filed away?"

"What, now?"

"Yes."

"But…"

"Enjoy your birthday!" he called back after he'd passed me with his laptop.

I was left open-mouthed. The fucking wanker!

I sent out the emails fine, but I hated going to Accounts.

Beryl.

She was a large lady who wore her clothes a few sizes too small. She thought it looked sexy. I felt sorry for her arse, stomach, and boobs that were all being strangled. I'd heard her boast how all the men loved her boobs. The truth was they were big because she was fat. Had she been even slightly plump then they would be hardly noticeable.

She also stayed late. Rumour had it that she'd had sex with a number of lonely accountants after hours in the fax room. No one faxes anymore, so it became a quiet and abandoned room. Beryl's sex dungeon, in fact.

I walked up the stairs, flashed my badge, and entered Accounts. I scanned the area for witnesses but saw no one. I thought perhaps luck was on my side as I put the report in the orange plastic tray.

"Well, hello!" a voice rang out. "What are you slipping into my slot!"

"Hi." She made me nervous. "Nothing. Well, a report."

"Come, come!" she said, calling me over with a wiggling finger.

I walked over. She began to fan her blouse.

"Phew, it's hot in here, isn't it?"

"Yeah," I agreed, and she grabbed my hand and placed it on her left boob. "Feel my heart." She moved it all around the nipple area.

"Yes," I said trying to pull away, but she had a vice-like grip.

"Sit," she demanded, pushing me into a chair but still holding onto my hand. She used the momentum to pull my hand down her body, and suddenly whipped it up her dress.

"I'm so hot," she purred, but the second I felt her panties I yanked my hand with everything I had.

"Okay, good luck with that!" I said and walked out a lot more quickly than I had arrived.

I got back to my desk and was about to go when my phone went. I looked at it, but knew I had to take it. It was one of the guys I'd sent the email to.

It was half an hour before I finally left the building.

I should probably explain something about the house. We researched it with the Land Registrar, and it was repossessed by one of the smaller banks. They had it on a long list of properties that were up for selling off cheap. It was surrounded by forest and would be a great project for us.

We'd visited it a couple of times before getting the keys, and it was a place I could truly see us calling home.

I really didn't want to stay much longer in my job, and Megan could work from home with hers. Well, I am sort of glossing over something. Megan sometimes doesn't like to leave the house. She gets bad anxiety. She's been signed off from work for a few months now. I think the country air will do her good.

It was a twenty-minute drive before I turned into the single track lane, leaving civilization behind me. I grew up in the country so could never get used to my flat. Megan shared with her friend and was also keen to escape the rat-race of town. Her friend was beginning to get annoyed that Megan would only leave the house with me, so this would help their friendship, too.

As Megan had made me drive here, I thought I would surprise her, instead. I parked my car in the lay-by just before the turn into the long drive to the house.

I smiled to myself and got out. I could already see cars.

This was definitely a party. They truly sucked at surprises!

Like some sort of undercover agent, I tried the quick sideways running. My legs tangled, and I fell over. I really hoped nobody had seen me.

Then my mobile went again. They were probably wondering where I was.

It was that number again. I ignored it again. *It was my birthday! Didn't they know that?*

The house was three storeys. It was beautiful. It was a country house although it had the design of an American Plantation House from deep Georgia. The ground floor was squared off with a surrounding porch, and the third floor was deep into the attic.

It truly was a beautiful house. I stopped for a second and took it all in just like it was the first time. It took my breath away. We weren't there fully in the sale, but it still felt like a dream.

I thought about going in via the back entrance, but I had a feeling that I had to play this surprise thing out. Megan had gone to a lot of trouble.

I walked up the steps fully aware that I could hear nothing. I could picture excited faces and suppressed smiles as they heard each footstep. It was like playing to a bunch of kids.

I opened the door and like some lunatic jumped in with my arms and legs out like a starfish.

"Surprise!" I shouted.

But nobody was there.

I looked ahead and saw a large banner that was ripped. The words Happy were twisted one way and Birthday another.

This was very strange.

I looked around at the lounge and there behind the sofa were some feet.

But these were not the feet of a hider. They were pointing up and belonged to someone laid on their back. This was not considered a normal hiding pose.

I walked tentatively towards them, expecting them to move, wriggle, or someone else to jump out.

I heard the sound of dripping.

I looked around the sofa and saw a female body drenched in blood. I suspect the reason for this was the head that had been smashed to a pulp.

It was Joanna. She was an old friend and one-time lover. She had certainly looked a lot better than this the last time I'd seen her.

A pool of brain matter and webs of blood-drenched hair artistically painted the wooden floorboards. It was the crimson liquid seeping through the cracks in the floorboards that caused the drip-drip sound.

Instinctively, I stepped back and took a breath.

I could imagine clawed fingers reaching up and cupping the blood as gravity helped it on its journey to hell.

I whipped my head around. I felt eyes on me but saw nobody.

The devil was watching, and I was now part of his game.

Perhaps the sensible thing to do when faced with a situation this was to turn and run back to my car.

But Megan was here somewhere. I had to find her.

Chapter 2

My heart was beating fast, and the front door – which was now behind me – seemed a mile away. I took a breath to steady myself and instead walked around in the opposite direction and towards the kitchen.

Someone had gone to great lengths for me. Snacks and bottles of alcohol were all over the counter top. Glasses and plates sat in anticipation of greedy hands with partially licked fingers grabbing and groping at anything considered free. That was standard party participation, greed over hygiene.

I saw the large walk-in cupboard door slightly ajar. A red, pooled liquid spoiled the scene. I reached for the handle, but at the last moment decided not to touch it and instead pulled the door open at the side.

The grinning face of my sister was there in front of me. She was smiling so broadly because her lips and part of her cheeks had been removed. Her eyes were deep bloody holes. The eyeballs had at some point been evicted of their home and were currently listed as MIA. As a reaction I glanced at the floor just in case they'd rolled to a stop at her feet.

My hand shot up to my mouth, and slowly my finger then reached and smoothed away her auburn hair. She was a year younger than me. At one time we'd been close, but recently we'd grown apart. It looked very much like neither of us would have to endure the awkward telephone conversations anymore. So that was something, I guess.

She was propped up. It was hard to tell how, but I didn't want to look at her any further.

With little other option, I closed the door on her walk-in coffin, almost pretending I'd never seen inside.

That's when I heard a movement upstairs.

Fight or flight they say. However, I was paralyzed rigid and in no position to contemplate either choice. I had always been of a sensitive nature. My father was quick to rename me Sissy-Boy, though I had no recollection of these words being on my birth certificate. At times he'd repeat the words to me in a sing-song chant that did nothing for my self-esteem. I would've preferred for him to have been in the cupboard. Perhaps with his throat slit and his dick in his mouth.

Slowly, I was able to move the muscles in my arms and legs. I had to concentrate and literally push the message down from my brain in order for them to respond and move.

But this did not help my confusion. Part of me still wanted to leave, but another part wanted to find Megan.

My sweet, sweet, Megan.

This was our house (sort of) and I'd be damned if I was going to be forced out of it before it was officially mine. I had been bullied around too much in my life to allow it.

I then saw the door in front of me. It wasn't quite open, but it was not fully closed either. Beckoning me towards it. Wanting to swallow me whole.

I realize that this is neither the time nor the place, but I should probably tell you more about this house. You see it belonged to Dr Jasper Olsen. He was an outstanding doctor and scientist specialising in memory loss. He was able to reach into the minds of the most forgetful of people and pull out what was once thought to be lost forever. Having secured funding, he was spearheading research into Alzheimer's when he disappeared.

Eventually, after several weeks, somebody raised the alarm, and the police broke into his house. They found him sat crossed-legged in a meditative state. He was in a circle surrounded by dead bodies.

This was in the cellar of this very house.

Various rumours tore around the medical world, with some suggesting that whilst he had found a cure for Alzheimer's, he had also found something a lot darker.

The ability to wipe and keep wiped somebody's mind. It was said that he had gone as far as developing a pill. However, other reports suggested that he had taken such a concoction of chemicals in testing that he had driven himself mad.

He now resides in a psychiatric facility and has no clue who he once was. In fact, some say he thinks he's actually Sir Cliff Richard. Such a shame. Nobody deserves that.

So, to look at the cellar door now was to bring on an uncomfortable fear.

Again, I heard a noise upstairs.

Like some macabre book on diseases and ailments I was drawn to it, even though I didn't want to discover what was up there. It might be Megan needed my help and was unable to call out.

I grabbed the bannister and slowly made my way up the stairs. I felt slightly light-headed with each step. The staircase wrapped around, and I ended up in a large landing area.

Tentatively I walked up to the first door. It was slightly open, and I believed that's where the sound originated. Noises can often play tricks on you.

Ever so gently I pushed open the door.

I saw nothing.

I walked further into the room, taking in the old furniture that we were debating whether or not to keep.

That's when the door slammed closed behind me. I turned around and saw my boss standing there. One arm stretched out towards me and another clutching his throat as blood sprayed out of an unseen wound.

He was gargling and trying to speak.

"What is it?" I said in a raised voice. "Where is she? Is she alright?"

Once again in typical fashion he only seemed to care about himself. His eyes were wide in shock.

"Talk to me!" I shouted. He removed his hand and blood poured from an ugly, raw, open wound. He wobbled and then fell flat on his face.

I couldn't believe what was happening.

The carpet in this room was one of the few that didn't need replacing. Now, it was covered in blood. It was always frustrating when added costs appeared in your budget. Especially when they were so unnecessary and easily avoided.

Just then something caught my eye. I turned towards the window and saw my cousin Pete stumbling away from the house and deeper into the woods.

He must know something.

I quickly ran down the stairs and out of the house. For a moment I stopped and looked around. If this had been a movie the camera would pan around me showing that, despite the number of cars, the place was quiet. There should be loud music and party people getting drunk, but it was eerily silent.

I looked over to where Pete was still making his way further from the house. I started to walk and broke into a slight jog. I caught up with him easily.

Pete was older than me and once had thought it funny to hold my head under water down at the river. I'd swallowed a lot of liquid and threw up the swamp-water before falling to the ground crying. He'd laughed at me for weeks after that. All I'd managed to do was humiliate myself further by soiling my trousers. I was fifteen. He thought I was a pussy.

"Pete!" I called. For a second, he came to a complete stand-still but remained facing away from me.

"It's me!" I said grabbing him and forcibly spinning him around.

"Urgh…" he said as blood bubbled out of his mouth.

"Jesus!" I said once again surprised. Someone had done something to his mouth. "What's happened!"

He tried to speak again but the sound was nothing more than frustrated grunts and nonsensical in my understanding.

He pointed back towards the house. That told me nothing. He was such a fucking simpleton at times.

Just then, and quite unexpectantly, a gust of wind blew up from nowhere sending a shower of leaves at us. Already shaken, Pete squealed and turned quickly. He tripped and fell straight into a tree trunk. There was an awful thud from the sound of his head hitting the wood and he fell in a heap onto the ground.

"Pete?" I said again. "Pete?" I nudged his body with my foot, but he didn't move.

Just what the hell was going on here? And where was Megan?

I turned and walked back towards the house. I was following the path that my footfalls had made. Just then I heard a sound like sobbing.

"Hello?" I said, "Who's there?"

There was a beat of silence before I heard some shuffling in the bushes. Whoever it was, they had a feminine body, and she had decided that she didn't want to be found.

"Megan?" I called just in case it was her and she was too scared to come out.

I heard a movement again. I looked carefully within the bushes. I crept closer. I saw her crouched down and hugging her legs.

"It's okay," I said in a voice I hoped was calming. "You're alright now."

"Who are you?" a small frightened voice said.

"I'm Matt. This was meant to be my surprise party." I paused and took a breath and chuckled. "It sure was a surprise!"

I could see that her head had turned towards me. She remained covered, but I could see she was hardly wearing anything.

"You're the birthday boy," she said with little or no expression clearly deciding that everything was alright.

"That I am," I replied.

She came up and out of the bushes. She was wearing nothing but a small pair of panties. She made no effort to hide her modesty. Her breasts wobbled with each step.

"I'm your stripper," she said. Her voice sounded younger than she looked, although she couldn't have been any older than twenty.

"Where're your clothes?"

She gave me a funny look. "I'm a stripper. We generally don't wear much."

"That's as may be," I said. "But I'm sure you turned up wearing something. Unless you're a naturist, and then that sort of spoils the fun of stripping?"

"What?"

I was confusing her. I often did that with women. "Your clothes, were you wearing any?"

"I was, and then I removed them."

"But I wasn't even there yet!" I realized I was whining. I know it hardly seemed important now, but I didn't understand why you'd book a stripper for a birthday party and not wait for the birthday boy to arrive. I bet they blew out my candles and ate my cake, too. That really pissed me off.

"It was my fault," she said, noticing my hurt voice. "They asked me to wait for you and I said I couldn't. I have… had another booking."

"Oh," was all I could think of.

"You, er, look nice," I said. I'm not sure why. I'm sure she knew that. She was young, smooth, and pert. Her raven hair looked slightly wild now, but I knew that an hour ago it would've looked perfect. There wouldn't have been a man at the party who wouldn't have wanted to fuck her.

"Thanks," she replied.

We stood there. It was an awkward exchange. I was still confused with the whole situation, and standing with a near-to-damnit naked woman didn't help matters.

"So, what happened here?" It was the question I'd been looking to ask since I had found the first body.

"It was weird," she said. "The music was playing and people were standing around. It was actually a pretty good party. I kept looking at my watch 'cause that other booking, and in the end, I had to start. That's when it happened." She gulped and took a deep breath. "Why were you so late?"

"Work," I said, letting it be known that it wasn't by choice.

"Ah, okay."

"So?" I encouraged her to speak on.

"It was like some horror movie. I was just about to step out of my panties and do the rest of the show when…"

"What's the rest of the show?" I was suddenly intrigued. I figured once she was naked there was little more she could do. Maybe jiggle and dance a bit, but that was usually it.

"I grab someone, usually the birthday boy, and go down on them."
"Really?"

She nodded. "It's what gets me return bookings."

"I'll bet."

"Then, well, let's just say I do other things," she then winked at me. "I hate heights, and they told me to…"

A gun blast was heard the same time as her head exploded. Or it felt like it had exploded. I was showered in her blood as something penetrated her head. Her body crumpled like a released marionette, and she buckled to the ground.

I looked at the broken body in shock. Then, I swung around and jumped behind a tree.

I peeked out at the dead woman. Such a waste. The mouth that could've been bobbing up and down on my lap was now lifeless. I'd not even had time for the dirty thoughts to form in my head before she was wasted.

Some fucking surprise party this!

Chapter 3

Somebody was picking off people one by one. I didn't even bother to look at my mobile phone. One of the main reasons that Megan and I loved this place so much was when we were here the world was cut off from us.

I began to walk back towards the house again.

By my calculations if the person doing this wanted me dead then I would already be laid out and leaking blood.

I felt a little like Clint Eastwood walking along without a care. I was cock-sure, and if I died today then so be it.

That was until a gun went off and the ground erupted a few feet away. It was hard to tell the trajectory or direction so I picked up the pace and suddenly ran with everything I had towards the house. That will teach me.

I had to find Megan.

This time I went around the side of the house and towards the garden behind. I stayed close to the house using it as protection from one way. I felt like I was in some computer game.

I stopped still. When I no longer heard anything, I looked out and scanned the garden.

There was a loveseat and a couple were sitting, swinging blissfully together. It was hard to imagine that amongst the bloodshed and gunshots a pair could be lost within their own world.

I admired that. There had been a time when I'd been lost in a world of me and another. A time when we had stood outside together despite the evening chill as the sun had dropped, and we refused to leave each other knowing that to get warm would mean us having to be apart. We'd stood smiling and teeth chattering, stealing kisses of hot breath and warm tongues, but slowly we'd lost colour in our faces and shivered involuntarily. Cold hands snuck up under T-shirts, partly for warmth, and partly for a sneaky feel of an unfamiliar body.

This had been Megan and me. This had only been a few months beforehand. I smiled at this teenage behaviour that seemed so natural at the time. I remembered the tag line to a book I'd once read: *Love can make you do strange things*. That it can.

I walked up behind them and noticed it was my parents. They were snuggled in to each other like lovers. I'd not ever known them to show such public affection. In fact, my dad had a crude way about him, and my mother was always slightly embarrassed by his advances. Of course, this was not true the one time I came home early from a school trip to find my mother on all fours and making what seemed like yapping sounds to each of my father's thrusts from behind. I had been shocked, but not as shocked as when she shouted, "Harder! Harder!" And then if that wasn't bad enough, she bucked and screamed, and then panted, "Cum on my tits!" I'd not looked my mother in the eye since that day.

I had scurried off, although there was something that told me that my father knew I had been standing there. The relationship that had been threadbare to start with was now gone for good.

"Mum? Dad?" I said but my voice no longer held the strength. In fact, a pitiful quiver was audible. I knew right away that something was wrong. My father would've made some sarcastic comment by now, and more than likely tried to belittle me with a cutting comment. But he remained tight-lipped.

As I walked in front of them, I saw that they were bound together. A single gunshot wound now decorated each forehead with single lines of blood spilling from the wounds but making different patterns in its descent.

I fell to my knees and felt my throat constrict. I wasn't sure what I felt.

I was numb. But there was something else. I suppose it was shock and a sense of loss, but dare I say a wash of relief, too?

It was hard to believe that they would be at a party that involved strippers and blowjobs. There was a slice of irony that wasn't lost on me. I'd never had a party of any nature before, and here I was with one I'd never forget. That would've been in very poor taste to have a stripper sucking me off whilst my mother looked on and clapped encouragingly. I imagine my father would be trying to get some sort of action after me, too.

Of course, part of me felt cheated. The whole point of a party such as this was that the birthday boy was the important person. Everything revolves around him, and yet for the first time in my life when I got the party I'd always craved, this happens. Somebody had decided to kill the guests.

They were my fucking guests!

I lay a hand on the shoulder of both of my parents and gave them both a final kiss.

With a heavy heart I walked away. I really wasn't in the mood for funeral directors and undertakers. That's the problem when someone shoots your parents, suddenly it's your responsibility to get them picked up, shipped out, and measured for boxes. I know I'll be footing the bill for that, too.

Maybe I could slip them into one coffin. My father could take her from behind one last time and they could be forever attached like some erotic jigsaw puzzle.

And then something caught my eye.

I looked up and saw swinging from the chimney-stack, my best friend Gordy. My first thought was surprise that the chimney held his weight. He was a big, sturdy lad, egg-shaped but with a large square head like a more human version of a Lego-man's. I felt bad, not only was he dead but he had clearly pissed himself, too.

My legs went weak, and I had to sit down on the floor with my back up against the stone wall. I had so many questions now. To get Gordy up there would've taken some doing. It would've taken… and then I thought back to what the stripper had said.

"I hate heights, and they told me to…" It's a shame the bullet ended her life like that, but I wonder if she had been the one to coax poor Gordy up there with a promise of a hand job or something. He'd have gone up there, too, even if she'd just said she'd flash her tits again or stick her finger up his arse.

I looked up again and saw that his belt may well have been undone. It was a long way away but it certainly looked open. Oh, Gordy. I remember the Russian model that was coming over to meet him. He'd already paid for her plane ticket before I told him that it was a scam. It was more than likely some fifty-year-old bloke trying to string him along and get his cash. He had been heartbroken. It was a shame. I went to the airport to catch the scammer and saw that she was real. She looked lost, searching around for big chubby Gordy. Gordy was more than likely at home masturbating to her picture at that exact point in time. Isn't it funny how these things happen?

Then suddenly I saw another runner.

It was Megan's friend and flat-mate Sheena. She was more of a flat-mate than a friend. The way I saw it, she was one of those stuck-up bitches who thought the world loved her. All she did was make Megan feel like shit. I was surprised to see her here. But then there had been a lot of surprises here. Maybe she was going to give me a birthday blowjob, too

She was now screaming in a way that was like nails down a slate-board. She was also running in a crazy zig-zag fashion. Her long blonde hair fanning out behind her. Her tight butt looked amazing in her skin-tight leggings. Like two balls bobbing up and down.

"Sheena!" I screamed but she was getting further away. I set off after her, although I was somewhat tentative. Experience of this party had already told me that the victims were often the runners.

Sheena was fast. She was a gym-rat and used to working out, hence her wonderful arse. She also had incredible cardio. It was probably down to the amount of sex she had. I'd heard her. She went for it. Maybe she liked it rough, but there was always something bashing and smashing when she was fucking whichever meathead had followed her home. I saw them, head down and trailing behind like some lost puppy. Arms bulging and veins popping unnaturally. They might nod to me as they silently followed her to her room and then BANG! All hell would be let loose. An hour or so later they would both appear sweaty and red-faced. She would be flashing an evil grin, and he would normally look a little embarrassed and slink off out the door.

I wasn't in such good condition. Megan had sex only when there was no one else around, and then she would only pull her clothing to the side. She favoured knee-length dresses, and silently she'd beckon me over, remove her knickers, and only pull my trousers down enough for my manhood to sneak inside her. Somebody could walk in and assume we were just cuddling. She liked to move her hips slowly herself. I would stand silently whilst she sat on her dressing table and moved back and forth. I had plans to spice things up, but I had to go gently with her. You never just spouted out your intentions.

This lack of movement meant that Sheena easily got away from me.

I stopped for a second and wondered whether she would be able to raise the alarm and get help. The trees went on for a mile or so, and the road was off in the other direction. I couldn't be sure but the next house was almost a mile away.

And then I heard the sound. It was sudden and scary, and completely unexpected.

But this time it wasn't a gunshot but the sound of a motorbike being kickstarted.

Then with crash a shed door burst open and a rider dressed in black biker leathers tore out on the scrambler-bike. The loud screaming engine suggested a low cc engine being pushed to its limit.

I jumped to the side as it roared past me and headed out towards the runner.

It was a sad time, and yet there was something that drew me to a person with such ability as to be able to work through killing these people. I was pragmatic about it all. I had a feeling deep down that I would be a victim. I was a rat caught up in a huge maze. Wherever I turned people were being picked off and murdered. I had a feeling the grim reaper was walking around and eventually would get to me. There really was nowhere to hide.

I watched the bike easily catching up with Sheena. An arm swung out and I thought that Sheena had been hit with something when I saw that she was grabbing her throat and falling to the ground.

Blood was spraying out of her.

"Megan!" I shouted towards the house, safe in the knowledge that the biker would not be able to hear me. Nothing came back.

I ran past a wall that had seen better years. I leapt over it and hid as the motorbike returned.

I looked at my phone. There was one bar, but it flickered.

I don't know who I was going to call. Maybe the police. Maybe a vicar. Maybe myself to suggest I get a grip.

I broke into a jog and ran towards the new fresh body. It was a sad fact that even in death her body was amazing. It was inappropriate for me to look at it, but there you had it.

"Sheena?" I said, my voice shaky. "Can you hear me?"

I saw her hand twitch, and suddenly she mumbled, "Why?"

And that, of course, was the million-dollar question!

Jim Ody

Chapter 4

I turned my back on her. I couldn't bear to see her take her last breath. Perhaps it was selfish of me, or perhaps I knew she was a selfish bitch so deserved to die alone.

There was now a stillness in the air. I walked back towards the house from another angle. It was obvious where everything came from. The house was clearly the epicentre of all that was evil.

I had to face it at some point.

I knew that somewhere in the house I would find Megan, and there was more than a chance that she would be dead. It had all come down to this. The late nights that we had sat up in her room staring at each other and waiting for the other to speak.

I wanted more from her, but I felt I couldn't push.

She would look up at me with eyes filled with such sorrow. A face that should be on the cover of a magazine smiling and looking like she didn't have time to stop even for this quick photo, she had a world of adventure that longed for her to be a part.

But instead, life had somehow come along, and an invisible vacuum had sucked it out of her. Perhaps it had then been injected into someone else with melancholy as their only friend and, as if by magic, had been cured.

I needed her though. She was an empty vessel, but the potential was there for all to see. She was gorgeous. She sunk into me and soaked my T-shirt with her tears.

At times she would remove her shirt and sit there in front of me topless. She'd pull my hand to her chest and hold it there. I would comply, unsure whether this was as an act of compassion or a prelude to something more. Being direct I would go to speak, but she would hold a finger to my lips and shake her head. She had done this first time we had made love. Silently she undressed and folded up her clothes. She slipped under the sheets before beckoning me over and requiring me to do the same. It was an act of silence but for quickened breaths and stifled noises. And when it was over, she smiled almost apologetically and took a shower, ridding herself of any trace of me.

At times she would be loud. We would travel to London to hit the bars, and she would grin and shout. She came alive. One time she pulled me into a back street and for no reason started to kiss me deeply before giving me a hand job there and then. Then we went into a wine bar where she was idolised by many, but it was me she clutched on to all night, and at the expensive hotel she uncharacteristically fuelled up a passion that started in the lift and exploded in the hotel room. She ripped open my shirt and constantly told me exactly what she wanted me to do to her.

I'd held onto those memories for dear life. I'd tried to coax them out with promises of other trips away, but Megan was often too tired or suddenly worried about money. I was doing all I could to light that fire again, but I was left sitting on the bed fondling a boob in silence like a boring game of brail, the one nub repeatedly touched for longer than the moment deserved.

So here and now I looked at the cars that would never be driven again by their drivers. The land surrounding the house that would now become infamous, and of course the house that may never be ours once the authorities swarmed the place. You could feel how everything had changed.

Above me birds circled like they knew something. They could smell death in the air and wanted to help themselves to the cadavers.

I walked to the back door and noticed the bloody hand-print smeared on it. I pushed it open and saw the body of my next-door neighbour face down in a pool of his blood. From the back he looked like he had either fallen or was perhaps just taking a nap. His hands down by his sides and palms facing up. He was in his sixties, and his wife had left him years before for reasons he had never shared, but deep down I had a feeling there was something to it. I had caught him looking through my windows when Megan and I had been on the sofa kissing. One of the times my hand was down her trousers when she screamed. That was why she no longer came around to mine, and also why she suddenly clammed up around people. The old guy had blue-balled me big time.

I spat on him. *Fuck you, Peeping Tom!*

I walked around him into the utility room and past another body. This looked like Dee, the buxom teen from my work. The bag on her head was still there, but I could tell from the marks on her throat that someone had used force to suffocate her.

My heart beat hard and fast.

I wanted to remove these scenes from my memory. The irony not once was lost on me.

I saw other bodies, but now I closed my eyes. I heard screams of pleading seconds before their deaths. This house was evil.

Pure evil.

I saw it there in front of me. It could well have had a light streaming from the inside and calling me to enter.

The cellar.

I walked up to the door and opened it.

Chapter 5

A week earlier…

I opened the door to the psychiatrist's office. He looked up from his desk and pretended that it was a surprise to see us. For a clever guy he must think us to be simple. Why else would we be here? We had an appointment.

His smile was false and meant to put us at ease. His clothes were smart casual, but there was no doubt that his fees paid for him to have a better life. I already resented him.

"Hello, and how are you both?" he said politely, first shaking hands limply with Megan before adding a touch of steal to his grip when faced with another male. I'm hardly an Alpha, but he was taking no chances.

The office was sleek with metallic fine lines. A simple and yet happy décor specifically chosen to put clients at ease. I deliberately refused to call Megan a patient. She was here by her own volition. Perhaps on the advice of others, but still should she decide to leave there was nobody to make her return.

We both liked that set up.

I forced an amiable smile whilst Megan was more forthcoming with her words, "Fine," she said, but we knew she was anything but.

"Please sit," he said pointing to the chair for Megan. He couldn't care less about me. I was her distraction.

"So," he began touching together the tips of his fingers as if preparing us for some revelation. "How are you really feeling, Megan?"

She shrugged.

"We still sit and…" I began, but he held up a hand that halted me in my tracks.

"Megan, please. I wish to hear her words."

Scolded, I nodded, my head lowering in defeat.

"I still see him watching me," she said. "The man. He's looking through my window."

He nods encouragingly the way he's been trained to do. Say little and let them lead the talking. Let their words tumble out and trip themselves up. You just listen, twist them back, and make up some Googled diagnosis.

I see him glance at me when she talks about being naked. He knows he's better than me. He's telling me this with his eyes. He gloats with his moisturized skin and his clipped beard. He knows that he would heat up a cauldron of passion, and it wouldn't just be flames that would be licking at her.

He disgusts me. I want to punch him full in the face. Feel the crack of bone and cartilage giving way as blood splatters and his eyes water in pain.

"You think he's watching you still?" he asks, but really, he's planting seeds. He's repeating what she's saying but he's reinforcing it. The clever bastard.

She nods. "I have to confront him."

"Good. Good." He grins. He's pleased with this answer.

"I just want the pain to stop. I want to be in control of my life again."

He nods slowly and deeply and touches her arm. "Then do it, Megan. Take control of your life."

And that is exactly what she did.

But she didn't go and see him in the institution. She thought that he was too far gone. He no longer was the man she recognized.

Instead, she found something much more personal and bought it.

His house.

She admired the man who peeped on his own daughter. The guy that could've had the world but gave it up for madness.

I pushed open the door to the cellar and descended down into the bowels of the house.

"Stay where you are!" The doctor said to me. He held a gun. Megan was on her knees and stripped to her underwear. Around her were half a dozen bodies in a circle. All of them covered in blood and looking the worse for wear.

This was of course a replication of how her father was found all those years ago. She had been sitting in the corner. A scared little girl.

"Why?" I muttered.

"She's crazy!" he shouted desperately, his arm wobbling.

I half grinned. "I'm not sure you're allowed to say that about a client, doc!"

"Just look around you!"

The knife slipped into my hand, and in two moves I flipped it open and threw as hard as I could at him. He spun at me and the gun went off, missing me wildly.

His body, now with a knife sticking out of his right eye crumpled to the floor.

Megan got up and grinned at me. "Surprise!" she grinned.

I held open my arms.

"This is by far the best birthday I've ever had. I can't believe you did all of this for me!"

"You're welcome." But her head dropped. "Sorry, I had to kill the stripper. You'd have liked her!"

I nodded. "We met. She was sweet, but she's nothing compared to you!"

"Really?" she said seductively and began to gently sway. She danced around the dead bodies, touching them as she went. She removed her bra and then her panties and rubbed blood all over her naked body.

"Did anyone get away?" I asked.

Her hand slipped under my shirt. "I don't know. But everyone had a drink. We toasted to you. Each

shot had my father's serum in it. Non-diluted.
They won't remember anything."

"Good girl! Now come here, I need you now!" I
said unable to control myself any further.

"I know you do, baby. I know you do."

And there in the cellar of her father's house we
fucked with so much passion I'm sure the
electricity flicked as we both climaxed.

Fuck the world. Fuck everyone else in it. She is
my kind of crazy!

The End

The Orphans

'The Orphans' was first released in 2018 by Crazy Ink. The anthology was called The End?

Jim Ody

Chapter 1

Darkness came thick and fast. Wisps of fog floated eerily through the air. The brash sounds of glass smashing and the odd scream pierced the silence of the evening. Really, it was a typical soundtrack to a typical day.

The house at the end of the street appeared lonely and dark, but that couldn't be further from the truth.

It was a foster home for four parentless teenagers who called it The Orphanage. They had all lived there for around five years, having previously come from separate foster homes that none of them were able stay at. Eventually they wound up here.

Toots was the first to arrive. She had stood outside the house with her antique suitcase at her feet staring up the path towards the large house. A social worker with a pained but professionally painted-on smile was speaking to her new foster parents, trying to convince them she was as sweet as pie. For the most part she was.

This was true if you forgot about the time she burnt down the last family's garden shed in a fit of rage. Toots thought perhaps this nugget of information would be cut from the woman's frantic conversation.

Her new foster parents were called Bob and Janet which was fitting as they were as plain and normal as can be. There was no edge to them, and they were average at best. She'd smiled to herself as she was wearing a beautiful dress and her hair was pulled back into two bunches. She'd agreed to this awful attire on the condition they would stop at a fast-food place on the way there. Finally, the woman had agreed. It hardly seemed worth it now. In years to come she would dye her hair and collect piercings all over her body. Both Bob and Janet would have a shit-fit but would be unable to do anything about it.

A week later a buzzing livewire of a lad called Jof arrived. He grinned permanently like the fucking village idiot. He was a gangly string of piss and had a big heart but the brain the size of a pea. His hair was always stuck up on end like he was a young mad professor. He couldn't stay still and needed constant attention. He acted up until the arrival of a lad called Tommo. This calmed him down.

Tommo came a few months later. He wore a cap that he often had turned backwards. Toots had explained to him about the design and function of the peak, but he was uninterested. He and Jof hit it off instantly, and a strange brotherhood was built between them.

Lastly, and a good few months down the line, Parker arrived. He was contemplative. He often had his head in a book or was flicking through comic books. He was polite but risk-averse. With neat hair that was always parted precisely down the middle, he happily sat watching Tommo and Jof goof around like his own 3D reality series.

As the years came and went, the teenagers were still very close and formed a bond between themselves. Other kids would try and give them shit, but soon enough Tommo would lose it, and somebody would end up in tears. And Tommo would be grounded.

The problem was they had grown together too closely. Each, not wanting to admit it, was anxious about stepping out into the wide blue yonder of life without the others. They knew the time was not so far into the future, and that was a scary thing.

The future isn't always something that needs much worry. Often in hindsight we realise just how useless anxious thoughts are. Painstakingly, each of them battled with the demons ahead. However, if they had all been able to see into the future then they would know that a dark cloud loomed ahead. Not just for them, but for the whole of mankind.

This could be the end.

Chapter 2

Toots had got to the age where she was fed up with the orphanage. Not forever, just for today. Bob – Safe-Bob. Or, Sucks-The-Fun-Out-Of-Life-Bob kept speaking to her about her clothing and how a young woman should dress. He meant well, but she wanted men to notice her. She wanted that attention. What was so wrong with that?

He looked at her disapprovingly and with regular disappointment, but so what? He wasn't her dad. She wanted to live her life.

Her parents had died years ago, and foster homes were a norm to her. They were all a little bit unruly in their own way, so it was inevitable that she would feel a little neglected. Tommo and Jof especially required stimulation, and a desperate attempt at one of them becoming successful, Bob and Jane latched onto Brainiac2000. Perfect Parker. The comic-book boy genius.

Normally she wore black, but today she wore a summer dress. It was light and flowing with spaghetti straps. A floral design gave it a more

- 299 -

sophisticated look. It hugged her figure and she was able not to wear a bra with it. Perfect.

Her bright pink hair was down apart from the one braid against a small shaved area. Her nose was pierced, and she had a small heart tattoo on her shoulder that she'd been given late one night by Tommo using a needle and a jar of Indian ink. It had hurt like hell, but she loved it.

She hung around the park on the swings. It was her place. She could daydream at being a film star. Maybe some modelling agency would come around and sign her up. Maybe she'd model and get put into adverts or a movie.

She liked to look at the boys who appeared not long after she did. It was like there was some sort of beacon that could only be seen by horny boys. She'd swing back and forth letting the wind billow up her dress. The flash of skin grabbed the attention the boys pretended not to give. But teenage boys are not poker players and have no concept of subtlety.

First a couple of guys came over and shared some beer with her. Just a bottle, which was thrust at her in a clumsy way.

One of them was okay if the light was slightly in your eyes, and the other one would take a lot of bottles of beer and a huge imagination to become anything other than disgusting. They offered to take her to a party, like it was some celebrity shindig rather than what it was: a few testosterone-filled males wasted and looking to cop a feel. There were about a dozen things that stopped her. Their smell mostly. The wonders of hygiene were lost on them. It was strange. She quite happily went off with any one guy, but if there was more than one then she preferred to stay in the park.

They got bored with her quickly when she refused to go with them and disappeared arguing between themselves.

She swung back and forth with her head down, hoping and praying that some gorgeous guy would come along and swoop her away in his car like that old guy did in that *Pretty Woman* movie. The one where the tart gets the rich guy.

It was six in the evening before a tall pale guy walked over with a large bottle of something. It was unusual to see someone like him around there. He had an air of confidence and was a duller version of Jack Sparrow if he were in normal clothes.

"What are you doing hanging around here?" he asked, his voice almost a whisper. He seemed high.

She had metaphorically danced this dance before. This wasn't her first disco. "Waiting for you, I guess," she said with a twinkle in her eyes.

"Want some?" he said nodding and offering her the bottle. It was some sort of spirit.

"Sure." She shrugged and took a swig, almost choking as the fiery liquid hit her throat. She never turned down free alcohol and she wasn't going to start now.

"It's strong rough stuff," he grinned. "It'll put hairs on your chest."

"I like strong and rough." She winked. "You can check my chest to see if this stuff works!"

"That right?"

She was already off the swing and they walked over to a grass bank. They sat down and drank more and more.

After a while she struggled to remember what they talked about – if indeed they talked at all. She had memories of him being on top of her – maybe checking for hairs – but her head started to get dizzy, and at some point she blacked out.

It was after ten when she woke up underneath the slide, her dress around her waist, her chest stinging and covered in blood.

She felt empty. She had been attacked. There was a little relief when she realized that she hadn't been raped or had her underwear removed at all. That she could tell anyway.

She walked away slowly. She felt different. It was as if she had changed.

That walk home was surreal. There were flashes of things in her mind, and her thoughts were dark.

Chapter 3

Tommo always wanted more. He watched movies and listened to song lyrics, and he wanted *that*. He wanted excitement. Okay, scratch that. He wanted a little more Toots in his life. The other lads saw her as a sister. They had all appeared here at The Orphanage five years ago within months of each other and had grown up together as if related. Jof was madcap and always doing stupid things but Tommo loved that. He was often seen drooling over girls way out of his league. He set his sights high and refused to lower them. That would probably be the death of him.

Parker was quiet. He'd had a girlfriend once called Beryl. She was small and round and was quick out of her clothes. Parker reddens up easily, and the others would burst into his room every so often to see him red in the face and her covered in nothing but a duvet. Parker doesn't like to talk about those times, but it was clear that whilst he now reads novels and comic-books, for those months he had become a man.

They were all seventeen (apart from Toots who had just turned eighteen) but Tommo was sure that Parker could've done better than Beryl. He had a quiet way about him.

No matter what he tried, Toots only saw him as a friend. She often disappeared down the local park sneaking whatever alcohol had been smuggled there by others. Tommo felt like he was the only one who seemed worried when she wandered off with some guy. Okay, not so much worried as jealous, but he still didn't want any harm to come to her. He couldn't help it though. It just didn't seem fair. He'd hinted, but he was never taken seriously.

But then it happened.

Tommo and Jof had been watching a movie last night. It was some old slasher movie from the 80s. Some masked guy walking purposefully around a group of sex-starved teenagers and picking them off one-by-one as they made out or showered. Even the ones that appeared to have a head start managed to make the wrong decision or fail in any attempt to escape. Jof was snoring before the end. For a hyperactive guy, when it got late in the day his batteries were the first to run out.

Tommo heard Toots come in. He thought that she might've been caught by Janet or Bob, but he'd heard no shouting – and Toots was a shouter. In fact, he knew she was a screamer.

Toots had then gone into the bathroom and run a shower. This told him everything he needed to know about how her evening had gone. She was cleaning off the residual traces of evil from her skin.

Tommo wasn't sure whether the feeling that he had growing was one of concern, one of jealousy, or one of lust. Hormones were a confusing thing.

He felt like he was out-growing this place, and there was a good chance that within a couple of years he would be gone. Jane and Bob were okay, but they weren't his parents. They were too distracted with what the others were doing to care. He wanted more. He was a boy, but he was beginning to feel like a man.

Listening carefully, Tommo heard Toots come out of the bathroom and then the door to her room close. He got up to leave his room but thought he should give her a minute. Bursting in would never be a good idea. It was a desperate act.

Jof was still asleep. The two of them shared a room, and this was another reason why he wanted to leave. Jof was like his brother, and he still wanted to hang out with him, but he wanted privacy now.

He walked quietly out of the room and gently knocked on Toots's door.

He heard a scramble of movement and her voice slur, "Who is it?"

"It's me," Tommo said. "Tommo."

"Okay…come in."

She sat with her long T-shirt on. She smiled sadly. He tried not to look at her nipples poking at the thin fabric. He was a teenage male, so this proved to be a challenge.

"Good night?" he asked, but in a way that suggested he hoped it wasn't.

"Not especially," her eyes were hooded. She was intoxicated. She looked a little rough. No wonder she had taken a shower. *You can't clean your actions away that quickly*, he pondered in his head.

He was staring, so quickly asked, "What happened?"

"Some guy." There was always some guy. Most remained nameless. Often this was because she never asked them their name. The mixed teenage feelings were confusing. He was sorry she felt the need to go out with whoever showed her attention, but he was also hurt she'd never wanted him. He had always treated her with respect, and this had backfired every time.

"You've been drinking," Tommo stated rather than asked.

"Ding-ding! Ten points to Sherlock over there!"

He walked over and sat on the bed next to her. "Toots… Look, I'm not sure why you do it?"

"Do what?"

Tommo noticed the bruising on her arms and scratches on the top off her chest. He had glanced, and then seeing her smile, had lingered.

"Go off with those monsters. What did he do to you?"

She shrugged and winced a little. "This was different. He wasn't filled with lust… it was like he wanted to kill me. You should see the rest of my chest."

Tommo wanted nothing more than to do that, but he also felt sorry for her. "You don't have to show me," he said which was said in the same way as someone might say, "Please show me." Of course, she hadn't said it in a way that suggested it was what she had in mind.

Toots looked at him and slowly removed the T-shirt.

Tommo didn't know where to look. Her breasts were medium-sized with over-sized areolas around both nipples making them more forbidden to look at. They had large welts on them, with cuts all over, some of which looked deep. He was caught between seeing the beauty and the horror simultaneously.

"Who was he?" he said quietly, his voice lost into the night.

"A monster, I told you."

"I'm so sorry," Tommo said as he touched a scratch lightly. He looked up, and their eyes locked. The distance between them was suddenly gone, and then their lips touched.

The chemicals of alcohol and lust exploded as clothing was lost and the two teenagers slowly and gently came together as one. It was done carefully as Toots winced every so often but at no point wanted to stop.

An hour later and they were covered in her blood and sweat as the wounds were opened. A lot of bodily fluids had transferred between them both.

Jim Ody

Tommo went back to his room extremely happy, albeit sore from a few scratches on his back. Life would never be the same again.

If only he realised exactly what this meant…

Chapter 4

The house was quiet this morning. Too quiet.

It was not the most rational thought, but when Jof noticed that Janet and Bob were not up and about he burst out of the house. Not to find them, but to buy breakfast.

It was Saturday morning, and Janet was famous for her big Full English breakfast that would be cooking when they woke. Jof always woke up like he hadn't eaten for days, and today was no different. The news that his breakfast was not just delayed, but potentially absent for the not-too-distant future was almost too much to bear. He pulled on his jogging bottoms with a slightly creased white T-shirt and made his way out to the local café.

Jof couldn't help but be a little self-centred. In his experience you never got what you wanted if you didn't go and grab it for yourself. There were four of them so if you sat back and waited, then you missed out. Jof was not going to miss out on breakfast.

It didn't occur to him to ask the others whether they might want to join him. A teenage boys' mind can be selfish at the best of times.

Wind whipped up an empty crisp packet into a dancing spiral. Leaves tried to follow suit but failed, barely able to get off the ground. They lacked the flare and finesse of the empty snack bag.

Jof rubbed his hands. It wasn't cold, but the air was still a little fresh. At the end of the road, he walked along a couple of streets before coming to the café. It wasn't an old greasy spoon affair but now a newly furnished hipster place. The guys wore beards, and the girls had piercings and dreadlocks.

Coming out of the door was Elle, a girl a few leagues above him in terms of attractiveness. She had hair that always looked perfect and breasts that even she was proud of. Embarrassed, he smiled at her and fully expected her to screw up her face and tell him to piss off. She'd done it before.

But this time she stopped.

Perhaps he had something on his shirt. He looked down but saw nothing.

"Hi," she said in a loud seductive whisper.

"Hey," he replied the way he'd seen cool kids do in American movies. He was still only half-engaged, expecting to be humiliated at any moment.

"Wanna go someplace?" she purred, tossing her long blonde hair back and looking at him with seductive eyes. He wondered what she was up to.

"What, like France?"

She grinned. "I don't mean on holiday, silly!"

He half smiled and pretended he was joking.

"I came for breakfast…" the words slipped out before he could stop them.

"I know," she nodded and grabbed his hand. "I've got something warm you can sink into."

She was hot, but he still glanced into the window at a plate of fried breakfast that had just been served up. The smell of bacon aroused his senses and made his mouth water. He never thought that he would struggle with a decision between a woman and a fried breakfast. Perhaps this was a case of probability. The food was there whispering silently towards him. Teasing him to come closer without a chance of suddenly laughing in his face. Elle could well do this. She could get him all hot and bothered and then laugh at him.

Again, he'd experienced this before.

He followed her as she turned down an alleyway next to the shop that served as the deliveries entrance and stopped.

He had so many questions running through his mind but was too fearful to speak them.

"Come here," she said and pulled him close, slipping her arms around him. He actually felt scared. He wondered whether she was on drugs.

He closed his eyes and tried to remain calm when for no reason she pulled aside the neck of his T-shirt and bit a chunk of skin deeply near his collar bone. Jof screamed and pulled away. Not just with surprise but like a small girl having her toy snatched away. He was expecting soft and sensual, not quick, sharp and painful.

"What? You don't like it?" she grinned, blood dripping down her chin and splattering her lowcut sweater. It was his blood. A lot of blood.

Jof backed away. She came at him, but he sidestepped and pawed her away in desperation. Almost falling off balance, he turned and ran back home as fast as he could.

He'd check in the kitchen for food a little later, he thought.

When he got to the house, he thought he'd go in through the backdoor. As he slowed up, he noticed something in the garden, just behind the garage. A body.

He walked up slowly, and when the body came into view, he closed his eyes tightly and looked away.

Immediately, he wanted to erase the images.

It was Janet and Bob. They were dead. But not just that, they were in pieces.

There was blood everywhere splattered over body parts.

For a second, he wondered whether he had lost so much blood that he was hallucinating. But he realized that his cut had finally stopped bleeding.

He was stunned for a second and stood with his heart beating fast and his eyes closed. He was like a child hoping his eyes were lying.

He prayed that he was still asleep and this was a nightmare. He'd wake up in a sweating mess and a sudden relief, gasping for air.

He opened his eyes.

The horror remained.

Jof ran into the house and straight up to the bathroom and locked the door. For ten minutes he sat there on the side of the bath panicking. What the hell was going on?

He bathed his wound and put a bandage on it. Thankfully it wasn't noticeable through his clean T-shirt. His white one had a large blood stain on it now and was screwed up in the hamper. Jof never considered that it might stay there forever.

"Tommo!" He said shaking him awake.

"Hey Sweet-pea." He was clearly still dreaming.

"Tommo!" He repeated, until Tommo's eyes shot open.

"W-what?!"

"Janet and Bob are dead!"

"In bed?" Tommo was still confused.

"No, not in bed. They are *dead*!"

"Is this a joke?"

"Does it sound like a joke?"

Tommo sat up. "It sounds like one of your jokes. A bloody unfunny joke, so yeah, it does sound like a joke."

"It's not a joke."

"So, what are you saying?"

Jof wanted to strangle him. "I can't spell it out any more, Janet and Bob are dead! I know this because their bodies are laid out in pieces behind the garage."

"Why were you behind the garage?"

"Pretty irrelevant," Jof said to the wall. "I was coming back from the café."

"You had breakfast in the café, knowing they were dead?"

"No, no! I didn't see them until I got back from the café. I didn't go into the café."

"So how did you eat if you didn't go into the café?" Tommo was now getting frustrated with Jof.

"Listen, Tommo. Don't worry about the bloody café or my breakfast. Let's concentrate on the fact that Janet and Bob are dead!"

"Who's dead?" Toots said walking in.

"Don't bother knocking!" Tommo said to her, grinning.

"This is like Groundhog Day," Jof said, throwing his hands into the air.

"Not really," Tommo said sarcastically. "That was a movie for starters."

"The door was open. Besides there's not a lot I've not already seen before…" Tommo went red.

Jof looked confused. "*O-kay. Kind of irrelevant Again.*"

"Do I have to repeat the question?" Toots said, her arms crossed and with a serious look on her face.

"Janet and Bob."

"Really?" she replied but with little conviction.

"Not just that though," Tommo added, encouraging Jof to say the rest.

"No," Jof said quickly. "They were mutilated. Into pieces!"

"Really?" she repeated. "I'll get Parker." She called back as she ran off.

"What's he gonna do? Resurrect them?" Jof said, and Tommo almost smiled.

They stood in silence neither knowing what to say. Tommo felt rough. Not just stay-up-late rough, nor drunk-too-much rough, but was aching all over. He smiled at what had happened the last night, but he'd never felt like *that* before...

Chapter 5

The night before, Toots had come home feeling pumped. There was something inside her that pulsated through the whole of her being. She felt like a moth must feel when about to break free from its cocoon.

Her aches were still there, but the feeling of being violated had gone. Somehow, she'd shrugged it off. Her mental wounds quickly healed.

As she got to the gate and tried to slip around to the backdoor, she saw him. Bob came storming out the front ready for a fight.

"Where've you been?" he shouted, looking her up and down like she was covered in muck. Those judging eyes bore through her, knowing the wanton desires she'd harboured and then indulged in. *What was his problem?* She thought.

"Leave it!" she snapped. She had felt smothered by his worries before. There was a part that understood his concerns, but she was a girl looking to be a woman. Why couldn't he just let her live her life?

"I asked you a question." He came at her, but she side-stepped him to around the side of the house.

He caught up and grabbed her as she got behind the garage. In doing so she scuffed a spade which made a loud noise as it hit the ground. Something in her mind clicked with rage.

"Stop!" he demanded. Toots turned round and elbowed him straight in the face. He went down holding his nose. Blood poured out.

She looked at him but not with pity. The love she'd had for him was gone. It was like all the sympathy and empathy had drained from her being on the walk back. A trail of it most likely left on the path from the park to the house.

"What's going on here…?" Jane panicked as she came around the side of the house and saw her husband covered in blood.

Jane was a woman with little fight at the best of times. Toots knew that Jane would take his side. She always did. Who wouldn't when faced with your husband injured on the floor.

Toots felt the rage inside her again build up to a dangerous level. It was nothing like she had ever known before. She ran and punched Jane full in the face. Jane went down hard and hit her head. By this time Bob had got to his feet, but Toots grabbed the spade that had fallen and swung it like a cricket bat. There was an awful dead thud sound as he went down hard, too.

Looking around, and still with a red mist fogging up her mind, she grabbed an axe from the woodpile and set to work at relieving the bodies of their limbs. It started as a frenzy, and at some point just became another obsession. A job that had to be done well.

By the time she had finished she was hot, sweaty, and out of breath. Her head had cleared, and she walked into the house. Her beautiful summer dress drenched in sweat and blood. She felt nothing. She was completely dead inside. Nothing registered that what she'd done was wrong.

She went up the stairs and straight into the bathroom.

Removing her clothes, she looked at herself in the mirror. The bite marks were now obvious, her blood and her foster parents' blood were now mixed together.

She stared. The smudged blood over her naked breasts suddenly filled her with a desire she'd not felt before.

This was something new that had awakened inside of her.

She scrubbed herself hard in the shower, as hot as she could bear it. She still felt different. She had no remorse, only the want to change others, too.

Was this a bad thing?

She dried herself and walked back to her room. She put on clean knickers and her long T-shirt and sat in her bed looking around. She felt like she had a new purpose. Life would never be the same again.

And then there was that knock at her door. It was, of course, Tommo sneaking about like some pervert. She smiled.

It starts here, she thought and let him in.

Chapter 6

They had all changed.

"What happened?" Parker asked. He was the only one that really felt unsure about things.

Toots shrugged, knowing the truth and justifying it over and over in her mind. She still felt nothing.

"We're lucky that they didn't come into the house!" Jof said looking around at them all.

Tommo looked at Toots. "D'you think it was whoever attacked you?"

Toots gave him a death stare. "Shut up!" she scolded.

Tommo shuffled his feet.

"What's up with you?" Jof grinned. "Need a piss!"

Tommo went to speak but something small fell from Jof's hand. Jof looked at the ground and then quickly to his hand.

"What the fuck?"

"What was that?" Parker said, moving away as Tommo and Toots moved closer.

"It was my…" he started.

"Finger! Shit, mate!" Tommo said, still shuffling.

Parker pointed to Tommo. "And you?"

"And me, what?" Tommo replied.

"What's wrong with your leg?"

Tommo knew it felt different, and as they all looked closely, they saw that one leg was clearly pointing inwards.

"That's not right!" Toots said.

They all looked at her.

"What about you? Are you okay?" Parker asked.

Toots shrugged. "I feel like I've been fucked by an army!"

Tommo felt himself go embarrassed, although he felt no heat go to his face. In fact, his skin had grown paler of late.

The other two looked back and forth between Toots and Tommo, joining the dots but not saying a word. Parker was non-committal. If any one of them was going to have sex with Toots, his money would've been on Tommo. He wasn't sure how he felt about her, but there was something he found scary. Jof was a live wire buzzing all over the place.

They knew their foster parents were dead, but nobody seemed to outwardly care. There was little doubt that they all felt it inside. Things were a little more worrying within themselves. They all made the right noises but each one of them felt different.

Jof grabbed his phone and moaned about no signal. Someone put the television on and before them they saw the whole world was going to shit. It was small pockets of isolated shit, but there were too many of them all over the place.

The world was changing, and they were a big part of that.

Jof still joked around about not having to get a job now but cast a roving eye out of the window at the world around. This wasn't just happening on the television. It was happening on their street and in their town.

Something huge had started, and they were slap bang in the middle of it now.

Was this the end?

They acknowledged they were changing physically and used gallows humour to try to laugh it off. It was something they had always done. It was what made them such a team.

"Hey Peg-leg!" Jof shouted to Tommo who was looking out the window.

Tommo turned and flipped him off. "I'll give you the finger seeing as how you've lost yours!"

"Idiots!" Toots said, coughing and spitting out a tooth.

Each loss from their bodies became less shocking. The lack of pain helped. They were almost resigned to this being the end of the world, and as REM had agreed, they also felt fine.

They were teens, and as such they bonded together and shrugged it all off. If they pretended that everything was alright, then maybe it would be. They knew this was naïve, but what was the alternative? Curl up and cry? Admit defeat? Fight?

For now, they'd do nothing. They'd stay in the house and look at the world outside.

Maybe later they would make a better plan.

"Keep your eyes closed, Jof!" The shorter teenager said to the tall skinny lad with long hair and an empty cola can balanced on his head.

"You'll hit me in the face!" Jof whined as Tommo aimed with his one good eye at his friend.

"It's all about trust."

"That's my point. With you and me, there *is* none."

Tommo pulled back his arm like a baseball pitcher and swung what he thought was a straight shot. It was not. It was slightly off target and smacked straight into Jof's cheek.

"Shit!" Jof angrily said rubbing his cheek, not worrying about the can falling to the floor. "For fucks-sake!"

"Sorry, mate," Tommo said apologetically, and the two other teens giggled in the background.

Parker sat on a bed flicking through a comic about a girl called Lisa Lipstick. She was a crime fighter who walked the streets at night and rid them of bad guys. She was badass and hot as hell! He had all the comics featuring her.

He and Toots were mesmerized by the pair of clowns in front of them. They always acted like life was a reality television show and cameras were all around beaming their antics to people all over the world.

"I'm going to bruise," Jof was still rubbing his cheek.

Toots laughed then said pointing at him, "It's not your biggest issue though, is it?"

"What do you mean?"

"Your finger. You know, the one that fell off earlier."

Jof looked down at his right hand and wiggled where there used to be another digit. It was strange that blood had ceased to come out. It wasn't healed, and it hadn't really scabbed, it just looked black and dead. "Shit! I forgot about that!"

"Really?" Tommo said.

"It doesn't really hurt… like your leg."

Tommo looked down. His left leg was turned in, and when he walked, he'd begun to drag it awkwardly.

"Good point."

"Yer takin' the piss?"

Tommo held up his hands. "Poor choice of words."

"So, what's the plan?" Toots said looking between the two lads in front and at Parker who was trying to lose himself in the comic. He was staring a little too hard at the cartoon babe with bright red hair doing a round-house kick into some sleazy guy's head.

"You can close that thing, Parker. This is serious!" Her bright pink hair was pulled up into a large pony-tail that looked like a generous bright fountain. She wore mostly black clothes in contrast to her lipstick and fingernails that matched the colour of her hair.

Parker thought Toots would make a good comic book hero. Maybe she would be a friend of Lisa Lipstick's. Perhaps even have a super power!

"I'm not sure of our choices, Toots. We all appear to be going downhill," Jof mumbled. "And fast!"

"Speak for yourself!" Toots was quick to reply, although if she was honest, she was stiffening up. It felt like the time Jof had talked them into doing a fun-run. Those were two words that should not be put together. The day after she ached and could hardly move. This is exactly how her body had been.

It was Tommo's turn to point now. "Have you seen the colour of us? We are all getting paler by the hour."

The question was, how had it all started? Yesterday everything was fine, and now looking out of the window, you could see people dead. The media mentioned the odd attacks, but there was something that told the orphans that they were holding back on the full details. They know that people panic, and when they do ultimately people die.

Somehow the media had already started a death toll.

It was in the thousands. People who were beaten and murdered.

And some just found dead.

They touched on several people who roamed the streets in a strange viral state.

"You know what they mean by that?" Toots said swinging her arms to gesticulate.

"What?" Tommo said, more to encourage her to finish what she was saying.

"They're dead."

"They can't be. They're walking around!" Jof said and then proceeded to throw his hands out in front of him and walk stiffly, shouting, "Brains!"

Tommo looked down at his own leg again and then at his hands.

"Guys?" he said quietly at first. "Guys!"

"What?" Jof stopped and looked at him. Toots turned, and Parker put down his comic.

"That's us. We're the ones in a strange viral state."

"Zombies?" Toots grinned.

"Not sure how funny it is," he added.

She leaned into him. "You had sex with a dead person!"

He frowned at her. "Not the time or place, really."

"What? We can't be dead!" Jof spat back.

"Maybe we're not, yet?" Toots offered.

"We're in transition?" They all let these words and thoughts sink in.

Parker looked up and said, "I don't think it's safe out there."

"What, the undead people?" Jof said a bit of sarcasm thrown in for good measure.

"It's not the undead we have to fear," Parker added.

"I'm not scared of them," Tommo said.

"Look, if we go out there the zombie-things will not attack us," Parker stood up to make his point. "It's the people that are okay that we have to worry about."

"We feel okay, but we are slowly looking like the undead, before we know it they will be surrounding us and chopping off our limbs!" Parker swiped his hands in a sword-like motion.

"Okay then, comic boy, what do you suggest we do?"

"We sit tight. See what happens." They looked at each other as Parker sat back down and opened his comic again. Toots held up her hands in exasperation, and Jof and Tommo started a frowning-fest to see who could wrinkle up their brows the most impressively. They had both clearly been practicing.

"Really?" Toots said. "It's the bloody apocalypse, and am I stuck with some hunky blokes? No. I'm stuck with a comic-book-geek, and bloody Beavis & Butthead!"

"Who?"

"Never mind!"

"Cheers," Tommo said slightly down-hearted, although considering their current predicament it was a little misplaced.

Feeling guilty she slid up to him and rubbed the side of his head.

Tommo's ear fell off.

"Shit, sorry!"

"Fuck!" he said, made a motion to pick it up and put it back on, but gave up and lobbed it at the wall instead.

Chapter 7

"You think this is it?" Toots said an hour later as the first clump of her hair came out. "Are we going to die?"

"It's not looking g-ood. Shit!" Jof spat another tooth out onto the floor. It was the fourth one. By the time the third one had fallen out he'd stopped saving them. It appeared to be a lost cause.

Parker was quiet. He looked like death warmed up, and whilst there were no injuries that could be seen, everyone knew that something was happening deep inside him. Sometimes the quiet ones are the ones to watch.

He had left the room several times, and each time he'd come back looking paler. They assumed he'd been throwing up.

They had always been outsiders. They were the orphans. Everyone referred to them as that. The truth was that despite Tommo's wish to move out, he knew he never would. They were all shit scared of a life apart; a time when they would merge in with everyone else. They would not be a group of special children anymore but adults with issues in a world of millions of adults with issues. No one would give a fuck.

They'd probably all end up in group therapy, slouched on chairs, sharing feelings and munching down pills that they were all addicted to.

"I should be sad," Tommo said defeated, the vision in one eye completely gone. "But if we are dying, then honestly… this is how I'd like to go… with you guys."

They all looked around and slowly nodded.

They were dying. You could smell it in the air now. A fetid aroma floating around them like an invisible funk. Their own flesh rotting slowly.

Outside they heard tires screech and the loud crumpled sound of a car crash. A gunshot. A woman's blood-curdling scream. A siren passing. Hell had come to suburbia, and this time it was here to stay.

Toots suddenly grabbed her chest and wheezed. "My chest feels tight."

"Take it easy, Toots," Tommo said, placing an arm around her. Even that seemed a struggle as his limbs had lost elasticity.

"Should we go out there now?" Jof said, jumping on his toes. He slipped, and with a loud crack his ankle broke.

"Fuck," he said. "That's not ideal!"

Their eyes danced over each other. The anxiety that was nowhere to be seen earlier was now here, its magnitude growing by the minute.

And then they heard the roar. Like a football crowd spewing out from grounds on a Saturday afternoon with the nonsensical rumble of tribal chanting. The soundtrack to a riot was complete with car alarms and windows smashing.

"What is that?" Jof said going over to the window. "I think they're coming here!"

For the first time there was sudden fear amongst them.

"Are they... dead... or human?" Toots asked in barely a whisper.

"Hard to tell," Jof replied and walked back over to them. The hoards were at their driveway now.

They all sat in a circle together.

Toots thought about the attack on her the day before. That had been how she had been infected. She'd then killed her foster parents and had sex with Tommo. She'd more than likely passed on this... death to him. She began to wonder whether there was a hell. She had a horrible feeling she was going to find out soon.

"You okay, Parker?" Toots wheezed brushing a hand over his cheek. He pulled back suddenly as if shocked.

"What...?!" Toots looked at her hand, smudged with grey, and looked at the lines on his face wiped clean by her fingers.

"It's not..." Parker started backing away. He looked at them all. He felt their eyes on him and could only imagine what was going through their minds.

"You're not infected?" Tommo said, anger creeping into his voice. "How?"

"Make-up," Toots said and smiled. "There is nothing wrong with you at all, is there?"

"It all makes sense now," Tommo said with a blank face. "Toots and Jof were attacked. Toots and I, er…"

"Fucked!" Jof jumped in.

"Yes… but you, Parker? You never had the opportunity to contract anything?"

Somewhere something crashed and then there were people everywhere downstairs.

Parker got up. "I'm sorry… I'm…"

BANG! The sound of a gun was heard at the same time that Parker's head exploded into a red mass of skull and brain tissue.

"In here!" A voice shouted.

The people swarmed the room around them.

Grey sunken faces looked out at the intruders as guns appeared and lit up the room with gunshots.

Then there was a second of silence as gun smoke and souls wisped up into the air never to return.

The orphans lived together and died together, and in years to come, a large house will be built and they will haunt together, too…But that's for another story.

The End

Hide &

Seek

This is a brand new story.

Chapter 1

The woods got darker as the three boys entered them. They stood close together, almost holding hands. A year ago they probably would have done, but they were trying to be big boys now.

"I heard a child was snatched from here by a big man," my friend Colin said. "A girl."

"Nah, a boy," my other friend, Roy, said. He was six months older than us so he was smart.

I felt even more scared. This seemed like a really stupid idea. But we were ten, our lives were all about stupid ideas.

"They're just stories," I said, but I was trying to convince myself. Our parents watched the news, and we sat looking at comics not paying much attention to what was going on. Everything seemed to be sad. Even the sport focused more on teams losing than winning.

I didn't like the news.

"News stories," Roy said with confidence. "All truth."

That stopped us. The path led deeper into the woods. We were now so far in that all we could see were trees.

Roy liked to scare us. "There're snakes here, too. Did you know that?" He a little smile that always appeared when he saw we were uncomfortable with what he had to say.

"There aren't no snakes here," Colin said rolling his eyes, but I knew.

"Adders? Right, Roy?"

He was nodding like he was that Bear Grylls guy. "Yep. One bite and you turn black, shrivel up, and die!"

"Shut up!" Colin said.

"You don't turn black," I said, although I didn't like to argue with Roy. "I heard you just have to get to the hospital quickly. They get you the anti-bite stuff."

"Anti-venom," Roy nodded in agreement. "But if you don't get it then you shrivel up like a raisin! It's a slow and painful death!" He made dying noises, clutching his throat with his hands, a lolling tongue poking out.

I still wasn't convinced it was true, but it seemed pointless to argue.

Ahead we saw the abandoned van. Once white it now was covered almost three-quarters with a green tinge. Roy had told us that's what happens when things stay outside for too long.

"It'll probably turn into a tree," he said, although that claim seemed a little far-fetched.

Colin had been quiet. The talk of missing children and snakes had done nothing for his courage, which at the best of times was well-below average.

"You alright, Col?" I said, turning to him. He nodded, but I wasn't sure. We'd had to talk him into coming with us.

"Right, who's going to count first?" Roy said, but he was hardly volunteering. Colin looked at me, and I looked at Colin.

"Well, one of you has to?" Roy said, missing the point that he could easily do it himself, too.

"Maybe, I'll do it next?" Colin said, and suddenly two pairs of eyes were looking at me.

"What? Me?"

"Sounds like you're volunteering, Ian!" Roy grinned. I opened my mouth to argue, but it seemed like a losing battle. Colin looked scared and Roy looked determined.

"Um, I guess."

"Go in the van then, Ian," Roy said.

"Why don't we all check it out first," I said. We'd stopped a few feet away, and no one was making any movement to go nearer. There might be a dead body inside.

"What is it doing, here?" Colin asked, his voice small and almost stolen by the breeze. A whisper, barely audible.

"Some paedo," Roy said. "Dumped it here and brought kids here, and did stuff to them."

Of course, Roy would know. It seemed like the woods were filled with stories about bad things happening.

I felt worried. Roy had suggested coming here. He said that the park near our houses was for babies. The woods were where the big kids went.

It sounded like some of them never made it out alive.

"Why don't you take a look first, Roy?" I said nodding over to the van.

"What? Scared?" he goaded, but I wasn't biting. If he wanted me to go in there then he could look inside first.

For the first time I saw something that might have been fear flash momentarily in his eyes. He held my gaze a little too long, almost wanting me to challenge him. I stayed strong. He broke into a forced smile, and threw his hands up!

"Well, if you babies won't, then I'll just have to, right?"

Colin and I shared a look. It wouldn't take a lot for both of us to bolt out of there.

We walked slowly behind Roy as he walked to the back of the van. He tentatively grabbed the handle and yanked it open.

We peered around him, taking in the mattress and clothes.

"Paedo," Roy said, but the clothes I saw were underwear. Women's underwear. The sort I'd only seen in a girlie mag that Roy's big brother had hidden under his bed. Too big for children. I said nothing.

"Maybe we shouldn't do this," Colin whispered. "Come back to mine, we'll play Fortnite or something."

"Later, Col." Roy looked at me. "You ready?"

"Ready."

"Get inside and count to a hundred, yeah?"

I knew I was nodding, but I really didn't like the feeling of being left alone in the woods. I had an awful feeling that the other two wouldn't get to have their go, and if they did, hiding out in the woods on your own didn't seem much better.

I got inside.

That's when Roy slammed shut the door behind me.

"Hey!" I shouted. "Why'd you do that!"

"So you can't cheat!" He shouted back. "Now start counting to one hundred... slowly. Elephants and Mississippi, or whatever!" his voice got quieter as it was swallowed up by the woods.

Chapter 2

I tried not to panic. That's easier said than done when you are all alone with awful thoughts in your brain.

I turned on a horror movie a few weeks ago thinking I could take it, and in the end had to turn it off. Worse still, it gave me nightmares.

A cabin in the woods. Trees with branches and roots reaching out and grabbing people.

I couldn't tell anyone about it, and yet here I was slap bang in the middle of it.

I had got to thirty. I wished I was further.

I felt hot, and my breathing had become short. The smell was intoxicating. I didn't know what it was. Something sour permeating up from either the mattress or the clothes.

The numbers spilled out of my mouth. I didn't even know why I was saying them out loud. Maybe my own voice broke the silence, almost fooling myself into thinking I wasn't alone.

I hit fifty. Half way.

I tried to think happy thoughts.

A few days ago, Nina had held my hand. It doesn't sound like much, but she's cute. I sit next to her and she shares her milk with me. Mum forgot to pay for it again, and Nina said she's not bothered. Everyone had milk except me and Paul. Paul's a traveller so he's not often in.

Anyway, it happened at breaktime. She came and sat next to me. Our hands touched and then they were gripping together like it was meant to be. I'm not sure what it means, but I know I like it.

I'm at seventy. Nearly there.

But I look at the off-white walls inside the back of the van and the lines of smudges that look like they're from desperate fingers clawing to get away. My thoughts of Nina are gone. They're completely replaced by fear.

Eighty.

I hear something outside. It sounds like footsteps. Is it Roy? Is he messing around? Doing the old trick where as soon as I jumped out and went around the van, he'd jump inside without me seeing? It was a classic move, and one that needed skill.

Ninety.

Then nothing. Silence. I'd stopped counting out loud and was finishing off the count in my head. Small creaks could be heard all around. Birds flapping in the trees. Some sort of animal screeching.

One hundred!

"Coming! Ready or not!" I shouted and kicked the door.

But it remained closed. I grabbed the latch but it moved without doing anything. It had been broken off so that it could only be opened from the outside.

I panicked. I'd already been inside here for longer than I wanted to be. Would they come back for me?

I looked behind me and saw there was a large wooden bulkhead with scratches in it. I scrambled over to it and managed to get my fingers into the gaps. With everything I had, I pulled back. A gap opened up to where the front seats were. I stood up as best I could, and used all the force I could muster in my legs to push the gap wider so as I could get through.

It was awkward, and my heart was beating fast as I was determined to get out.

I fell into the seats like the bulkhead was giving birth to a large baby. As I fell, my arm reached out and caught the door. That released the catch, and it swung open sending me tumbling to the ground below.

I ached. Laid there on my back, the trees peered down over me like adults.

Slowly, I got to my feet.

I turned and looked all around.

Trees everywhere. As far as the eye could see.

I scanned for movement but saw nothing.

Where are you? I said to myself. *Where would I go?*

I headed back along the trail. If it was me then I would've hidden along the perimeter nearest the entrance to the woods. That way, if I was scared or worried, then I could step out. I know it sounded weak, but I had a feeling Colin would've had the exact same idea.

I felt better the further away from the van I got. To the side was a pile of logs we'd sat next to once. That had been the first time we'd ventured in to the woods. It was a perfect hiding spot.

Crouching slightly and walking carefully so as not to make a sound, I crept around the edge.

"Found you!" I shouted.

But no one was there.

Up ahead I could see the clearing, and further on from there were the houses that led to our little town.

I thought I saw movement from a clump of trees. I headed that way, but again I found no one.

I looked back behind me. The woods were such a large area. I didn't even know what was on the other side, but there was no way I was going to go all the way there.

I'd had enough.

I just wanted to go home.

Chapter 3

I gave up. I felt bad for Colin but wondered whether he'd given up too. We had no way to communicate. Roy had a mobile, but Colin and I didn't. I asked my mum for one and she looked at me like I'd just asked her to buy me a house.

"You don't need a phone," she said not even entertaining the idea.

"What about for safety?" I tried.

"I've lived here for over thirty years, and I didn't need a phone at your age."

"But my friends go on Apps," I argued, although I had no idea which ones, or even what they did on them. I just felt like I was missing out.

"You're too young," was all she said and that sounded final.

I could imagine Roy staying out there for hours. His dad was in the army, and he thought of himself as some action hero.

I tried, I thought. My watch told me I'd been looking for half an hour.

"I give up!" I shouted. "You can come out now!"

I stood and turned all around expecting them to suddenly show themselves.

But there were no movements.

"I give up!" I repeated, but nothing happened.

The only movement came from a man walking his dog. He walked with his head down whilst his dog zigzagged around, clearly overwhelmed by the smells around it.

I looked up at him expectantly, but he only took a further path around me.

I sighed. I wished there was some way I could tell my friends the game was over. I thought about walking back to the van but I really didn't want to go back there. I couldn't get the feeling out of my mind that bad things had happened there.

Instead, I left the woods. I walked out into the small open grass area that led to a path that connected to the first street of houses.

I was going to go home but felt guilt. A lot of guilt. What if they were both wandering around looking for me? What if something happened to them? I could never forgive myself.

I knew that Roy's house was closest, so I could pop by and see if he was there. If not, I'd leave a message with his parents. That was the least I could do, wasn't it?

I tried to hum to myself. I didn't know who sang the song but I liked it. I didn't know all the words.

Roy's house was at the end of the street. A car was in the driveway up on bricks. The wheels were missing. We liked to pretend that his dad was going to turn it into some James Bond-style car, replacing the wheels so it would turn into a plane or something. Maybe add some guns. Roy would smile but didn't share the same fantasy. Come to think of it, I'd not seen his dad for a while.

I walked up the path and knocked on the door.

I heard shouting from within but couldn't make out whether it was the happy or sad type.

The door swung open, and a shaved-haired guy in a dirty vest said, "Yeah?"

"Is Roy there?" I tried to be polite.

"Does it look like he's here?" he said, and I wasn't sure whether or not I should be responding. It felt like a negative response was what he was looking for.

"Er, no?"

"No in-fuckin'-deed!" He slammed the door shut and left me open-mouthed.

I quickly walked away, suddenly feeling embarrassed. I had turned right and was walking through an alleyway that would eventually take me to the street where Colin lives.

His street was nicer. The houses seemed bigger and there was colour all around from gardens that looked lovely. I didn't know much about them but I could see that the grass was thick but cut short, the hedges were trimmed, and colourful flowers were all around. I wondered whether you had to sign some agreement or something. Not one house looked like it wasn't owned by a gardener!

Colin's house had a caravan outside. I wasn't sure I'd ever seen it before and had to look at the house number to confirm it was the right house! How silly!

I almost skipped up the path towards the door.

I rang the bell, and took a step back. My mum told me never to stand an inch away from the door when someone opened it as it scared them.

The door opened slightly and a voice asked, "Can I help?"

"Is Colin there?" I said.

"Colin?" she sounded unsure. She probably expected him to still be with me.

"Yeah? Has he not come home yet? It's okay. Just tell him, I've gone home, okay?"

"Um, yes, okay," she said. I really hoped I'd not worried her.

I stopped at the end of his driveway and thought about going back to the woods. It was clear neither Roy nor Colin had gone home so they must still be waiting for me. But on the other hand, I'd spoken to their parents so they would know soon enough that I'd gone home.

It was time to go home.

It was Saturday night, so we'd get fish & chips. I loved that.

Thinking about the food, I walked back to the end of the street and turned further from the woods, along past the school and eventually towards my house.

I was humming the song again.

As I got close, I went to get the house key from my pocket but realised I didn't have it. I wasn't sure, but I had a feeling I'd forgotten to take it when I left the house earlier.

I went through the garden gate and around the side of the house. There was washing out on the line, and the back door was open.

"Mum?" I called as I walked into the house. I heard movement from above.

With a smile on my face, I ran up the stairs.

"Hey mum! We had ace fun!" I shouted.

A woman stepped out and suddenly screamed!

I jumped. It scared the hell out of me. What was she doing in my house!

"Who are you?" I said, "Where's my mum?"

"W-what are you doing in my house?" she looked scared. She was grabbing for a phone and backing into the bedroom.

"This is my house," I said. Now the initial shock had gone, I was angry. She was like some sort of imposter.

"No…!" she said, and slammed the door behind her.

"Hey! That's my mum's room! Get out!" I pounded on the door.

I could hear her talking to someone. Maybe it was on her phone. Was she like Goldilocks? Breaking into people's houses? Eating porridge, breaking chairs, and sleeping in beds.

I pounded again. "Get out!"

I turned and went into my own room. I was ready to hide until the strange lady left us alone.

Except, it didn't look like my room. Someone had changed it.

"What have you done?" I muttered. I looked around and everything had changed. No more football posters; they'd been replaced by posters of Winnie the Pooh.

"What have you done!" I repeated, this time louder. I was getting frustrated. I fell to my knees. My legs gave out. My head was spinning. I just couldn't tell what was going on.

I heard the door to my mum's bedroom open, and there was the sound of someone running down the stairs.

"Hey!" I shouted, getting up and running after them.

She was out of the front door before I was even at the top of the stairs.

"And don't come back!" I shouted, feeling brave now she was gone.

Who was that woman?

Chapter 4

It was all still confusing though. I walked down the stairs and into the lounge. Everything was different.

The TV was now on the wall where the large mirror used to be. My mum's figurines were gone.

Everything was different.

I walked into the kitchen and it was completely new. Like really new. The once brown cupboards were now sleek and black.

I was scared. Really scared.

"Mum?" I shouted. I hoped she'd suddenly jump out and tell me it was all some huge joke.

"Mum?" I repeated and walked slowly towards the front door.

I opened it up just as a car pulled into the driveway. It had barely come to a standstill when the door swung open and a woman in a suit got out, her hands held out wide.

"Ian? Are you okay?"

I shook my head. "No. Where is my mum?"

"It's okay, Ian. It's okay." She walked up to me and pulled me in to her.

"This isn't your home anymore. Remember?"

I continued to shake my head, but this time more slowly. Unrecognisable pictures flashed in my head.

"I was playing hide & seek," I said as a response. "With Roy and Colin…"

"I know," she replied. "But you couldn't find them, could you?"

"No! I searched everywhere…"

"It's okay. They were found."

"They were?" I think I was pleased but she looked sad. Then I saw a police car pull up.

"You were taken," she said, trying to explain, but the words might've been foreign. I was struggling to take them in. "What d'you mean?"

"A man in the woods took you in his van. You were found two years later."

"I was taken by a bad man?"

She nodded. "Yes, a very bad man."

"And Colin and Roy?"

She sighed, and I think she was making gestures towards the police. "I'm afraid they didn't make it."

"What? Why?"

"We don't know, but the bad man was caught and he's in prison."

"What, today? You arrested him today?"

"I'm not the police, Ian… this happened twenty years ago. You're being looked after at an institution. It's a nice place, you like it there, but every once in a while, you walk away and search for your friends in the woods."

I'm sobbing. The feeling from back then comes flooding back. The pain of never seeing my parents again. The back of the van. Being kept in a dark and smelly room. Then the day I was found. A tsunami of emotions has me holding on to her tightly. I remember seeing my parents again but they seemed like strangers. Within six months I was taken into care unable to adjust back to normal life.

I look down at myself. My small child-like hands are no longer what I see, but larger man hands aged with the scars of life.

I'm no longer ten but thirty years old.

I want to play with my friends again. I want to go and play hide & seek, but my life changed forever. Years ago.

The End

Psychological human sacrifice, I'm numb and
dead inside,
Nervous and paranoid, the feelings that I hide,
Once I was so popular, but now I'm cast aside,
The bright spark behind my eyes has gone away
and died,

Derogatory rumours spread like idle chat,
Sharp words of accusations that can't be taken
back,
Forced against the wall, he put me on the racks,
But now his bloody head sits nicely in my burlap
sack.

Virgin Women From Outta Space

This was originally released in 2018 by Zombie Cupcake Press. It featured in the sci-fi anthology 'Off Course'.

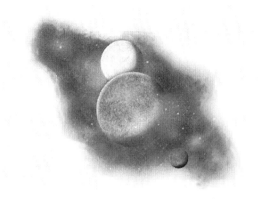

Chapter 1

We'd been sitting here shooting the shit for two hours. We were pretending to be rebels. Or rap-gang-members. I tried to rap once but a teacher told me that I was very poetic with my Pam Ayres delivery. She asked whether I was a fan.

I don't know who Pam Ayres is. She doesn't sound like a gangsta. When I looked her up I found out she was a poet in her seventies.

I don't rap anymore.

"Hey girl? Nice legs, what time do they open?" Trenton shouted. Boy, he was smart. I wish I had the balls to use such charm on women. He says they love it.

The girl had been one of those stuck-up sorts. You know the type, all nose-scrunching-up and looking like we were some turd pushed out from a dog's arse. We're not. We're humans. But she had been jiggling like she was in some shampoo commercial. Her hair was beautiful. Hell, all of her was beautiful!

Trenton was grabbing his crotch. I think he might've picked something up and be in need of that strong cream again. I'm not really allowed to talk about that previous 'incident'.

"This is what ya missing!" he was yelling again. I wasn't sure why he was suggesting that they might want itchy-balls. I certainly didn't, and I couldn't imagine anybody else did. He does that when women ignore him. They don't always. Sometimes they slap him hard across the face. He cried once. He said he had allergies, but I know he was crying. I don't like to see him sad.

It was after school. The sun was hot, and as generally was the case, people were not wearing a lot of clothes. We like this weather. Trenton plays a game called Count Women's Nipples. I'm not too sure of the rules but it appears it involves him looking at breasts. I thought it was a bit pervy, but he told me that next month he has a try out for this very sport to represent England Schoolboys in some championship. He's so bloody gifted. I sometimes think that he got all of the brains.

"Bailey? Ya, gonna do something 'cept sit there and scratch your arse?"

Trenton says things like this to me all of the time, but only once did he catch me itchin' my butt, and that wasn't my fault. He'd put something in my trousers when we'd been getting changed from PE. I guess it was funny. I came out in a rash which took nearly a week to go away. It was sore every time I sat down.

It could've been just a normal day, but I was kind of excited.

I had something to show Trenton. It was sort of a big thing. He's way clever so it will be nothing to him, I'm sure. We saw some career advisors last week. He told them that he wanted to be a spaceman when he grows up. They said he'd have to train very hard, and that he might be more suited to Data-Entry, some more administrative position or perhaps Security. I told them that I wanted to eat peaches for a living. I like peaches. That would be a great job.

"Hey, Trenton? Ya wanna see something?"

"Not your pecker, I don't!" He laughs in a rowdy way that shifts phlegm around his throat. He's so funny. If only I was just a bit of his funny then I'm sure I'd get a girlfriend.

"Nah, not that. I found a book."

"A book?" He said it like I had mentioned the man on the moon.

"Yeah, a book. I think it was my brother's."

"It got naked chicks in it?"

I shook my head. "Why would I have a book like that?"

"Then why would I care about some boring book? They are hard work. Everyone knows that people don't read no more."

"Really?"

"Yeah, they watch the DVDs on their Kindles."

"Makes sense."

"So what's in this old fashioned relic of yours?"

"My brother's."

"Whatever."

I took a deep breath. It was really hard to explain. I'm not good with words. Trenton has that gift of the gob, or whatever it's called.

"I'll show you."

He rolled his eyes, but I could tell that he wanted to know. We were bored and the women in town didn't seem to want to go on dates with us. Trenton has had loads of girlfriends. I've not seen any of them but that's because he says that they're so beautiful that my eyes would probably fall out of my face and roll onto the floor. You can say what you will, but Trenton is a very caring guy.

"Let's go, Arse-munch," he says deadpan. It's his little joke. Either that or he's forgotten my name again.

My house is not very far away from school. I'm lucky as I don't like the bus. I've heard all kinds of things that have happened on the school bus. I'm smart. I walk.

"I don't know why you don't ride a bike," he says in a whiny voice.

"I can't ride a bike."

"Shut up! I've known you what, like six years and you've never mentioned this?"

"You've never asked."

"But everyone can ride a bike."

"I can't."

"Don't you want to?"

"Nope. People fall off and die on bikes."

"People die eating grapes, too but you eat them, right?"

"Nope. That is why I don't eat them. They are a health hazard."

Jim Ody

We are silent for a while. I think he is mad at me. Or perhaps he's lost for words at my clever acts of self-preservation.

"Right. Let's see it then," he says as we get to my front door.

I ring the bell twice. Knock slowly three times and then open the door with my key.

"What the fuck was that?" Trenton asks. He's full of questions. That's what makes him so smart.

"Code. I once came rushing home due to excess bran in-take which brought on bowel-cramps. I had to go to toilet really bad, so I burst in and I…"

"What?"

"I saw something I shouldn't've."

"What was it?"

"I've blocked it out of my mind, but now when I come home, I do this secret code. I will never see those horrors again."

I don't wait for a response and usher him upstairs. My mum is out so I'm safe.

I reached under my brother's bed and pulled out an old book. I don't go into his room very often. Not since he left home and never came back. But last week I missed him so much, I came in and curled up on his bed. For some reason I fell off the bed onto the floor. I was rubbing my butt when I saw the book.

"Look," I said to Trenton, opening it up a little way to where I had turned over the corner of a page.

"What?" he said perplexed. "Read it then. I'm not."

So I did.

When I finished, I stopped and looked up with a smile on my face. I knew he'd be impressed, but I realised he was laughing at me.

"You dumb-fuck! Doorway into another dimension? Who the fuck are you? Dr Who?"

"Who?"

"Too easy."

"Huh?"

He stopped laughing at me. Well, in truth he had fallen about a little more, and had tears streaming down his face. But eventually he composed himself.

"Okay, okay," he said holding up his hands. "Let's check it out."

I grinned. See, I knew he wanted to do it, too!

We walked slowly to the bottom of my garden to where there was a brick building. I knew these to be the electricity buildings powering all of the streets in a small radius. But what if this wasn't one? What if…?

A few months back before my brother disappeared, an old door had found its way to the back of the building that faced onto our garden. I'd thought nothing of it. Old shit was always turning up. But then I read in the book how you had to enter the building from a non-conventional way.

"You are fuckin' more simple than I first thought, and that's saying something!" I wasn't sure this was a compliment.

We stood there next to a battered old door between bushes I didn't know the names of and pushing back the hanging branches of a tree.

"Let's get this over and done with," he said, glancing at his watch like he had some place better to be. We both knew he didn't. His parents didn't love him. That's what he told me, and I knew he never lied.

I opened the door and a bright light shone out. It felt like it had sucked us inside.

There was a great big flash, and then a boom! And we were suddenly sitting on the floor. I felt confused like after one of Mr McGregor's algebra classes.

I couldn't hear or see anything. I had begun to panic when suddenly I made out a figure. Sitting there beside me was an attractive female looking just as confused as I was. I couldn't help but feel suddenly better. She was pretty hot. I licked my fingers and ran them through my hair. Self-grooming was really important. Although my hair seemed longer than I remembered it.

"Hello?" I said, but I couldn't hear the words coming out of my mouth. She looked at me first in panic and then with a strange look.

I looked down at myself, and then as I'd tried to get up, I was shocked to have found out I had turned into a woman!

Chapter 2

"Jesus Christ, you've got tits!" The other woman said in the way that Trenton would normally address. Surely it couldn't be Trenton, right?

"Trenton? Is that you?"

"Fuck me, I've got tits too! What the fuck?" He was grinning at himself and bouncing his breasts in his hands. Left and right. Right and left. Both together and then individually again. I think if I walked off and returned in an hour, he'd still be doing it.

"How did that happen?" I couldn't believe it. It never said anything about this in my brother's book. Surely this would've been an important sidebar. Perhaps even a warning. Not everyone is happy about changing sex.

"Who cares! This is like the best thing ever, don't ya think?"

I really wasn't sure about that. It seemed somewhat inconvenient. I'd never had any desire to become a woman. They were… well, *different*, weren't they?

"I'm not sure I like it," I said honestly. I thought of all the inconveniences of being a woman. I couldn't cook, and I'd always been good at throwing a ball. I liked sports, too. I sighed deeply, that was bound to end now.

I looked back at the door like it was to blame. I saw a pile of something in a plastic leaflet holder. I reached up and picked it up.

"What's that?" Trenton asked, pointing at the paper. He laughed loudly, "Look at my long nails, bro!"

I ignored him. I couldn't give a flying flapjack about his nails.

The paper seemed to be a map, or rather our current destination. It had names of places on it. I supposed it had something to do with us getting back here again should we get lost. It was too much, so I ignored it for the most part and stuffed it in my pocket. I looked again at the door. What if my brother came here but that door never led him back home? What if he's lost out in this other world?

"We have to find him!" I found myself saying loudly.

"What, some hunky guy? You slut, you!"

"No. Pete, my brother."

Trenton shrugged skinny shoulders and tossed his long blonde hair. "Whatever… Let's explore!"

Pictures of my brother flashed through my mind. He was tall and skinny, slightly different to me. I was shorter, and whilst not fat, I was a little chubby. Pete had just got a large bullseye tattoo on his elbow and an eagle design on his neck. Mum had gone mad at him. When he disappeared, she blamed herself. I felt bad for her.

We pushed open another door which had taken us outside into an area that had hard sand on the ground and two red circles in the sky. Suns? Moons? Who knew?

We were both wearing vests, shorts and knee-length boots. It was strange that we had both looked so good. I couldn't properly see myself, but looking down my body it all looked in pretty good nick. I saw no chubby rolls whatsoever. Trenton said that I was hot, and he knew women. I hadn't been totally comfortable with that though.

I scanned the area. Most of it looked pretty bleak. It was how I imagined Mars to look like, or areas of Nevada. To the left I could see some buildings. There was a large almost skyscraper next to them, and a dome building behind.

"Should we head over there?" I asked Trenton, he was still checking himself out with his hands. I wondered whether he wanted me to leave him alone for a while.

"This is great!" He grinned again, completely ignoring me.

"We can go back through the doorway, if you want?"

"No chance. I think it is in our best interest to stay like this for a while, right?"

I was unconvinced. It had just felt weird to me. I shrugged.

"Think about it. If we walk around like this for a while, then we'll understand what it's like to be a woman. We'll have to think and act like a woman, and eventually we will totally understand what a woman wants, yeah?"

"I guess." There was some sort of logic to it.

"So when we go back we will be experts in women and they will fall at our feet!"

"That's a big leap."

"What?"

"It's a great feat."

"Feet? What?"

"No, a great feat, you know, like a challenge that you've completed. Conquered!"

"You talk in riddles."

"Sorry."

We walked silently towards the buildings. It was a longer walk than we had anticipated. The buildings weren't small, but rather a little way away. I'm glad we weren't wearing heels.

"That's the one!" Trenton had said pointing to a door with large neon flashing lights. He's always been attracted to bright flashy things.

The sign said *"C. Her Liquor & Poker"*

"Um?"

He slapped me on the back. "C'mon, yer pussy!" He laughed at what he'd just said.

The door must've had some incredible seal on it, because when he had pulled the handle, loud music blared out. It was a strange mix of jazz played with a banging beat and heavy guitar riffs.

"Wha!" Trenton shouted in surprise as something with green skin and four ears and sharp teeth grinned at us.

"Her? Her?" It said slowly looking us up and down

"Yes," Trenton nodded. He was showing his multilingual side again understanding this foreign tongue with somewhat ease.

The creature pointed to the back, shouted something to a large guy with an inbred forehead, and the patrons parted to let us through. There were a lot of strange people. They had excess fur, or pointed features, wings, or claws and as we walked past, they all grinned at us. It was most welcoming.

We'd been ushered out the back to where there were a handful of females. Some of them were naked. Some not altogether human. We froze. Even Trenton who has seen hundreds of naked women was suddenly paralysed. I suppose you never get used to seeing naked women in the flesh.

A large woman in an outfit that looked like a cross between a leotard and a bikini walked up to us. She scowled and had a whip that she looked ready to use.

"Greego be como reh?" She said in a gruff voice.

I looked at Trenton. He looked at me.

"Her?"

Trenton nodded and she stood to the side and showed us the door along the other side. Silently we walked through. A nerdy guy with a large clipboard and a headset waved us over.

"Stay cool, Bailey-Balls." I was a million miles away from cool.

"Greego be como?"

"Her!" shouted the woman from behind us.

"Her?"

Trenton nodded again. I guess whatever he was agreeing to seemed to satisfy everyone. He's so clever.

Then the guy opened the door and pushed Trenton out. I went to follow but the guy closed the door and held up his hand.

"Balbo, non-terrang bo cassin."

"What was that?" I said.

"Huh?" he replied.

"I'm afraid I don't understand you?"

"Earth?"

I nodded. "Yes."

"Why didn't you say that then, sweetheart?" he grinned in a cockney accent.

"Where are we?"

"C Her Club."

"Ah, okay."

"You ready then?" he said, looking me up and down.

"For what?"

"To strip."

"What!"

"That's what your friend said, yeah? Her – it means strip."

"What? No."

"Look," he opened the door just as Trenton was taking off his shorts, his underwear coming off, too.

However, as he became completely naked it appeared that he wasn't completely female. There in front of a man who had been whooping into what may've been a beer, was an extremely large cock. Trenton stopped. The music stopped. The crowed stared long and hard.

There was a gasp, and somewhere a glass smashed.

"You friend is part man!" the geeky guy almost whined. This sounded bad.

Trenton grabbed his clothes and ran to me. He stepped into his shorts, and wrestled on his vest. Behind him boos rang out and security did their best to stop punters jumping up onto the stage.

"You better get the fuck out of here!" the guy said, showing me another door with a light above it. "Out the fire exit, and run straight to the shuttle-station. I suggest you get the hell off of this planet ASAP. That was a highly illegal move!"

"Why?"

"False-advertising in a strip joint is a major crime. Keep that thing covered up and don't come back!"

We thanked him and ran out the fire exit as fast as possible.

"I don't know what to say," Trenton said as we burst out and saw the large building ahead. It had a picture of a small shuttle with smiling aliens in it.

"I thought we were women," I said slowly putting my hand down my shorts.

"I thought so, too."

My hands touched a strange furry area that was most definitely devoid of a penis. I'm not sure whether I was happy or disappointed. I also wasn't sure what I was touching. It felt weird.

"What's there?" Trenton asked. I could see that he hoped that we were both in the same boat.

"I'm not sure."

It must've looked strange to anyone looking at us. He looked mad and was clenching his jaw.

"Have you got a cock, or not? It's a simple question."

I shook my head. "No."

"Fucksake," he mumbled and set off running again.

I suddenly wanted to be back home. I didn't want this adventure anymore. I wanted to be sitting in front of *Call Of Duty,* talking to other people online, and knowing that my mum was there to give me a cuddle when I died.

We had burst through a door to what must've been an office. It had a big bright sign that had drawn us in like moths.

"Geelko," a woman with blue skin and a bright pink beehive hairdo said in a friendly way. She had a lizard tongue that poked in and out.

"We're from Earth!" I had said loudly, and a little desperately.

"Ahh, explains it," she winked to a guy sitting in front of a screen.

"We need a ship out of here, madam," Trenton said, taking over. He never likes me to speak for too long. He says I get flustered.

"How much have you got."

"Not much," Trenton said unconvincingly.

"Which would be? Come on, ladies. What are the figures?"

"Nothing," I added quickly.

"Ramone, you got anything for free?"

He got up. He was average size in height and weight but he looked like he wanted to eat us up. He also had an eye on a stalk coming out of the top of his head.

"I got something down here, for them?" All three eyes had winked. I felt a bit of sick in my mouth.

"Ramone, you cheeky thing!"

He grinned and then replied, "I got a ship that might be able to help you."

"Okay, we'll take it!"

"You won't take it anywhere. I have two learner pilots that need the experience. You have to sign a waiver though."

"A waiver?" Trenton said.

"Yeah, you know, if you lose a limb or die, something like that. It's all pretty standard stuff." He whipped out a piece of paper.

"You got a pen?"

"A pen!" The guy laughed looking at the woman. "These gals are cute, aren't they! Na, doll, just put your finger here. That's all we need."

Trenton did as he was told and suddenly like some magic trick a pair of teenagers walked out.

"Well, blow me the fuck away!" A lad with long wavy hair said.

"Hey, hey. Be respectful to these ladies, lads."

"Sorry, Ramone."

Ramone looked at us. "Here they are! Your pilots, okay?"

I looked at them. To be honest they reminded me a lot of us. That was not good. Then I looked out of the window and saw a number of people running.

"Fine. Fine. We need to go now!"

"Don't worry, babes, we got ya!" The other one said. He was slightly shorter and with a shaved head. He had ears that were slightly pointed and a slightly blue tinge to his skin.

They'd gestured for us to follow, and out we went.

In front of us there was something the size of a bungalow, and about as aerodynamic as one, too.

"This thing fly?" I asked as we got inside.

"Sure." Blondie said.

"He's a bit of a scaredy-pants," Trenton said. I thought that was a bit harsh.

We sat down, strapped up, and got ready to take off.

I wasn't a fan of taking the bus, and I'd only been on a plane once in my life when I was three. I didn't remember it. As we started to move, I grabbed the seat and went rigid.

"Are you crying?" Trenton asked.

"Probably," I said. This wasn't going to be good.

Chapter 3

"I'm Sandy," said the blonde one.

"Yes, you are quite fair haired," I replied feeling slightly better now.

"No, I mean that's my name."

"Oh, I see. I'm Bailey, and he's Trenton."

"She!" Trenton spat. "I'm a girl!"

The two pilots looked at each other.

"I'm just… a… girl!"

"Well, I'm Johnson," the other lad had said, smirking.

"That your first name?" Trenton asked, now calming down.

"I only have one name."

"Good for you."

The cockpit was fairly comfortable, and once we were up and out into space I almost relaxed. Behind us was a large area that was blocked out.

"Where are you girls going to?" Sandy asked.

Trenton and I looked at each other, this was not something that we had thought through.

"Where are you going?" Trenton asked in a way that sounded like he was sweet on them. He's clever like that. He was using psychology to hide his lack of ability to give an answer.

"We have to pop to Epiphany for a drop off, and then we are hoping to go for a bite to eat. Then back to Poontang, I guess."

"That sounds like it might be fun," Trenton replied.

"Does this have a massive engine?" I asked. I really had no idea how big an engine had to be to shoot a spaceship up and around the galaxy.

"Not especially," Sandy said, turning around to me. "We have a large area for storage!"

"Storage?"

"He means smuggling!" Johnson winked, and his ears wiggled.

"Shh!" Sandy scolded. "We're not meant to talk about it!"

Johnson looked Trenton up and down. "These ladies won't say anything, will you, girls?"

"Get your eyes back in your head," Trenton said shocked. "We're more than just a piece of meat!"

"Sorry," Johnson said looking Sandy for help.

"Have you two heard of SpaceConnections?" Sandy asked.

We both shook our heads. Anything non-Earth related was completely alien to us.

"It's a dating site. It's got loads of sweet chicks on it." He must've realised what he had said and quickly added. "Guys too, I guess."

"Really?" I said but more to be polite. I wasn't sure what to make of it. Dating on earth was hard enough, in space it seemed extremely complicated.

"Yeah. You make a date and then you get to go and meet them in sector 315a. You been there?"

"No," Trenton said, but I could tell that his mind was working overtime. He gets like this sometimes. He came over to my house once to watch telly. It was a while ago. He went to go to the toilet and instead of using the one downstairs he went upstairs and burst in on my mum in the bath. That was bad enough except she'd had her headphones on listening to Justin Timberlake and didn't notice him standing there for a long time. A really long time. Trenton didn't stop talking about it for two weeks. And that is why he hasn't been allowed back for a long time either...

"You wanna see something cool?" Johnson said with a grin. "Go look in the room on the right!"

I got up and Trenton followed. We walked towards the room, and I let him go first. He's a lot braver than me. He told me that, too.

I could see that he was looking for a handle. I saw the button and pushed it. With a swoosh the door opened and a light shone brightly. There in front of us were about thirty attractive women. All still and all staring ahead.

I put my head out the door and was about to shout when Johnson appeared. "Pretty cool, huh?"

I nodded. "What are they?"

He appeared to puff out his chest with pride. "These, ladies, are HB3000s, or HotBot3000 if you like. They are pleasure bots. Robots for the lonely man… or woman."

"They look so real," Trenton said in a slow way that suggested that his mind was already thinking about what could, and couldn't, be done with them. He was dribbling. I'd seen this happen before.

"They feel pretty real, too, if you know what I mean!" he said with a wink.

"Trenton does. He's had loads of women!"

"She! You're such a prick!" he hissed at me which was a bit rude. He turned back to Johnson. "Yes, I've had a few."

Johnson opened his mouth to say something and grabbed his chest like he might have a heart attack.

"You've been with other women," he stammered, which was strange. He almost seemed nervous.

Trenton nodded and then realised what Johnson was thinking. "You know, casual stuff. Blokes too, of course."

"Of course," Johnson was just able to reply.

"Can I take a closer look?"

Johnson almost pushed Trenton forward. "Please do."

I didn't want Trenton to be alone so I followed, too. Once he tried to make out with a shop dummy. We've not been in Ann Summers since.

"How about you?" Johnson asked me.

"How about me, what?"

"Have you been with a woman?"

"I've been to the shops with my mum," I said.

"Uh, not what I was thinking…"

I then got what he was saying. I shook my head. "I'm afraid not."

"Would you?" he pressed pulling something out of his pocket.

"I guess," I said, although I really didn't like to be questioned like this. I had felt my anxieties coming on again. This was all somewhat overwhelming for me. If this continued there was a chance, I'd break out in a rash.

Trenton was all over the first robot. He was touching and squeezing in a way that would be frowned upon had it been a real human being.

"Oh my," I heard and turned around to see Johnson looking through the small handheld device.

"Are you filming this?"

"I am."

"Could you not?"

"What? Film?"

"Yes."

"Erm… okay." He snapped something shut and walked off with a big huff.

"Trenton, come on!" I said as loudly as I could. He was still groping away and looking everywhere on the robots.

"Really?" he moaned, pulling his hand out from down the robot's pants.

"Yes, you're embarrassing me. We are in a strange place with persons that we do not know, and you are acting like a sex pest. It's unacceptable."

"Well, look who's found his balls! It's funny that when you had your own balls you were as weak as shit, but now they've been taken away, you're Billy-Big-Balls!"

"I'm just saying…"

"I know. Don't fuck the 'droids."

"Yes, if you wouldn't mind."

"Fine!"

We walked back to the other two like a pair of naughty boys who'd been caught pawing over a porn mag.

"They're pretty neat, guys. What d'you do with them?"

Johnson gulped. "What? Like sexually?"

"God no," Trenton said. "You can keep that to yourself! I meant, what are you going to do with the lot of them?"

Sandy tapped a few buttons, pulled up a lever and said, "We know a man. We pretend that we are a taxi service but really we smuggle these things around. Technically they're illegal."

"Illegal? Why?" I said.

"People have sex with them," Sandy replied like it was an obvious thing. "Sex and anything remotely sexual is banned on Poontang."

"I beg your pardon?" Trenton said in the politest way I've ever known.

"Poontang. The planet we just left."

Trenton looked at me and smirked. "We just left Poontang?"

"Do I speak in riddles?" Sandy said, a little annoyed.

"Sorry, please go on," I'd encouraged.

"*Poontang*," Trenton giggled to himself.

"As I was saying, anything sexual is banned."

"What about the club opposite your shop? That had strippers in it. Is that not banned?"

Johnson shook his head and had a serious face on. "No, that's okay on account of only showing titties. They aren't sexual, but functional."

"Let me stop you there," Trenton said again with a big old smile plastered all over his face. "Functional, you say?"

Sandy nodded. "Yes, milk for the babies."

"Okay…" I sort of got what Trenton was thinking. Surely if they were not seen as sexual then there wouldn't have been so many leering male-things at that bar.

"See, one time," Johnson grinned. "This girl got up and stripped completely naked!"

Sandy was shaking his head to this story, and then finished it off. "'cept it wasn't a girl. She had like man-parts swinging around!"

"She got pulled off the stage, and my uncle said she was dragged outside and had her man-bits cut off and shoved in her mouth on account of false advertising!"

"What was she advertising?" I asked.

"Not the point," Sandy rolled his eyes.

"Story-spoiler," Johnson agreed.

"Oh, no. Good story!" I said looking at Trenton. He looked nervous and was suddenly moving around his own man-bits.

Sandy pulled some levers again and pressed a couple of buttons.

"Okay," he said. "We are about to land."

It's funny but I had got used to being up in the air. The spaceship was incredibly steady so it was easy to forget exactly where you were. Now, however as we headed towards a large grey and blue planet, I began to feel anxious again.

"Here we go!" Sandy sang out.

Everything went dark, and then cloudy, and as if by magic we hit blue skies and a sprawling mass of lush fields and a city.

"Welcome to Epiphany, folks!" Johnson shouted. We slowed up and glided down into a port.

"Don't you have to introduce yourselves, or something? Ya know, get clearance to land?"

Johnson and Sandy shared a look.

"No," Sandy said. "They scanned our ship before we hit the atmosphere."

"I thought you were smuggling those robots?" I said.

"We are. But they are just androids marketed as house-maids."

"Yeah," Johnson added. "They can't tell that you can have sex with them too."

"Is that a problem?" I pressed.

"Yep, look, the thing is. There is this guy called Raymond. He owns that website that I was talking about earlier."

"SpaceConnections," Trenton grinned.

"Yes, over on sector 315a. He owns a lot of businesses in the sex industry. He sees himself as the Sex God of the Universe and has an army called Dickstroyers who get suspects and make them disappear."

"Aren't you scared about getting caught?" I said. It seemed to me that doing something that was seen as illegal was an extremely risky pastime.

They shrugged at once like this was nothing.

"Why would we?"

"It sounds dangerous!"

"Dangerous is our middle-name!" Johnson said.

"Good one," Trenton grinned.

"No, really," Johnson replied deadpan. "My middle name is Danger, and his is Russ."

Sandy nodded to this.

"I thought you only had one name?" I said, suddenly remembering what Johnson had said earlier.

"I do. One first name and one middle name."

"And your last name?"

"I don't have one."

I felt myself frown. "If you don't have a last name then your middle name is a last name not a middle name, right?"

"You girls!" Johnson said, winking. I had a feeling that as a woman I wasn't being taken seriously. As a boy I was used to this, but I had tits now. I thought that it would be better.

We walked out and were hit by the heat. I don't know what I was expecting, but a warm temperature was not it.

"Look, go and have a look round and meet back here in three-cubric-jarvs, okay?" Johnson said.

"I beg your pardon? Cubric-jarvs?" I said.

Sandy clicked his fingers as if to remember something. "Ahh, yes, an hour in your Earth time."

"There you go! Come on Bailey!" Trenton was already off exploring.

"Really? Shouldn't we stay near?"

A purple robot rolled by and wolf-whistled at us.

"Piss off!" Trenton said. "That's not right, surely?"

I shrugged. I'd seen Trenton attempt to wolf-whistle before. He had first done it to Donna Patsley and ended up spitting on her. She had called him Homer, or some such name. He had sulked for an hour after that.

Two men with full-faced helmets and guns were walking around, and they naturally made me nervous. They stopped and looked at us for a couple of beats, and then turned and marched off.

"Let's go in here," Trenton said pointing to a large looking stone igloo that blasted out some sort of electrical music in a slow beat.

"Hold up!" I said, "the last place I followed you into you ended up naked and swinging your ding-a-ling around like a weapon."

"I don't plan on doing that again!"

I thought about it. I suppose it didn't hurt to try it out.

As we walked in there was a green smoky haze and a smell like some sort of spice that hit me with some force. There was a bar in front of us, and to the right a seating area of booths, and then to the left a band was playing some sort of music. As far as I could tell there was a robot, a blue creature that was a cross between an elephant and a cat, a tall scaly lizard-type of person blowing something, and in front a woman with tentacles dangling down her back like dreadlocks, was holding the microphone in a quite sexual way. She purred some lyrics out to nobody in particular, but all around people were watching whilst pretending that they weren't. Trenton said this is what you do when you go out. You look, but you don't look. I had no idea what this meant or how you would execute it. I found social situations incredibly confusing.

"Problem…" I said.

"You can't help touching yourself?" Trenton laughed.

I rolled my eyes. "No, I hadn't finished my sentence. How can we buy a drink here? We have no money."

Trenton nodded. "A good problem indeed."

And that was when two guys appeared.

"I guess we could stretch to getting you fine ladies a drink!"

I looked at them. They looked slightly hopeless like us, and not too dissimilar to Sandy and Johnson, either. It was strange, we had travelled all this way and managed to attract the attention of two alien sets of ourselves.

"I'm Caloosh," said the first guy, wild curls flowing and rough stubble on his chin. "And this here's my sidekick, Robone."

"He's *my* sidekick, he means!" said the other guy who sported a dirty-blonde ponytail and a goatee. In 1991 he might have been considered cool.

"What are you having?" Caloosh asked.

Trenton as usual took charge. "We'll have the same as you."

The two guys looked at each other and gave this a nod of approval. Caloosh wandered off towards the bar and Robone sat down. It was strange, but I felt like we could do better than these two.

"What's nice girls like you doing in a place like this?" he said.

"Really? That's what you've got?" Trenton said, almost disgusted.

"What?" Robone looked hurt.

"I look this good, and you can't come up with a better line than that?"

Robone shrugged. "What would've been better?"

"I'm Fred Flintstone, and I can make your bed rock!" Trenton laughed.

"I don't understand."

Trenton held up a hand dismissively. "Forget it."

There was an awkward few minutes whilst we waited for Caloosh to return. Then suddenly he walked back with a 'droid following with our drinks. They were on a tray and green.

"These will put hairs on your chest!" Caloosh grinned. I hoped not, looking at his head I could only imagine what sort of forest was hidden under his shirt.

"Let's go!" Robone winked and gulped down a few mouthfuls.

I picked up the beaker, blew at the wisps of smoke coming out of it, and took a sip. It was cold and I was trying to guess the flavour when the fire of the alcohol kicked in.

Caloosh grinned and winked at Robone, and then turned to us. "You like these?"

Trenton had already drunk half of his glass, and I was feeling my head spin. I was nodding, and then I could see Caloosh press some buttons on the 'droid and it shot off towards the bar. I once drank a pint of cider, and Trenton says I grabbed a girl's boob. I'm not sure I did, but I have no recollection of the event.

"Then it calls for another round!!" He shouted and did a huge wolf-cry. It was apt as he looked somewhat primal.

I remember more talk about SpaceConnections and this section 315a. Then everything went really green. Everyone's voices slowed right down, and I was struggling to focus on anything. I swayed slightly to the bass from the music.

There was fire in my throat, white flashing lights, and then there had been liquid projecting from my mouth. There was a stinging sensation in my eyes and a definite case of sticky fingers.

And then everything had gone black.

Chapter 4

Later I had woken up to the sound of dripping water. I looked and saw Trenton through bars. He was sitting on the wooden floor pretending not to cry. He was hugging someone.

"What happened, Trenton?" I asked.

"I'm not sure, but I think I might've taken my clothes off again."

"Why would you do that?"

"Someone said something about my tits, and I remembered what it was like being a guy, and it would be nice if I commented about a girl's boobs and she showed them to me."

"What?! You thought getting your tits out on another planet would end well?"

"I didn't think."

"No shit, Trenton."

"You've got your big-balls again. I think I preferred you being a pussy rather than you having one!"

I then looked at the other person and realised that it wasn't a person at all but one of those androids from the spaceship.

"Trenton, what is that?"

He glanced at who he was hugging. "Portia."

"Portia is one of those robots, *yeah?*"

He was shaking his head. Then he stopped and nodded.

"I felt so good I wanted to show her to those guys, and how good she was."

"Did you go back to the spaceship?"

He nodded. "Yeah. I think they said some bad words to me and left."

"So they left us here?" My heart sunk. I felt like the kids from that *Dungeons & Dragons* cartoon that just wanted to get back home.

"Right. They're horrible people, aren't they?"

"Why were you showing off to those blokes? They got us drunk, the fucking assholes!"

"Hey," a voice from behind said. "We can hear you."

I turned around and saw them in another cell. One was laid down and the other was standing up resting against the bars. It then struck me how old fashioned this seemed to me from our world let alone on another planet that had 'droids as waiters, and 'droids as... er, sexual partners.

"Well, which part is untrue."

"The asshole part," Caloosh said. "We bought you drinks, and your friend repaid us by stealing some sex doll and then getting her tits out!

"You didn't seem to mind," Trenton mumbled, which only added to how bizarre this whole conversation was. Not in a million years would I have ever thought that I would be party to such talk. I suddenly wanted to hug my mum.

"You've traumatised Robone," Caloosh said. Robone had his head in his hands and was nodding.

"What?!" Trenton and I said at once.

"Traumatised. After seeing your tits, he was thinking that he was going to get lucky, and then you pulled your shorts down, grabbed that..." he nodded down. "Thing, and started swinging it around!"

"Not again!" I said.

"He, er, she's done it before?"

"It's a long story but yes."

There was then a fizz sound like an electric door before we heard a manual metallic clunk of a heavy lock. In walked one of the guards that we had seen earlier. Obviously he was still wearing a helmet so it may or may not have been one of the actual guards.

He stopped and his helmet turned towards all of us individually like it was scanning us. I had held my breath until my lungs burned.

"You are here for severe crimes of nudity. You will be taken up to the Higher One, where you will learn of your fate."

He clicked his heels, turned and marched out. I was unsure whether he was a person or an android.

"I don't see why we are all in trouble," I said. "Is it by association?"

"Could be," Caloosh said. "Or that Robone decided to join in and whip his manhood out, too."

"I didn't want your friend to feel left out," Robone muttered loudly.

"Left out?" Caloosh chided. "He was making whipping sounds and shouting *I wanna ride you like a cowgirl!* I'm not sure he really needed any further encouragement!"

"I suppose not."

"Shit, I wish I remembered it," I said. I couldn't believe that I had no recollection of it at all. One minute we were sitting down half listening to the band, and then we were downing drinks.

"You girls couldn't handle your drinks, is all," Robone grinned with teeth that had clearly scared away a toothbrush years ago.

"I still maintain that you were trying to get us pissed!"

Robone looked up to Caloosh who shrugged.

"We got ourselves a pair of fine women!" He grinned. Then Robone got up, and the two of them high-fived, spun around, clapped their knees twice, and grinned like a pair of fools.

"What the fuck was that?" Trenton said. "You a boy-band dancing to some silent music, or what?"

Trenton cracks me up sometimes. His face was shocked like the two of them had just made out.

"It's our thing," Caloosh said. "You wouldn't understand."

"Too fucking right, I wouldn't," Trenton turned his head in disgust. It was funny. I thought their little dance thing was cool.

"Funny thing," Robone said. "Coming from the woman with a large cock and a sexdroid!"

"He's got a point, mate," I agreed.

"Well, you can go and join their little dance squad then! And she's called Portia, not sexdroid!" He was in a huff. Like when I said he was no longer allowed to come to my house again.

Suddenly another guard appeared. He went through the same ritual of stopping and scanning us slowly.

"Soon you will be taken up to the Higher One. To find out your fate. For severe acts of nudity!" And then he was gone. The clipped speech had told us that he was definitely not the same guard.

"That's what the other one said," I pointed out.

"Why don't they just take us now?" Caloosh said. "I heard about this guy who went up and put slugs in the Higher One's face. The Higher One screamed and let him go.

"Have you got any slugs?" Robone asked knowingly.

"Sure, a whole host of them up my ass. No, of course I haven't."

"Not a very helpful story then, is it?"

"It was meant to be entertaining, not helpful."

"Good to know. Maybe next time you can say – *this isn't helpful, just trying to entertain you before you die*!"

"Stop being so melodramatic!"

Trenton piped up. "Not kissing and hugging anymore, are you!"

Caloosh and Robone grinned and went through their routine again.

"For fuck's sake!" Trenton grumbled. "What is wrong with you two?"

"Hey, tell me about these women," I said. I was intrigued. I had dreamed of being with so many different women that it was hard to imagine that there wasn't one out there that I had not fantasised about. Well, a few ugly ones, I suppose. They didn't venture into my dreams very often.

"Where do we start?" Caloosh pondered, his face pulling a weird sort of grimace that might've been something a little like lust. It made me feel a bit strange.

"At the beginning would be good," I said.

"Well, Robone and I were tinkering around and we found the SpaceConnections website…"

"The women on there were smoking hot!" Robone cut in.

"Anyway, I saw this real hottie called BigTitsWarbler, and the picture showed me she was everything that you could ever want…"

Robone laughed. "He meant it just showed her tits."

"They were big? And juicy?" Trenton said, serious. He took women very seriously. I wasn't ever sure how breasts could be juicy. That seemed to be a strange phenomenon, but it did seem to be a big requirement for a lot of men.

"Too right. They were juicy, and huge enough to get lost in for days…"

"That's good?" I asked. It seemed scary that you could get lost in a woman's ample bosom. Proportionately that would make her about thirty-foot-tall…

"The best, my friend. The best!"

"To be fair, she does look good!" Caloosh conceded.

"You've seen her face?" I said.

"No, her tits! Did we not just say that?"

"I'm confused," I admitted. Wasn't a face important anymore? Most women had them in my experience. Their breasts weren't often on show.

"Your girl is nice looking, too," Robone said patting his friend on the shoulder. "Nice hair."

"Yes, InsertItInMyWormhole has lovely hair. Nicely trimmed."

"InsertItInMy what?"

"Wormhole."

I shook my head. Whatever happened to sweet-named girls called Susie, or Heidi?

"What colour eyes has she got?" I asked and instantly regretted it. I was met by laughter.

Robone rubbed the tears from his eyes. "Good one. It was her hair from down below! You know?"

They all laughed again, even Trenton. He seemed to have heard something that I had not.

And then another guard appeared.

"You're all in big trouble," he said in a bored voice. "A severe act of nudity you are charged with. Soon you will be going up to the Higher One. There you will…"

"Learn our fate. Blah, blah, blah. Whatever," Caloosh said. "You taking us now?"

"Not yet… but very soon." He turned and marched out.

"D'you not find that weird?" Caloosh said when he was gone.

"Yes," Robone laughed. "A dark visor on a full-face helmet in a dark room!" They high-fived into their little routine again. All we could do was watch and wait.

"So, your women…"

"Ah, yes. We were off to meet them. They are in sector 315a, you know it?"

I shook my head. "Not really, but we've heard of it though."

"*Really?* From who?"

"The two guys that brought us here."

"Man, we gotta get there quick. The ladies won't wait forever."

"Shouldn't we be giving it some thought as to how we can get out of here?" I suggested.

Trenton sat his sexdroid up against the side and got up. He looked at the cage and pulled at the bars in the fashion that was clichéd but hugely expected.

"Pretty strong," he said. "I think we'll need the key to get out?"

"You think you need a key?" I said loudly. "What is this, 1901?"

"Haha! Ancient history ladies. It will be an automatic lock. This is 3069."

"What?" Trenton and I said at once.

"That's the second time that you have both done that together. It's pretty cute, you know!"

"Shut up!" We both said together again.

"Be still my beating heart!" Caloosh grinned flicking back his curly locks again. I didn't like it. He had that animal look in his eyes like he wanted

- 391 -

to ravish me. I didn't want to be ravished. Not by a male anyway.

I looked at Trenton who mouthed the year to me. That door at the end of my garden was a very powerful door. I don't think you can get them like that in Harrods.

Robone was trying to push through the gap in the bars. He was never going to do it but for some reason looked like he believed that he could. I admired his tenacity, but it was always going to end one way. He was a large lad.

"Too small," he said.

"You do surprise me," Caloosh replied.

"So what shall we do?"

There was a lot of puffing out of our cheeks and hands held up. It was a real conundrum.

"Why don't we sing a song," I said. Singing was known to relieve stress.

"What? Why would we do that?" Trenton said. He thought that I had gone cuckoo again.

"Morale. I read it somewhere," I said.

"You start."

I didn't like singing in front of other people. I tried to sing a few scales to get my voice warmed up when we heard marching footsteps again. I stopped singing.

"Here we go," someone muttered.

"A most heinous act is severe nudity. Not looked upon lightly. You…"

"Yeah, yeah… upstairs to the Higher One. Punishment dealt…"

"Fate learnt."

"Tomatoes, tomaytoes. You taking anyone now?" Trenton asked.

"Not now but soon!"

"Okay, nice chat. Fuck off. Goodbye."

The guard marched off muttering something under his breath. He didn't enjoy his job today.

I looked over at Trenton, who was fiddling with his 'droid Portia, the dirty pervert.

"Leave her alone!" I hissed. He couldn't be taken anywhere. He'd have his cock out in a minute again if we weren't careful. That was the whole reason why we were down here!

Then there was the sound of something starting up. A humming and whirring.

"Get off of me, you strange man/woman!"

"What the shitting-hell?" Robone eloquently said.

Trenton looked worried.

"I am a state-of-the-art 'droid companion. I have a number of uses but do not like to be touched." The droid spoke in a plummy upper-class voice.

"What?" said Trenton, his jaw dropping open. "You're a sexdroid and you don't like to be touched?"

"Madam, I am nothing of the sort. I agree that others of my kind have indeed been designed to perform and carry out sexual acts that are similar, if not completely the same as those performed by your human females…"

"But…"

"We even lie completely still and make false noises as if to fool you into thinking we are enjoying ourselves. Hah hah. That last bit was a joke. A quip. Humour. It's an added extra."

"You don't like being touched."

"I can see that you are one of the simpler types of humanoids, possibly with learning difficulties so I shall endeavour to simplify my speech accordingly in order to accommodate your smaller inferior brain."

"Huh?"

"Touch me and I will kill you. Simple enough for you?"

"But...?"

"You stupid idiot, Trenton," I grinned. "Of all of those sexdroids on the spaceship you chose the only one that doesn't like to be touched. That is funny!"

The 'droid turned to me, nodded and turned back. "Your friend is correct. I am the only one of the 'droids – and you will notice I dropped off the word sex from it – that doesn't like to be touched. It is indeed amusing – especially when I tell you that the one you almost took is known to be the best at performing these said acts that it appears you were looking to indulge in."

"Un-fucking-believeable."

Trenton looked completely crestfallen.

This sent Caloosh and Robone into their high-fiving once again.

"And may I ask what is up with those two? Really, of all of the male species that I have come in contact with, those two appear to be the least human!"

"I think I might have to turn you off now," Trenton said, still sounding completely disappointed like someone gave him a pie and then shat on it just as he was about to eat it.

"Before you do that, madam, would you like me to open the cage?"

"You can do that?" I said just before Trenton.

"I can, but it will amuse you to note that those other slut bimbos that you were looking to splash with your seed cannot. Not such a bad choice now, right?" Its eye actually winked. It was another weird experience.

Then there was a sudden *swoosh* sound and the cage opened. Trenton and the 'droid walked out.

The 'droid opened up my cage and then the cage of Caloosh and Robone. They, of course, did their dance again.

"Why do they do that? Is it a primitive mating ritual?"

"More than likely," I replied.

We looked down the corridor and thought about how we might escape.

Chapter 5

As we walked further down the corridor, things became more polished and clinical. It was like we had been held in a movie set that had been built to look like a group of cells. Now things were more futuristic. Clean lines and efficiency.

We entered a glass tunnel that was within some large structure. Quickly we ran to the large double doors at the end, happy that the 'droid was able to unlock each door as we made our escape. *It's a good thing that we didn't go back in time instead of to the future*, I thought. We'd have been burnt at the stake by now.

"Caloosh?" Robone said.

We stopped and looked behind us. He was gone.

"Where the fuck?" Trenton said to no one in particular.

"Look up," the 'droid said in a frustrated voice.

We looked and saw the silently screaming face of Caloosh as he was handcuffed and going up in a transparent elevator that Dahl's character *James* would be impressed with – although I also recall him being fond of over-sized fruit, too.

"Should I go without him?" Robone pondered out loud which surprised me.

"No," I said. "I'm not doing that dance with you, and you'd look even more stupid on your own doing it."

"Really."

"Really!" Trenton agreed.

"If you'll pardon me for interrupting these poor flirtatious attempts at courtship, might I suggest that if we take a left the other side of these doors, and then take the elevator to the right of us, we might meet your pea-brained cohort there."

"And what? Ask him to follow us like a puppy?"

"A puppy?" Robone looked confused.

The 'droid shook her head in disbelief. "A puppy is a baby dog, a creature commonly found on a former planet called Earth a thousand years ago."

"Former?" I was shocked.

"Puppy?" Robone repeated.

"Yes, and yes. Please do try to keep up."

"Well shit-fuck-fancy-pants and all that is goddamn sacred," Trenton muttered. The words tumbling out of his mouth like they were being quickly rejected by his brain. "There is no Earth?"

"Not unless you count the trillion pieces of it that are heading in different directions throughout the galaxy," the 'droid added matter-of-factly.

"I see," I said.

"So back to saving your friend." It was something when a robot was trying to motivate us into helping someone.

"I'm a bit worried that it might be dangerous," Trenton said after a fashion. "I mean, we didn't really know him, did we? His boyfriend here did, but not us."

"Funny," Robone muttered, eye-rolling his contempt. "We've been friends for a very long time."

"You'd better go and save him then," I added. Trenton had a point. This sort of thing never ended well. If nothing else one of the characters would die. The odds didn't look very good for Trenton or me. If Trenton died, I would never be able to look his mum in the eyes again. If I died, then Trenton might think twice about looking at my mum in the breasts again. Or perhaps not. He might even try to move in, taking my place in the family. He'd be sneaking into the bathroom willy-nilly. She'd be soaking in the bathtub and from beneath the suds his ugly face would pop out with a leering grin and his little grabby hands reaching for her womanhood. It didn't bear thinking about.

"We'll wait here," I said nodding to Trenton.

"Yep," Trenton agreed.

"Not exactly heroes, are you," the 'droid pointed out. "By my calculations you would be safer and better off to come with us. I can see you are both at an unhealthy level of anxiety, however you must face your fears to beat your fears."

"Fucking typical. I brought a 'droid to fuck and it spouts out philosophy and motivational statements instead. I'd have been better off to try and have sex with Ms Hammond in Home Ec."

I pulled a face. "She's old. She's been retiring for the last fifteen years!"

"My point exactly. She's old and wise."

I frowned. "I'm not sure about that being the right point."

"You need to read between the lines, Bailey. Geniuses speak in ways that are hard to comprehend by those of lower intellect."

I nodded. He was probably right. He was very clever.

"Hargh! Hargh!" The 'droid made a laughing noise and although the facial expression did change to a slight grin it looked more sinister. I couldn't help but think that technology of faces might've come along a lot more than this.

"You're a comedian, I see," the 'droid added, and then beckoned us to follow. "Come on."

As she advised, we walked through the doors, turned, and walked towards the elevators in a way that the *Scooby-Doo* gang might. A quick tip-toes walk.

"Why are you walking like that?" Robone said.

"Never you mind," Trenton replied. I sensed a bit of tension between them.

We got in and the doors closed behind us. I was looking for a large panel with numbers on, when it started moving.

"Mind control," the 'droid said.

"Eh?"

"If you had noticed, I pressed the sensor and told it where I wanted to go in my head."

Trenton and I exchanged glances. He looked like he needed a poo. He probably did.

The doors opened, and we tentatively got out.

"You two are acting in an extremely peculiar fashion. I can see danger ahead."

"What about in the bar?" Trenton countered. He is so damn clever.

"I was turned off before there was any danger. Or rather I was never turned on."

Robone giggled. "I bet all the girls say that to you, huh?"

"And all the men to you!" Trenton shot back.

"Okay, you two," I said, trying to be the peace-keeper. "Let's go and save Caloosh."

We walked slowly down the side of a corridor that had a number of signs with symbols I didn't recognize. The 'droid led us to a door on the right, and like sheep we followed.

For a second I did wonder about the 'droid. We were putting a lot of faith in her. She was a machine, albeit a bloody clever one.

We were met with a couple of stairs and I felt I had to say something.

"Hold on," I said. "You said down there that you could sense danger, but how come you didn't see Caloosh get taken."

Her face was blank. It was hard to read the face of a 'droid.

"Your friend was lagging behind. I was scanning in front. I cannot be held responsible for every turn of fate. Especially those that happen behind and out of range."

"Yes, but…"

"Do you want to save your friend or not?"

"Yeah, I suppose…" I started.

"Nope!" Trenton said emphatically. "I didn't down there, and I don't up here. I would very much like to go off and have some privacy."

The 'droid turned to him. "No matter the land, and no matter the year, you are a silly human."

"Harsh," he muttered though visibly hurt.

"Look," the 'droid said. "This is not going to be easy, so you have to trust me. Okay?"

"Fine," I replied and Robone nodded. He looked ready to get on with things.

"And you?" she said to Trenton.

"Okay, okay. Whatever."

We headed up the stairs. The 'droid was quite nimble for a robot. I guess technology had come a little way after all. Functionality over aesthetics.

We came out in a gallery looking down on a number of people. I could see Caloosh stood there, his head was bowed, and in front of him a strange man in dark-grey with a large horn coming out of his forehead.

"Sshhh!" the 'droid said with a finger raised to her mouth. It seemed a very earth thing to do. I don't know why. "We have to be quiet."

We were only ten feet above them, but it was like we had just snuk in to the back of a church.

"Who's up for a bit of running?" the 'droid asked.

"I guess," Robone said nervously as Trenton and I both shook our heads.

"Okay, listen very carefully. I do not have the speed to move as quickly, so two of you will need to run over and carry your friend back…"

"Not my friend," Trenton stated.

"Irrelevant comment."

"Just saying."

"I can stun the room in front of me for thirty seconds, and in that period, you will have to run over and carry him back here. When he comes round, he will be able to run himself, however so will everyone else."

"You can stun the room?" I said.

"It is a standard issue on this model. The normal functionality is to stun the aggressor trying to penetrate you, but I made a few adjustments which meant it stuns harder and longer."

"My sort of adjustments," Trenton grinned.

"Blimey," I said, but then questioned, "Why will we not get stunned too?"

"I've already scanned you all creating a forcefield over your bodies, therefore you will not be affected."

"Oh, okay." Sometimes it felt like the 'droid was just making these things up. For all we knew she was a chancer just us much as us!

She pointed to Trenton and Robone. "Okay, when you see the stun rays, start running after them. Grab your friend, and we will head out of here. Go down there, and we will meet you." She pointed to the doors below us.

"Question." I said.

"Yes?"

"Why have I not been picked to run? Is it because I'm a girl?"

Robone nodded. "Probably."

"No. You're wearing boots."

"So is Trenton."

"Exactly, and she's a girl."

"Mostly, but with a large cock." Robone giggled.

"Explains so much," the 'droid replied. "It's not important. Do you want to run and grab him?"

"Not really," I agreed.

The 'droid actually raised her eyebrows and tutted. "Really, I will never truly understand humans! So why are you questioning my decision?"

"Because…" I realised I just needed to shut up. "Forget it. As you were."

"Thank you!"

With that, a huge bolt of red waves shot forward and down. Robone and Trenton looked at each other and ran in a comical fashion down towards the people.

It was a strange sight to see a large room of people who previously had been moving, now as still as mannequins.

Robone got to Caloosh first, tipping him and then Trenton got there as Caloosh toppled over. Robone grabbed him and hefted him onto his shoulders whilst Trenton bolted away.

I saw this over my shoulder as we headed down the steps and out of the door.

Then as we met them we heard a commotion firstly of Caloosh wriggling and writhing on

Jim Ody

Robone's shoulders, and then shouting from within.

The 'droid clicked something as the doors locked, and we headed for the elevator.

We burst through the doors as they opened, and within seconds the doors closed and we were heading down.

"I will have to try the stunray again once the doors open. There will be a number of guards who have been called."

"You can put me down now," Caloosh said.

"Oh, sorry."

The doors opened with a *swoosh* and another red wave shot out. The angry faces that could be seen and the masked visors of the guards seemed evil as we pushed through them. It was like everyone and everything wanted us dead. A few fell down like dominos.

We headed for the exit and burst outside, the brightness burning my eyes for a while before I became used to it.

Once again, with a *whoosh* another red wave shot out at one of the many vehicles in front of us.

"Pull out the driver and let's go. This is our getaway!"

We did as we were told. Caloosh jumped in the pilot's seat, and with a shake and a slight tilt of the vehicle we were off moving forward and rising a few feet in the air.

We zoomed around a large building that looked like shops, and then I recognized the entrance to the bar. The one where we had drunk too much.

I looked around at all the people and creatures going about their business. Then we passed a group of women. One of them stood taller than the others. She was completely stunning. She had a tattoo on her elbow and what looked like an eagle on her neck.

But then she was gone; lost in the crowds.

My brother?

"Let's go over there to the pads. We need to get off of this planet before the scanners come out."

"Scanners?" I said, still thinking about the woman.

Robone was nodding. "Yep, they can pinpoint exactly where you are."

"Shit, what are we going to do, Trenton?" I said in desperation.

"As we saved their arses, maybe these gentlemen will give us a ride."

"You didn't want to save him," Robone pointed out.

"Snitch. Anyway, that's not the point. The point is that I did save him, right?"

Robone slapped Trenton's thigh. "Yes, you did."

"Watch it," Trenton replied swatting his hand off.

Caloosh stopped the small craft, and as it lowered to the ground we jumped out.

"Welcome to our spaceship!" he said. "This is MyGirl!"

Robone rolled his eyes. "HeapofShit, more like!"

We walked in. It was as big as the ship we'd been on before but there was something a little old about it. The chrome was tarnished, and there was a funky smell likened to incontinence. I visited my granddad every week at an old folk's home – or senior residential housing facility, as it was also known – and that place smelt like piss and shit. It was like a bodily fluid punch that had been sprayed around the place as some sort of air de-freshener.

"Nice," I said politely.

"It's alright, I guess," Trenton said, not wanting to agree with Robone.

"Don't listen, my sweet!" Caloosh purred, rubbing the controls before setting the thing in motion.

We took seats that had seen better days and got ready for take-off.

"So where are you going?" Caloosh said as we took to the skies.

I looked at Trenton who shrugged. What the hell was the name of the planet that we had left?

"Okay, where did you come from?" Robone asked. "You must know that, right?"

"Funny fucker," Trenton scowled. "Earth. We come from Earth."

"Not originally," Robone said. "Earth exploded years ago. Where did you come from earlier?"

"Ahh!" I clicked my fingers and reached into my pocket. "The leaflet!"

"Ha-ha!" Robone laughed. "A leaflet. A planet that still has paper must be ancient!!"

"Why don't you come with us to sector 315a?" Caloosh said. "You might find someone, too?"

I shook my head. "I just want to go home now. This has been an incredible experience, whilst also being extremely overwhelming and anxious. I would very much like to return to a familiar place where I feel comfortable."

"And you Man-Woman?" he said to Trenton.

Trenton looked at me and then back at Robone. The two of them were pretty similar.

"Nah, I'd better go back with Bailey before she cries, or pisses herself!"

Caloosh looked at the leaflet and nodded. "You've not come such a long way."

"Planet Poontang. Not been there for a while!' Robone said.

"What?" I said.

"Poontang. That's the planet."

"Oh, yeah," Trenton laughed.

"You both have a strange sense of humour," Robone said, frowning.

"Robone almost got us killed there. He was swinging his manhood in a bar. Again!"

"Trenton, want to tell them why we left?"

Trenton laughed. "I might've done the same."

I had to laugh. "You two are like brothers from another mother!"

"No one says that," Trenton muttered. That wasn't true, I'd seen it said on the television before.

After a second or so, Caloosh pressed a few more buttons and then turned to us.

"Let's get you girls home."

"What's with the 'droid?" I said. "She's been quiet ever since we got on here?"

"Probably the smell!" Robone laughed.

"Take that back, Robone!" Caloosh said, a little hurt.

"Nope!"

Caloosh grabbed him in a neck-hold and started to rub his head with his knuckles.

"Okay, okay. I'm sorry!"

They stopped and looked at the 'droid.

"You think she needs recharging?" Robone said.

Caloosh got up and walked over. He glanced over her and found what he thought to be a power socket.

"Hold on," he said and grabbed a cable of sorts. He untangled it, leaving a couple of knots, and plugged it in. He leant over and clicked something.

"I've turned her off whilst charging. I reckon all of those stunwaves drained her power."

We sat back down for a while. There was no doubt that Caloosh and Robone were thinking about their dates. Trenton and I just wanted to be back home. I guess it's true what they say about not knowing what you've got until it's gone!

"Here we go," Caloosh said as we were drawn into the planet. We slowly entered the atmosphere and were met by the brightness of Poontang. We flew around for a while as Caloosh followed the coordinates to take us to the correct area.

When we touched down, we saw the familiar large buildings of the shops, the large tower, and then the bar.

"Ladies, you are here!"

"Thanks guys!" I said. Without any thought we all did the silly routine. High-fiving and spinning around. Perhaps it was the hysteria of going home. Perhaps we wanted one last blast of silliness before we left.

"Unplug Portia, Bailey," Trenton said.

"We taking her?" I asked.

"I don't see why not!"

And so we did.

"Good luck with your dates, guys!" we said as we left the ship, stepping onto the sandy ground. My heart beat hard as I felt my anxieties heighten. I really wanted to be home now.

"Thanks for saving me," Caloosh called.

"Anytime!" Trenton said. I guess they were friends after all.

We walked slowly towards the doors from where we had first appeared. It seemed like weeks ago. So much had happened since. I felt like I'd experienced more in the past few hours than I had in a lifetime.

Then we heard shouting. We looked over and a mob was running at us.

"I suggest we get out of here," the 'droid said.

We burst through the doors to the first room that we had ever seen when we had got to the planet.

"Now through here!" Trenton shouted, as we headed towards the door.

Jim Ody

We all fell through in a pile, and with a flash
we were in a tangled mess.

Chapter 6

When we opened our eyes, we were back in my garden.

"We're home," I said looking down at myself. I was a boy again. Everything was back to normal.

"Trenton," I said.

He looked up, and then quickly down at himself. Instantly his hands shot to his chest where before there were breasts. He then shot his hand down the front of his trousers.

"We're what we were," he said and then looked around.

There was no 'droid.

Instead, there was a dog.

The dog looked at him as Trenton stood up. It ran purposefully at him and attached itself to his leg. It started humping for all it was worth.

"Get off!" Trenton said in a voice full of panic.

I grinned, and then laughed long and hard.

"You must see the humour here?"

"What?" Trenton said. "I fail to see anything humorous about a dog trying to rape me!"

"Think about it. The dog was a 'droid that was used to having sex against its will. Back through the portal, it turns into a dog that tries to have sex with those that wanted to have sex with it before. It's a complete reversal."

"How ironic."

"No, not really. An easy mistake to make."

"Shut the fuck up, dickhead." He was back name-calling so must've been feeling better!

He was then kicking his leg frantically, which sent the small dog tumbling off. Undeterred, it ran back again.

"Piss off!"

We ran to my house, and Trenton shut the dog out with a slam.

The dog started to whine.

"Bloody bitches," Trenton said.

"It's a male dog."

"Same thing."

"Not really."

***

"And that, class, was what happened in the summer holidays," Trenton had said proudly. I had stood awkwardly beside him trying not to look embarrassed. I wanted to be in a million other places than there at that point.

There was a sea of shocked faces in front of us. Little Daisy Webb was sobbing, and at some point Rupert Donegan had thrown up. Chester Ball had his hands over his ears, and Johnny Randle was singing a song from *Oliver!* and rocking back and forth. Teachers were consoling individual members of the class, and the headmaster was repeating something in a mantra-like fashion." If you don't stop you will be expelled! If you don't stop you will be expelled!"

Trenton had carried on unperturbed by such benign threats. You cannot punish someone for a remarkably in-depth presentation. He had a story to tell and he was going nowhere until it had been told.

It was impressive that he had carried on with such gusto not bothered by the threats from first the teachers, and then when he had arrived, the large and imposing figure of the Head.

Luckily for Trenton, teachers were no longer allowed to lay a hand on a child.

As we looked over the class one final time, a policeman came through the door. But by then we had finished.

It was a strange summer.

And now the class, school and local residents knew all about it.

If I got nothing else from this whole adventure, the one thing I did know was that I never wanted to be a woman again.

Ever.

The End

Delirious with hysteria, my heart is beating fast,
I'm completely narrow minded, how long will this last?
Re-changing my clothes, and adding more cologne,
Staring at my mobile I know she will not phone,
Papa says I'm ugly, and the reason Mama left,
He says that I'm a failure even when I've done my best,
So how could she ever want me, and not let me go?
I swallow, my smile is nervous, and of course, I know!

When I hold her in my arms, I don't want this feeling to stop,
The innocent pools of her eyes, the soft lips I forgot,
Submissive to my desires, does she feel what I see?
Unlike my Mama, I know she will never leave,
Her skin is so pale, and her touch is so cool,
I kiss her so deeply, the room flashes red and blue,
I stole her heart, but they will never understand,
As the police burst in the room, it's just stopped beating in my hand...

Acknowledgements

A big thank you to my family and friends. Your support is massive and continues to motivate me.

A huge thanks to the members of *Jim Ody's Spooky Circus* - my street team, and specifically my group of advisors Simon Leonard, Angela Hill, AJ Griffiths-Jones, Cheryl Elaine, Dee Groocock, Terry Hetherington and Ellie Shepherd who listen to all my crazy ideas and advise me whether or not they are worth pursuing!

Thanks to my BETA readers Deb Day & Sue Scott.

A nod of appreciation to the hard work of my admin team: Donna Morfett, Zoe-Lee O'Farrell and Kate Eveleigh.

A special thanks to the wonderful Mel Comley who has given me such great sage-like advice.

Thank you to Caroline, David and Jason for your continued support. Also, to Andy Barrett, Maggie James, Sarah Hardy, Valerie Dickenson, and Kerry Watts who also try to steer me in the right direction. Or try.

Thank you to Matt Rayner for your friendship, design and support with Question Mark Press. Everybody else at Question Mark Press: we are a great family!

A special mention to Emmy Ellis @ studioenp for her wonderful design direction. You truly bring my book covers to life! Not to mention being a great author, and a wonderful friend.

And a huge thank you to Shelagh Corker for adding the final polish to my books.

And finally thank you to you, the readers. For reading, for enjoying, and for getting behind me. Without you there would really be no point!

ABOUT THE AUTHOR

Jim writes dark psychological/thrillers, Horror and YA books that have endings you won't see coming, and favours stories packed with wit. He has written over a dozen novels and many more short-stories spanning many genres.

Jim has a very strange sense of humour and is often considered a little odd. When not writing he will be found playing the drums, watching football and eating chocolate. He lives with his long-suffering wife, three beautiful children and two indignant cats in Swindon, Wiltshire UK.

He is also the owner of Question Mark Press and enjoys helping new authors.

JIM ODY
Stories with a Twist

Connect with Jim Ody here:

Facebook: www.facebook.com/JimOdyAuthor
Jim Ody's Spooky Circus Street Team:
https://www.facebook.com/groups/1372500609494122
/
Amazon Author Link:
https://www.amazon.co.uk/Jim-Ody/e/B019A6AMSY/
Email: jim.ody@hotmail.co.uk
Twitter: @Jim_Ody_Author
Instagram: @jimodyauthor
Pintrest: https://www.pinterest.co.uk/jimodyauthor/
Bookbub: https://www.bookbub.com/profile/jim-ody
www.questionmarkpress.com

Want to read more books by this author?

Here are details of three more books for you to get your hands on!

A Lifetime Ago (Hudson Bell Book 1)

This is a tale about how the events of one day have such catastrophic consequences on the future.

Hudson Bell is a consultant for the police. A former DI, he spends his days helping to find missing children.

May and her son go on a road trip to celebrate his birthday; Robert and Nadia buy their dream house by the sea.

But as each look to enjoy a new life, none of them can shake off what happened on that fateful day. One of them blames the others and will stop at nothing to seek revenge.

One accident and five lives changed forever.

Question Mark Press

The Place That Never Existed

For Paul and Debbie it was meant to be the happiest time of their lives.

A small village wedding in front of their family and friends, followed by a quiet honeymoon in Devon. Not everyone had been happy to see them together. A woman from their past refused to accept it. Her actions over the previous year had ended in tragedy, and had almost broken the happy couple apart.

Now, away from it all in a picturesque log cabin, Paul and Debbie look forward to time spent alone together... But she has found out where they are, and she will stop at nothing to make sure that the marriage is over... forever.

But Huntswood Cove isn't just a beautiful Devonshire fishing town, it has its own secret. Recently, people have begun to disappear, only to turn up dead in suspicious circumstances. The locals begin to question what is going on. Soon everything strange points to the abandoned house in the woods.

The house that nobody wants to talk about. To them, it is the place that never existed.

Question Mark Press

The Crazy Season (Joel Baxter Book 1)

Joel Baxter is infamous for solving weird and bizarre cases that others avoid. So, when he receives an email from a teenage boy Tim saying his town is cursed, he cannot turn it down.

"...I will more than likely be dead when you read this. There is nothing I can do about it. It's the curse, and we've hit The Crazy Season." Every 20 years, there are a handful of unexplained teenage deaths and it's started again.

With the help of his straight-talking friend Melody, they set out to get to the bottom of the alleged curse. Everybody in Black Rock has secrets and nobody wants to speak.

The closer they get to truth the more Joel and Melody realise that their involvement is far from coincidental.

Question Mark Press

How many have you read?

Other books from Question Mark Press

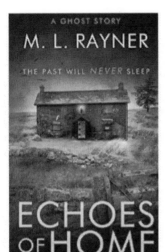

A GHOST STORY

M. L. RAYNER

THE PAST WILL *NEVER* SLEEP

ECHOES OF HOME

The Führer cannot protect them now

AMALIE

E.J. WOOD

COMATOSE

...AND HER NIGHTMARE IS JUST BEGINNING

JANE BADROCK

DNA IS

RECKONING

MARISA NOELLE

Coming soon:

Question Mark Horror

A new series of YA Horror books. One series by a handful of authors.

Are you ready?

1 – Camp Death
2 – Ouija
3 – House of Horrors

Printed in Great Britain
by Amazon